Unlocking the Scriptures for You

PHILIPPIANS— THESSALONIANS

Gary Weedman

**STANDARD
BIBLE STUDIES**

STANDARD PUBLISHING
Cincinnati, Ohio   11-40110

Library of Congress Cataloging-in-Publication Data:

Weedman, Gary.
  Philippians—Thessalonians / by Gary Weedman.
    p. cm. — (Standard bible studies)
  ISBN 0-87403-170-2
  1. Bible. N.T. Philippians—Commentaries.   2. Bible. N.T. Colossians—Commentaries.   3. Bible. N.T. Thessalonians— Commentaries.   I. Title.   II. Series.
BS2705.3.W44 1988
227—dc19   88-2915
                                                  CIP

CONTENTS

Part One

Philippians

INTRODUCTION TO PHILIPPIANS

Destination

Philippi was a Roman colony in Macedonia, perhaps the most important eastern European city near the continent of Asia. Though far from Rome, the citizens of Philippi were considered Roman citizens; many were retired Roman army men. Located on the famous Egnatian Way—a road stretching from the Adriatic Sea to Byzantium—Philippi was a strategic city for political and commercial purposes. It was to become a strategic city as well for the Christian gospel.

Here, for the first time in Europe, the gospel message was preached less than twenty years after the death of Jesus. (See Acts 16 for this account.) Paul and Silas, having separated from Barnabas and John Mark, were joined by Timothy and, after visiting churches in Asia Minor, ended up in Troas. They were undoubtedly disappointed upon their arrival here, since they had been prevented from preaching in Bithynia. But, nevertheless, Paul was challenged in a vision by "a man of Macedonia" (whom many believe to have been Luke) to "come over to Macedonia and help us" (Acts 16:9). The four men (Paul, Silas, Timothy, and Luke) set sail and ended up in Philippi.

It was Paul's practice upon entering a Gentile city to visit the local synagogue first to preach to the Jews and the "God-fearers" (Gentiles who attended but had not become full proselytes). Apparently, however, there was no synagogue in the city. (There had to be a minimum of ten Jewish males in order to form such an organization.) Instead, Paul found a group of believers who assembled on the Sabbath day "down by the riverside"; the group was led by a business woman named Lydia, "a worshiper of God" (Acts 16:14). When she heard the message of Jesus, she and her household accepted the message and were baptized, thus becoming the first recorded converts to Christianity on European soil.

9

Another event of significance also occurred in this city at this time. Paul and Silas were thrown into jail after casting out a spirit from a slave girl. When they did not grab the opportunity to escape the prison following an earthquake, the jailer was moved by their actions, heard the message of Jesus along with his household, and was baptized with them. The second recorded convert in Europe, then, was a Roman jailer.

Having later been released from the prison, Paul and his company then visited the church meeting in Lydia's home, encouraged them, and left Philippi. Some believe that Luke stayed behind at Philippi since the first "we" section of Acts comes to an end here. (Luke resumes his use of the first person at Acts 20:5.) Luke joined Paul and several others on their way in what would be a fateful trip to Jerusalem. Thus, the believers at Philippi became the first in Europe to embrace the gospel and the last to bid Paul farewell after his last recorded missionary trip. Even during his imprisonment, they remembered him and responded to his needs. Even fifty years later, the church at Philippi was still responding to the needs of leaders. Ignatius, a bishop from Antioch, passed through Philippi on his way to Rome and to martyrdom. They apparently aided him on his way, and later wrote to Polycarp, bishop of Smyrna, for some of Ignatius's letters. Polycarp wrote them back *(Letter to the Philippians)* reminding them of their kindness to Paul and commending them for continued concern for Ignatius. At least for some time after Paul's association with them, they observed his admonitions to them and were widely known as a loving and caring people.

Author

The apostle Paul is early identified in the letter itself as the author. This claim is generally accepted. In the mid-nineteenth century, F. C. Baur questioned the Pauline authorship. However, his views are not readily accepted today. In the 1960s, A. Q. Morton questioned the Pauline authorship based upon a computer-assisted statistical analysis of certain linguistic characteristics. Again, however, his methodology and assumptions have not generally been accepted. The tone and content of the letter are similar to other Pauline epistles. The overwhelming testimony of the early church attests to the Pauline authorship. Polycarp (A.D. 150-160), Clement of Rome (A.D. 101), Clement of Alexandria (A.D. 150), Irenaeus (A.D. 140-202), Tertullian (A.D. 160-230),

Hippolytus (A.D. 170-235), Origen (A.D. 185-254), and Eusebius (A.D. 371) all directly or indirectly support the Pauline authorship. There is no compelling reason, then, to question that the apostle Paul was the author of this letter.

Date and Place of Composition

Next to the issue of the structure of the letter (whether there are one, two, or three letters in the document), one of the most difficult questions to resolve is the date and place of its composition. Wherever Paul was when he wrote the letter, it is clear that he was in prison. There are four imprisonments mentioned in the book of Acts: in Philippi (Acts 16:23-40), in Jerusalem (Acts 21:33—23:30), in Caesarea (Acts 23:35—26:32), and in Rome (Acts 28:16-31). Philippi and Jerusalem are easily ruled out as the site for the composition of the letter; Paul did not have time to write at either place. Therefore, Caesarea and Rome remain. The traditionally held view of its origin is Rome during Paul's imprisonment there (Acts 28). There are many reasons to support this view.

1. Paul said that the gospel had spread "throughout the whole praetorian guard" (Philippians 1:13, NASB), an apparent reference to the Roman imperial guard established by Augustus and numbering nine thousand strong.
2. Paul was not held in favor by some of the local preachers (Philippians 1:15-17). It is known that Paul was not so close to the church at Rome. Furthermore, the large number of preachers would be more characteristic of Rome than of other smaller cities.
3. Paul expected a decisive verdict with regard to his case (Philippians 2:17, 23).
4. It appears that some time had passed since the founding of the church in Philippi, thus giving him enough time to complete his third missionary journey and be sent to Rome from Jerusalem (Philippians 4:15).
5. He warned the Philippians of experiencing "the same struggle" that he was undergoing (Philippians 1:30), a conflict likely to happen in a Roman colony as well as Rome itself.
6. Paul sent greetings from "all the saints ... especially those who belong to Caesar's household" (Philippians 4:22). This greeting certainly sounds as if he was writing from Rome.
7. For 1700 years, the view of the Roman origin predominated. There are many early church fathers who held this view.

There are, nevertheless, some difficulties with this view, though they are not necessarily insurmountable.

1. In Acts 28, Paul seems to have had a relative degree of freedom, accepting visitors in large number and preaching to them without restriction. Throughout Philippians, however, the conditions seem to have been worse.
2. If Paul wrote this letter from Rome, he would have visited Philippi once after the founding of the church there (Acts 16:1-6). Yet, there is no apparent acknowledgement of this second visit. Instead, he talked about the early days with them: "... because of your partnership in the gospel from the first day until now" (Philippians 1:5); "in the early days of your acquaintance with the gospel, when I set out from Macedonia, not one church shared with me ... except you only" (Philippians 4:15).
3. The distance between Rome and Philippi is great, 730 land miles plus a two-day sea voyage. There are a number of journeys back and forth between Rome and Philippi: (A) Someone went from Rome to Philippi to tell them of Paul's imprisonment. (B) They sent Epaphroditus to Paul with a gift. (C) Someone traveled back to Philippi telling of Epaphroditus's illness. (D) Someone journeyed from Philippi to Rome communicating the great concern over Epaphroditus's illness. The issue is, does such a great distance between Rome and Philippi preclude this number of trips?

There are plausible explanations for these questions.

1. Though the conditions in Philippians appear to have been worse than in Acts 28, there is no reason to believe that the latter conditions continued throughout his two-year stay in Rome. No such affirmation is made. In fact, Philippians 1:12 may imply the opposite. (See page 24 below.)
2. While it is true that Paul did not mention the second, the brief visit there, the very fact that he referred to "the early days" seems to imply that enough years had passed for Paul to have had time to get to Rome.
3. At the most, the journey would have taken no more than six weeks; the two-year stay in Rome would present ample opportunity for at least four trips between the two cities.

Because of the lack of absolute data, therefore, it is impossible to be certain from what place Paul wrote this letter. The traditional view of Rome, though, seems to have the fewest problems and is still to be preferred.

Purpose

The immediate occasion for Paul's writing this letter was to send an acknowledgement of the gift received from the Philippians (Philippians 4:14ff). He sent this message with Epaphroditus, their minister who had come to help Paul while he was in prison (Philippians 2:25ff). Furthermore, Paul set the stage for the sending of Timothy to them since he would be able to report to him of their condition (Philippians 2:19ff). Ultimately, Paul wanted to visit them himself (Philippians 2:24).

Beyond this immediate purpose, Paul's confidence in and love for these Philippians just bursts forth throughout the letter. They had stood by him without waver; they had demonstrated their commitment to him in concrete ways. All throughout the letter, then, he expressed his appreciation for them. They appear to have been never far from his memory or his prayers (Philippians 1:3, 4). He exuded a confidence in them that they would continue in the same fine manner demonstrated by their past. Even though they were about to undergo the same kind of hardship as Paul was experiencing, they could do so with *joy*. Fourteen times, Paul mentioned *joy* or *rejoice;* the letter deserves the title, "The Epistle of Joy." There is a joy that triumphs even amidst suffering (chapter 1). There is a joy that comes through service (chapter 2). There is a joy in having a worthwhile goal (chapter 3). There is a joy that comes from fellowship (chapter 4).

In spite of their coming hardship, Paul was confident that they could experience the same joy he knew if they held fast to their faith and heeded his exhortations to them in this letter.

Literary Structure

Unlike some New Testament letters, Philippians does not readily lend itself to an obvious literary structure. This characteristic has led some to believe that there is actually more than one letter embedded within this document. Polycarp, a disciple of John who lived in the second century, refers to "letters" that Paul wrote to the Philippians. Some have seen such a change of tone and content within the letter that they argue that such disconnectedness could not have been in a single letter. For example, in Philippians 3:1, the tone is positive and upbeat: "Finally, my brothers, rejoice in the Lord! It is no trouble for me to write the same things to you again." But in Philippians 3:2, the tone is alarming: "Watch out for those dogs, those men who do evil, those mutilators of the flesh." Some commentators see as many as three separate letters within the document. Although there is not complete agreement among them as to the exact parts of these letters, they are generally identified as follows:

1. *Philippians 4:10-20.* Paul sent a brief thank-you note to them for their gift sent to him in prison.
2. *Philippians 1:1—3:1; 4:2-7; 4:21-23.* Paul was in prison and, while hoping to be reunited with his dear friends in Philippi, did not know for sure that he would ever see them and wrote to them a final word, a "last will and testament."
3. *Philippians 3:2—4:1; 4:8, 9.* Paul wrote a short, forceful letter warning the church to beware of attacks from those outside the church who are trying to destroy it.

Of course, even if there were two or three letters, they still have the force of Scripture if they were written by Paul. But our *understanding* is significantly affected by this question. A careful look at the literary structure affirms the unity of this letter and informs our understanding of it.

The letter is structured around admonitions or exhortations generally focusing upon thinking correctly and acting appropriately. These admonitions are extended by the use of examples, usually positive, though occasionally negative. This series of admonitions is preceded by the typical sort of opening and followed by a personal conclusion. The following outline demonstrates this literary unity:

I. Chapter One
    A. Opening salutation and thanksgiving (Philippians 1:1-8)
    B. First series of admonitions (Philippians 1:9-11)
        1. Love abound so that ... *discern* what is best (mind)
        2. and be *pure and blameless* (actions)
    C. *Example* of love abounding *to discern ... and to be pure and blameless* (Philippians 1:12-26) (Paul's discernment of mind and blameless actions)
    D. Admonitions repeated (Philippians 1:27-30)
        1. Conduct yourselves in a manner worthy ... (Philippians 1:27) (actions)
        2. Stand firm in one spirit (Philippians 1:27) (mind)

II. Chapter Two
   A. Second series of admonitions (Philippians 2:2-4)
      1. Be like-minded, having the same love, being one in spirit and purpose (Philippians 2:2) (mind)
      2. Do nothing out of selfish ambition or vain conceit, but in humility consider others better than yourselves ... (Philippians 2:3) (actions)
   B. Example of Christ (Philippians 2:5-11)
   C. Admonitions repeated (Philippians 2:12-18)
      1. Work out your salvation (Philippians 2:12) (actions)
      2. Do everything without complaining (Philippians 2:14) (actions)
      3. Be glad and rejoice with me (Philippians 2:18) (mind)
   D. Examples of Timothy and Epaphroditus (Philippians 2:19-30)

III. Chapter Three
   A. Third series of admonitions (Philippians 3:1-3)
      1. Rejoice in the Lord (Philippians 3:1) (mind)
      2. Watch out for those dogs! (Philippians 3:2) (actions)
   B. Positive example of Paul (Philippians 3:4-14)
   C. Admonition repeated (Philippians 3:15-21)
      Join with others in following my example (Philippians 3:17)

IV. Chapter Four
   A. Fourth series of admonitions (Philippians 4:1)
      Stand firm in the Lord (Philippians 4:1)
   B. Example: Euodia and Syntyche (Philippians 4:2-3)
   C. Admonitions repeated (Philippians 4:4-9)
      Summary of admonitions
   D. Conclusion (Philippians 4:10-23)
      1. Thanksgiving for Philippians (Philippians 4:10-20)
      2. Final greetings (Philippians 4:21-23)

CHAPTER ONE

Joy in Suffering
Philippians 1:1-30

Opening Salutation (1:1, 2)

The form of letters written at the time Paul writes this letter is much different from modern form. Contemporary letters end with the author's name; ancient letters begin with the author's name. Then follows the name of the recipient of the letter, generally followed by a thanksgiving and sometimes a prayer, then the body of the letter, followed by concluding remarks such as personal greetings and a benediction. This pattern is characteristic of all letter writing in the ancient world and not merely of religious writing. Thus, Paul is not creating some specialized form for his messages.

As he does in 1 and 2 Corinthians, Colossians, and Philemon, Paul includes Timothy in the greeting. Timothy, the son of a Jewish mother who was a Christian and a Greek father, had joined Paul on the second missionary journey and had sailed with him to Philippi (Acts 16). He apparently stayed in Philippi, perhaps with Luke, after Paul and Silas went on to Thessalonica. At the time Paul writes this letter, Timothy is in Rome attending to Paul's needs in prison. He may even serve as Paul's secretary in the writing of this letter. Paul clearly used secretaries for other letters (cf. Romans 16:21-24; Galatians 6:11; Colossians 4:18); it is not incredible to assume Timothy may be acting in that capacity for this letter. Furthermore, Timothy will soon visit the Philippians again, bearing this very letter (Philippians 2:19-23).

Paul calls himself and Timothy "servants [literally "slaves"] of Christ Jesus" (Philippians 1:1). In none of his other letters does Paul include others alongside himself with a common title. It is he alone to whom he attaches such descriptive phrases in the introductory sections of his other letters. *Apostle, prisoner,* and *slave* are usually descriptions of him alone. Why, then, the change from the norm here? It is true that Timothy is his companion in his imprisonment, but he is not included in a similar title in the other prison epistles. Even though Timothy is familiar with the church at Philippi, that alone does not seem sufficient explanation. While Timothy may be Paul's secretary for this letter, Paul is not in the habit of including his secretaries under such titles. The reason is certainly not explicit, but may relate to the themes of humility and service that he will build upon throughout the letter. While there apparently is no significant problem within the church, humility and service are stressed throughout. (For example, see Philippians 2:3: "in humility consider others better than yourselves"; and the reference in Philippians 2:7 to Jesus' "taking the very nature of a servant.") Thus, Paul implicitly sets the tone for one of the important emphases in the letter by including himself on the level with Timothy. In this way, they are equal and co-workers. They are both slaves of Jesus Christ.

While the concept of slave is a common one in the Greek world, and it may be that image that Paul has in mind, the word was also used in the Septuagint, the Greek version of the Old Testament with which Paul is familiar, to refer to God's leaders. Neither in the Greek world nor in the Hebrew mind was the relationship between a worshiper and his god ever described as that of a "slave." It is unexpected, then, that the Septuagint uses this word to describe the relationship (see Jeremiah 25:4; Ezekiel 38:17; Amos 3:7; Zechariah 1:6). At any rate, the use of the term in Philippians 2:7 certainly seems to have more of the Greek understanding of slave in mind than some sort of special leader. Perhaps Paul is cleverly combining the two meanings to form a paradox here.

The letter is addressed, first of all, to "all the saints in Christ Jesus at Philippi" (Philippians 1:1). The word *saints,* of course, does not refer to persons with some sort of extraordinary moral superiority. *Saints* is usually taken to mean ordinary rank-and-file Christians who make up the constituency of the church. While this may be the meaning in a some of the passages in the New Testament, there is substantial evidence that much of the time, *saints* especially means Jewish people who have accepted Jesus as Messiah and have been incorporated into the church. However we understand the word generally, the phrase *all the saints* here seems less to be a title with the inclusion of *all.* With this phrase, Paul includes Gentiles along with the Jews.

18

Paul also addresses this letter to the "overseers and deacons." Nowhere else in Paul's epistles does he address these particular persons. The overseers are not mentioned anywhere else by Paul outside of the Pastoral Epistles. The word for *overseer* (or *bishop,* as the NIV footnote suggests) was a common one and was not used in an exclusively religious connotation. It could describe any person who exercised any kind of oversight of others. The Hebrew equivalent of this word was used to describe men who were leaders of the Essenes, a Jewish sect contemporary with Jesus, though there is no reason to think that this became the model for the bishops in the early church. It appears that these "overseers" are also called elders (Titus 1:5, 7). The first term undoubtedly describes their function, the latter their maturity.

Deacon also did not have an exclusively religious meaning, but was a quite generic term describing any person who performed a service. With a few exceptions (e.g. the Pastorals and perhaps Romans 16:1), the New Testament does not seem to have used it as an official title.

Just why Paul includes these persons here is by no means clear. Some have speculated that he really is referring to a single group: the bishops, who are servants. This understanding is a possibility grammatically and is consistent with the tone Paul has set in calling Timothy and himself "slaves." Be that as it may, the church in Philippi, even at this early stage, has identifiable leaders (plural), and that should not be surprising.

Grace and *peace* combine the Greek and Hebrew form of greeting. Paul uses this formula also in Romans, 1 and 2 Corinthians, Galatians, Ephesians, and Philemon. *Grace* takes on a particular Christian content here, describing that quality of God in giving undeserved good will to His people. *Peace (Shalom)* was and is a Jewish greeting that means more than the absence of war, but rather describes a state of life in which the whole person is at peace and functioning as God intended.

Thanksgiving (1:3-8)

It is customary for the Greek letter-writing form to include a thanksgiving and often a prayer following the greetings. It is often Paul's practice to include in his thanksgiving section some of the major themes he intends to deal with in the letter. There are three that are outstanding here. The first is joy: "I always pray with joy" (Philippians 1:4). His love for the Philippians just bursts out

19

in this thanksgiving. Second, it is their "partnership" *(koinonia)* with him that is the immediate cause of Paul's joy here. Philippi was the scene of the first church in Europe, and they have continued their support of Paul's ministry since their founding (Philippians 4:15; Acts 16:12-40). Paul expresses no greater love for any church than this one because of their continued support. Fellowship is more than church dinners. Paul used this word in Romans: "For Macedonia and Achaia were pleased to make a contribution *[koinonia]* for the poor among the saints in Jerusalem" (Romans 15:26). The elements of the Lord's Supper represent a "fellowship" with the death of Jesus: "Is not the cup of thanksgiving for which we give thanks a participation *[koinonia]* in the blood of Christ? And is not the bread that we break a participation *[koinonia]* in the body of Christ?" (1 Corinthians 10:16). Furthermore, Paul also speaks of "the fellowship of sharing in his sufferings" (Philippians 3:10). So fellowship is not just good times and warm feelings; it is a full participation in the life of Jesus and in the lives of others with whom work and worship is accomplished. Third, there is need for perseverance: "He who began a good work in you will carry it on to completion until the day of Christ" (Philippians 1:6). The Philippians, who have been Paul's partners in the gospel, will continue in their good work until Jesus returns. The responsibility of continuing the work of the gospel is underscored. It is interesting, however, that it is God who does this work through them. This paradox of their work's being God at work is continued in Philippians 2:12, 13: "Work out your salvation with fear and trembling, for it is God who works in you...." It is through God's grace that Christians can continue until judgment day itself.

Although Paul has been forsaken by some since he has been imprisoned, the Philippians have continued to support his ministry. It is for this reason, especially, that Paul is so drawn to these his friends. The word translated "feel"—"It is right for me to feel this way about all of you" (Philippians 1:7)—is characteristic of Paul. Of the twenty-six times it occurs in the New Testament, twenty-three times it is used by Paul, and ten of those are in Philippians. It includes the idea of thinking as well as feeling. Likewise, the metaphor of the heart—"have you in my heart" (Philippians 1:7)—does not merely focus upon the emotions, but on the intellect as well. He not only feels strongly about them; he also carries out those feelings in concrete actions for their good will.

They have supported him whether in prison ("chains") or "defending and confirming the gospel" (Philippians 1:7). *Defending* here is a technical word used to describe a personal testimony and defense in a court of law (literally, *apology*). It was through his "apology" in his trial that he was able to "confirm" the gospel. The Philippians supported him in that endeavor.

First Series of Admonitions: the Prayer (1:9-11)

Embedded in this prayer for the Philippians is the beginning of Paul's pattern of admonitions focusing upon how one thinks and how one acts. (See the comments above on the "Literary Structure" in the Introduction to Philippians, pages 13-15). Earlier, Paul has said he prayed for them (Philippians 1:4); now he reveals the content of his present praying for them. It is a simple prayer: "That your love may abound more and more" (Philippians 1:9). He does not specify the object of that love—God, others, or himself. Undoubtedly, he uses the admonition in the broadest sense. As is frequently the case in these introductory sections of Paul's epistles, he reveals part of the problem in the church. In this case, it appears to be a lack of harmony with some persons or groups in the church. The problem has not yet approached a critical situation, but it has the potential of developing in such a way. Paul tells them, therefore, that their love should "abound more and more." The problem is not a lack of love; they merely need to exercise it even more.

This "abounding" love is to be accompanied by "knowledge and depth of insight." The Philippians have already demonstrated love, but as their love increases, they will gain a greater understanding as well.

This relationship between love and knowledge is an emphasis made elsewhere by Paul. In Colossians, he describes a relationship between being "united in love" and in having the "full riches of complete understanding" (Colossians 2:2). The words used here denote a kind of knowledge and of understanding that go beyond the ordinary, and these characterize a love that increases.

There are at least two admonitions, then, that follow from Paul's prayer about their love—two purposes that are to govern thought and action. They are to "discern what is best" and to be "pure and blameless" (Philippians 1:10). One of the goals of their abounding love, and Paul's admonition to them in this prayer, is not only to judge right from wrong. That task is relatively easy

21

most of the time. Rather, they are to distinguish the best from the good. While it is true that "to the pure, all things are pure" (Titus 1:15), the Christian who has this abounding love does not insist on this principle to act in disregard for others, especially those in the church who might be harmed by actions that are in and of themselves not evil. This newfound freedom in the church could prove to be heady wine. Apparently, the Corinthians had also been prone to use their freedom in disregard for others. Paul wrote to them, quoting their own teaching and then responding to it: "'Everything is permissible'—but not everything is beneficial. 'Everything is permissible'—but not everything is constructive. Nobody should seek his own good, but the good of others" (1 Corinthians 10:23; cf. 1 Corinthians 6:12). For the Jew, this discernment of the best is done on the basis of the law (Romans 2:18); for the Christian, the discernment is done on the basis of love, an *agape* love that seeks only the best for others.

The Christian life, then, is lived in this tension of liberty and love. As far as the gospel is concerned, nothing can indict the freedom it brings. When it came to circumcising Titus, Paul refused. Titus was a Greek, and the truth of the gospel was at stake (Galatians 2:3). With Timothy, however, who was half-Jewish, Paul had him circumcised so as not to hinder him in his work with Jews (Acts 16:3). Liberty is exercised in defense of the genuine gospel; love is exercised in deference to the good of others.

Not only are the Philippians to discern the best; they are also to be "pure and blameless" (Philippians 1:10). Actions follow thoughts. The call to purity is a call to stand before Jesus without mixed motives ("for" the day of Christ rather than "until" the day of Christ as in the New International Version). The word comes from the word *sunlight*. As the Christian stands before the Son, the sunlight reveals the inner motives and purposes. If this love abounds, then there is confidence that love will prove the Christian as pure in the sight of Christ; "love covers over a multitude of sins" (1 Peter 4:8).

As the Christian is pure before Christ, he or she is also blameless before others. In the discussion of liberty and love in 1 Corinthians, Paul admonished, "Do not cause anyone to stumble, whether Jews, Greeks or the church of God.... For I am not seeking my own good but the good of many" (1 Corinthians 10:32, 33). Liberty is not license to ignore concern for others.

Paul makes it clear, however, that this right thinking and right acting are not self-generating; they do not come solely by human effort, but rather represent "the fruit of righteousness that comes through Jesus Christ" (Philippians 1:11). It is ultimately *His* righteousness, and not self-righteousness, that occasions such thought and deed. He reminded the Galatians of similar fruit (Galatians 5:22, 23)—"fruit of the Spirit" and not of human righteousness. The result, then, is not to glorify the individual, but "to the glory and praise of God" (Philippians 1:11).

An Example of These Admonitions (1:12-26)

In a passage remarkably revealing of Paul's personality, he gives an example of right thinking and right acting from his own life. In doing so, he moves from the introductory section of the letter to the main body.

Paul has come to understand something of his imprisonment. Apparently, he had anticipated an acquittal of the trumped-up charges against him when he arrived in Rome. Such was not to be. Instead, he has lingered on in prison. Unfortunately for inquiring minds today, Paul does not go into great detail about his circumstances in prison. There apparently has been a change in his status, and that has caused distress on the part of the Philippians, if not for Paul himself. Since he is "filled with the fruit of righteousness that comes through Jesus Christ," he is able to understand how these circumstances have worked out for the good of the gospel. To see through unfortunate circumstances to God's providence takes the filling of the Spirit.

Paul has come to understand at least two benefits of his imprisonment. The first is that it has become clear to the whole palace guard that Paul is not there because he has committed insurrection, but merely because he is a Christian (Philippians 1:13). The story of Paul's arrest and imprisonment, first in Caesarea and then in Rome, is chronicled in Acts 21—28. Paul was falsely accused by Jews of starting riots. Later, to avoid a trial—or an ambush—by the Jews, he appealed on the basis of his Roman citizenship to Caesar himself.

God revealed to him that he would testify in Rome as he had done in Jerusalem. After approximately two years in prison in Caesarea, he arrived in Rome, fully anticipating to be set free and having opportunity to preach the gospel unhindered in Rome. But such was not to be. Instead, he was at first put under house arrest and could speak only to those who visited him. It is possible that his conditions of imprisonment then worsened, that the reference to "what has happened to me" (Philippians 1:12) means that he has been placed under the palace guard themselves instead of "in his own rented house" (Acts 28:30). On the surface, then, Paul's hope for a witness in Rome has not materialized as he had hoped. However, Paul can see by this time that he has, in fact, been able to testify in Rome and has done so in a significant way. His honor has been cleared, at least in the minds of the guards, and his suffering is for Christ—not for a criminal act. Instead of Paul's being a prisoner of the guards, it seems almost as if they have become *his* prisoner. They are a captive audience; they cannot get away from him or his preaching. He has thus been provided an audience by his imprisonment he could not have had otherwise.

A second benefit he has come to see in his imprisonment is that others have been emboldened to witness more enthusiastically (Philippians 1:14). It might be supposed that, seeing what has happened to Paul because of his preaching, others would be more hesitant to speak openly about the Christian faith. But such is not the case. Perhaps, like Paul, they see God's hand at work, even in Paul's imprisonment, and are encouraged in their part in this kingdom work. Because they are able to preach where Paul cannot, they are all the more determined to do what they can to take up the slack. Whatever the reason, more people have heard the gospel because of the imprisonment.

It is remarkable that Paul even rejoices when some preach for the wrong motives. There is here another example of his discerning what is the best. They preach out of "envy," "rivalry," and "selfish ambition." It cannot be said with certainty who these are. Surely, they are not the Judaizers; they preach the wrong message. Since Paul contrasts them with those who know Paul was put in prison "for the defense of the gospel," some have supposed them to be ones who preach a gospel of success. How could Paul be acting within God's will and by faith if such a fate has befallen him? For them as for many today (especially with so many television evangelists), earthly success is seen as evidence of faith. If Paul were so unsuccessful as to end up in prison, surely there must be something wrong with his character. They find themselves at odds, not with the gospel Paul preaches, but rather with the apostle himself. That they are mistaken about him and that they demonstrate wrong attitudes does not prevent Paul from rejoicing that the gospel is preached nonetheless. He understands that it is the message ("the word—*logos*—of God"; Philippians 1:14) that has the transforming power and not the character of the speaker. Paul demonstrates here a tremendous confidence in the power of the gospel.

It is further remarkable that Paul does not care who gets the credit for preaching and success. In the contemporary age, with its spirit of competition and rivalry, his attitude bears imitation. The church has been, and is, hampered when some of its leaders envy others with whom they have some disagreement, and would actually rather see them fail than succeed. Differences over style, over words, and over human loyalties should not prevent God's servants from rejoicing when those who differ preach the gospel. The church needs to rise to the stature of Paul.

After giving as an example his own understanding of "what is best," he next turns to his own commitment to be "pure and blameless" in his actions (Philippians 1:19-26). One reads this remarkable self-revelation of his inner struggles with some embarrassment; such a thing is too personal for just anyone to hear. Yet Paul is quite willing to share them with his dearest of friends, the Philippians. He quotes a passage from Job 13:16: "What has happened to me will turn out for my deliverance" (literally, "salvation"; Philippians 1:19). In the same way that Job knew that he would be vindicated when he stood before God, so Paul asserts his faith in this "deliverance." He mentions two reasons for this confidence. One, he has the prayers of the Philippians; he believes in the power of prayer by the faithful (Philippians 1:19). Second, he has help from the Spirit of Jesus. Just as he has admonished them in his prayer to be pure and blameless, he expects that when he is put to the test, he will demonstrate such character himself: "that I will in no way be ashamed, but will have sufficient courage" (Philippians 1:20). If he is to face death, he wants to do so in such a way that Jesus will be exalted by that death. If he is to live and face trial and vindication, he wants "fruitful labor" (Philippians 1:22) for the sake of Jesus. Thus, he cannot lose; whether in death or in life, he will be able to demonstrate the pure and blameless behavior that is characteristic of the Spirit-filled life.

If only his own concerns were the question, he would far rather "be with Christ" (Philippians 1:23). But since his principle is that "nobody should seek his own good, but the good of others" (1 Corinthians 10:24), he thinks it "more necessary" for him to be vindicated and to return to them and to his missionary endeavors. The phrase *be with Christ* has caused some speculation with his teaching of the resurrection of the dead in Christ at the last day (1 Thessalonians 4:13-17). While there is no exhaustive and systematic treatment of this doctrine in Paul's writing, there need be no contradiction seen in the available data. Paul consistently teaches the resurrection of the body at the last day (1 Thessalonians 4:13-17; Philippians 3:20, 21; 1 Corinthians 15:51-55). But he is equally assuring that death does not separate the Christian from Jesus Christ (Philippians 1:23; 2 Timothy 4:6). While there are many unanswered questions about what happens at death, his teachings do not contradict themselves. At death, the Christian is "with Christ." At the second coming, Paul affirms, Christians will receive a new and imperishable body.

In Philippians 1:25, Paul states his confidence that he will remain on this earth for a while longer. Such confidence is a paradox given the wrestling with life and death he describes in Philippians 1:20-24. Furthermore, in Philippians 2:17, he may be alluding to the possibility of martyrdom. And in Philippians 1:27, he says, "Whatever happens [that is, whether I live or die], conduct yourselves in a manner worthy of the gospel of Christ." How can he say, then, "I know that I will remain, and I will continue with all of you" (Philippians 1:25)? It must be remembered that the struggle of living or dying that Paul describes was not his choice to make. It was made for him. He faces the reality of death as one who, at least at one point, believed it to be imminent. Such an experience gave cause for reflection on his own life and contribution. In that reflection, he realized the pressure and could say, if the experience occurred again, "I eagerly expect and hope that I will in no way be ashamed" (Philippians 1:20). The struggle he describes was real; the choice was out of his hands. But now, by what means cannot be said, he has knowledge that the decision of life or death has been made, and he understands it to be life. This decision will mean progress and joy for the Philippians.

Admonitions Repeated (1:27-30)

Paul closes this first series of admonitions by restating the same basic ones as he began in Philippians 1:9-11. There, he focused on right thinking ("discern what is best") and then right actions ("be pure and blameless"). Here, he reverses that pattern and focuses first of all on right actions. The word here translated "conduct yourselves" literally means to live as a good citizen. One might wonder whether Paul has his own Roman citizenship partially in mind. As noted earlier, it was because of his citizenship that he was taken to Rome in the first place. God had used that circumstance for His own purpose. Therefore, Paul might reason, it pays to be a good citizen.

Nonetheless, Paul certainly has more in mind than that. Their citizenship is to be "in a manner worthy of the gospel of Christ" (Philippians 1:27). He will remind them later that "our citizenship is in heaven" (Philippians 3:20). If it is advantageous for persons to be good citizens of an earthly kingdom, if God can use that to His own glory and to the benefit of those citizens, how much more important is it to be good citizens of the spiritual kingdom?

Paul then turns to the attitudes of the mind with several descriptive phrases: "stand firm," "contending ... for the faith," and "without being frightened" (Philippians 1:27, 28). In the face of opposition and possible persecution, if they only stand in one spirit, acting as one person, not demonstrating inordinate fear, then they will succeed in their task. It is possible for them, with newfound freedom in Christ Jesus, to be not of "one spirit" (i.e., human spirit and probably not Holy Spirit here). But if they "discern what is best" (Philippians 1:10), they will understand the need to be of one spirit.

Though they will be victorious by right thinking and right acting, they will not escape suffering. One can only reflect, again, on the contrast of Paul's observation here and the false teaching of the success-oriented messages today. Their suffering does not prove an uncaring or absent God. Rather, it proves that God is in control all the more since He can still effect His will and their victory, even through suffering. Jesus, Paul, and the Philippians all experienced suffering. Yet there is a joy made possible through that suffering.

That is the great message of Philippians 1.

CHAPTER TWO

Joy in Service

Philippians 2:1-30

Second Series of Admonitions (2:1-4)

Paul continues in this second series of admonitions by first of all focusing upon how one thinks. The language he uses is concise and pointed. In chapter 1, he focused largely upon thoughts and actions with regard to those outside of the church; here, he turns to the thoughts and actions with regard to others in the church. The problem of disunity within the church becomes increasingly apparent now as he moves through this letter.

The admonition to them is to "think the same thing" (literally) or to be "like-minded" (as in the NIV). Ten times in this letter, Paul uses this word (almost half the number in all of his writings). It is the same word as in Philippians 1:7 ("It is right for me *to feel* this way about all of you"). It is a word that involves both thought and emotion, both head and heart. Paul is not saying that all must hold exactly the same thoughts or opinions on every issue that they might encounter either in their common life together or in the relationships to the world. Such an expectation would not contribute to the unity and harmony he wishes for them, but rather detract from them. What he does mean by this admonition is that they are to strive for a unity with head and heart; they are to have a disposition of will that works toward a unity of purpose and understanding. Rather than occasioning some sort of mechanical and wooden uniformity, this word describes a circumstance where there could be differences of opinion, but there would still be a unity of mind and spirit.

Paul expands the meaning of this admonition by adding phrases that further define his meaning. One is "having the same love" (Philippians 2:2). Since they have all been incorporated into the body by one Spirit, and since love is one of the products of that Spirit they all possess, it follows, therefore, that they have the same love. He means, of course, a love for one another. If there is the kind of love present that is produced by the Spirit, there will be unity. Furthermore, they are to be "one in spirit and purpose" (Philippians 2:2). He repeats the same word he used in the initial admonition, adding to it even more explicitly the idea of unity in intellect and emotion.

The next admonition, at least by force if not by grammar, focuses upon actions. "Do nothing out of selfish ambition or vain conceit.... look not only to your own interests, but also to the interests of others" (Philippians 2:3, 4). It follows that, if they are "like-minded," they will act in ways consistent with that thought. Paul has already referred to this "self-ambition" as characteristic of some of the preachers in Rome (Philippians 1:17). There, the gospel message was strong enough—it had enough integrity of its own—to be effective with those outside the church in spite of this unworthy motive. But as this characteristic impacts the life of the church, it simply is disastrous. In addition to breaking the unity of the church, it leads to "vain conceit" (literally, "empty glory"). The two ideas here are in contrast to the ways that Paul uses them elsewhere in the letter. Several times, he mentions "glory," usually as an attribute of God (Philippians 1:11; 2:11; 4:19, 20). Once, he uses it with regard to Jesus' resurrection (Philippians 3:21). Therefore, those who exercise selfish ambition divert a "glory" that belongs to God and to His mighty work in Jesus. Furthermore, it is described as an "empty" glory. In contrast to this kind of emptiness, Paul describes in the next section the "emptying" of Jesus (Philippians 2:5-11), who divested himself of His rights to draw attention to God. It is not, then, the empty glory that comes from self-ambition that is to be sought, but rather the emptying of rights that leads to a focus on God's glory.

One further dimension of this section is the meaning of *glory*. It comes from a root word that means appearance. It came to mean, then, something very akin to character. Thus, "the Word became flesh and made his dwelling among us. We have seen his glory [character], the glory [character] of the One and Only, who came from the Father" (John 1:14). The person who acts from selfish ambition, then, ends up with an empty character; that person is ambitious without any reason to be so, given the nature of his/her character.

The converse of this vain characteristic is to "consider others better than yourselves" and to "look not only to your own interests, but also to the interests of others" (Philippians 2:3, 4). This characteristic was not considered a virtue in the ancient world of Paul. In fact, the noun form is not found outside the New Testament. As an adjective, it describes, in quite negative terms, the character of a slave. It is Christianity, through the example of Jesus, that made this a virtue. In this current age of narcissism, the church needs to rediscover this truth.

The Example of Being in Christ Jesus (2:5-11)

Paul here gives the perfect example of the previous admonition; it is Jesus himself. He is the example of acting with regard to the welfare of others and in disregard to His own legitimate rights. It is the consensus of scholarship that this passage represents one of the most magnificent and poetic descriptions of Jesus in all of the Bible. Many believe it to be a hymn sung by the early church and either quoted by Paul or actually written by him. Beyond these two positions, there is a very little agreement concerning anything else about the hymn. Issues such as the original author (whether Paul composed it or is quoting a well-known hymn), the exact structure or versification, and the purpose for which it appears here in the text have all generated much writing. Those who want to study these issues in greater detail than this present work is able to do should look at the lengthy book on the subject by Ralph P. Martin, *Carmen Christi: Philippians 2:5-11 in Recent Interpretation and in the Setting of Early Christian Worship* (Grand Rapids: Eerdmans, 1983).

While many of the technical questions go beyond the scope of this study, there are some important considerations to study before the individual verses are examined. First, whether Paul originally composed the hymn or not does not affect its place in Scripture. He was certainly capable of such rhetorical ability; whether he is quoting a contemporary hymn or composing one anew may ultimately be impossible to answer. Second, the precise structure of the hymn may be equally impossible to determine, though such an inability need not prevent its understanding. A rather cursory review of articles and books on this passage reveals at least eight variations of structure suggested.

Third, some attempt to determine the overall purpose of the hymn is necessary since it affects the understanding of the parts. To a great extent, the answer to this question is tied to the translation of Philippians 2:5. The complexity of this problem is obscured by the English translation. A rough and literal translation of the verse is as follows: "This think in [or "among"] you which also in Christ Jesus." As is apparent here, the verb of the second clause of this verse is missing and must be supplied by the reader. Unfortunately, there is no great agreement as to what that verb should be. The usual one is *was,* either explicit or implied. Thus the New International Version, "Your attitude should be the same as that of Christ Jesus." The New American Standard Bible translates it, "Have this attitude in yourselves which was also in Christ Jesus." The King James has, "Let this mind be in you, which was also in Christ Jesus." And Phillips translates, "Let Christ himself be your example as to what your attitude should be." But what if *was* or some synonymous translation is not correct? What if another verb is meant to be implied by Paul?

Another possible verb to supply is the one in the first clause, *think.* Thus, "Think [or "Have this mind"] in [or "among"] yourselves, which mind [or "thinking"—the verb supplied] you have [as ones who are] in Christ Jesus." It is in this way that the Revised Standard Version takes it: "Have this mind among yourselves which is yours in Christ Jesus."

The difference in these two translations has significance for the understanding of the hymn. If the first is what Paul intended (i.e., "Your attitude should be the same as that of Christ Jesus"), then the hymn is seen as a call to imitate the humility of Jesus described in the hymn. If, on the other hand, the second understanding is what Paul intended (i.e., "Have this mind among yourselves which is yours in Christ Jesus"), then the call is not primarily to imitate Jesus, but rather to "think" in a way that is consistent by virtue of being "in Christ." It is this latter view that is taken here.

In spite of these technical difficulties, some attempt must be made to get at the meaning. Perhaps the most convenient way is to consider the main verbs of the hymn. There are three actions that Jesus took:

1. He *did not consider* equality with God something to be grasped (Philippians 2:6).
2. He *made himself nothing* (Philippians 2:7).
3. He *humbled himself* (Philippians 2:8).

There are two actions that God took:

1. He *exalted him to the highest place* (Philippians 2:9).
2. He *gave him the name that is above every name* (Philippians 2:9).

Each of the three actions of Jesus described here, as well as other affirmations about Him in this passage, centers around the very heart of the nature of Jesus—both His relationship to God the Father and His human-divine character. Wars have been fought and thousands have died because of the difficulty of defining these dimensions of the person of Jesus. The mistake is not the attempt to understand; the mistake is imposing upon others a human, therefore possibly fallible, understanding. Each of these actions is now considered in turn.

He Did Not Consider ...

First, it is said of Jesus that He "did not consider equality with God something to be grasped" (Philippians 2:6). The difficulties of understanding this passage are immense. Who can be equal with God? Satan tried to be "like the Most High" and was cast away from His presence (Isaiah 14:13-15). The serpent's temptation to Eve was to eat of the fruit and "be like God" (Genesis 3:5). If being "like God," that is, equal to God, is such a horrendous evil, how can it be said that Jesus was "equal with God"? Furthermore, how is it that this equality was not "something to be grasped"? Thousands of words have been written in answer to these questions.

The Greek verb for this first action of Jesus is *hegesato,* meaning think, consider, or regard. That which He "did not consider" was a double object: (1) equality with God, and (2) something to be grasped. He did this "considering" while "in [the] very nature [of] God." The understanding of any one of these parts of this affirmation affects the understanding of the rest of the parts.

What does Paul mean by saying that Jesus was in the "very nature [of] God"? (The NIV note has "*form* of God," which might be more accurate for the word *morphe*). There are at least three possibilities:

1. The essence or basic nature of a thing. This is one of the primary uses in ancient Greek philosophy and is so used by both Plato and Aristotle. If this is the meaning in this text, then Paul is saying that Jesus in His pre-existent state shared the same essence as God. What God was, Jesus was before He became flesh.

2. The outward form or appearance of a thing. This meaning of the word is synonymous with *image (eikon)* and is found in Colossians 1:15: "He is the image *[eikon]* of the invisible God." This meaning of the word occasions two possible understandings

33

of the phrase. Paul could mean that Jesus in His earthly existence was the image, "the form," of God perceived by the physical senses. It was that form that He was willing to forsake for the form or image of a servant. If *form* and *image* are synonymous terms, as they seem to be in the Septuagint, then Paul could be drawing an analogy between Adam, made in the *image* of God (Genesis 1:26), but then trying to be equal with God, over against Jesus (the second Adam—Romans 5:12ff), in the "form" of God, but then not wanting to gain or maintain that equality with God.

3. Both the inward nature and the outward form. The Jewish understanding of the nature of man did not compartmentalize mankind as did the Greek understanding. There was not the separation of form and substance; in Jewish thought, the real essence of anything included its appearance. A frequent description of this characteristic in the New Testament is the word *glory* (*doxa; see* the discussion of this word in another context above). Paul spoke of the "glory *[doxa]* of Christ, who is the image *[eikon]* of God" (2 Corinthians 4:4). In this same vein, Paul wrote that "we, who with unveiled faces all reflect the Lord's glory *[doxa]*, are being transformed into his likeness *[eikon]* with ever-increasing glory *[doxa]*" (2 Corinthians 3:18; see also 1 Corinthians 15:49 and Philippians 3:21). These words, *glory (doxa), image (eikon), and form* or *nature (morphe),* are used rather interchangeably and refer to an essential quality of Jesus that existed even before His earthly existence. Jesus, in His poignant upper-room prayer to God, spoke of "the glory *[doxa]* I had with you before the world began" (John 17:5).

While the meaning of *very nature (form) [of] God* is hard to understand (used only here and in Philippians 2:7 in all the New Testament), this third understanding seems to fit the context of the passage best. Jesus was the very character and nature of God in His pre-existent state.

The next phrase to be considered is *equality with God.* The language of the text implies that the phrase is meant to be parallel to the phrase that precedes it, namely, *the very nature [of] God.* In this pre-existent state, Christ is said to be equal with God. This affirmation is contingent upon understanding the double object, the second of which is discussed in the next paragraph.

The phrase *something to be grasped (harpagmon)* (Philippians 2:6) has been described as one of the "most thorny" problems in all of the New Testament. There are three basic understandings:

1. Something not possessed, but desirable to own, even if by robbery. Thus, Adam tried to possess that which was not his to own (Genesis 3:5). Satan, too, tried to rob God of what was uniquely His own (Isaiah 14:12, 13). With this meaning of the word, Jesus was not equal with God and did not consider trying to grab this equality. It is in this sense that the New English Bible takes the phrase: "He did not think to snatch at equality with God." This understanding, however, does not correspond with previous conclusions made above about the other phrases in this passage.

2. Something possessed that could be held on to as one's very right to maintain (thus, the New International and Revised Standard translations). This understanding is consistent with the interpretations of the other phrases of this passage. Jesus was equal to God in His pre-existent state; He was in the very form of God. But He did not consider this state something to maintain a hold on; He was willing to let it go for a higher purpose. While this understanding is consistent with the context, there may be a better one yet.

3. The right of possessing by good fortune. The slight variation between this and the previous understanding is that the focus here is upon the *act* of holding on to or obtaining what was rightfully one's own, whether presently possessed or not. Plutarch says Alexander the Great had Asia as his own; he could do with this land what he wanted. It was a part of the spoils of war. Yet he refused to engage in this act of taking what was his (the same word is used of him: *Alexander* 1:8). Paul was a Pharisee by accident of birth, and as such had certain privileges; he was willing to refrain from the act of claiming those privileges, however. "I consider [them] as loss," he could write (Philippians 3:7). The point is not that Jesus refused to seize what He did not possess. It is not that He merely refused to hold on to what was rightfully His and He already possessed. Rather, He refused to engage in the *act* of obtaining or holding on to any status. It was not the nature of God, it was not equality with God to do so. Rather, the nature of God was to do just the opposite—to give up what was rightfully His.

In summary, Jesus Christ demonstrated the inward nature and outward form of God himself; He did this in His pre-existent state. Having the "form of God" made Him equal with God. Equality with God meant that He forsook the very act of holding on to what was rightfully His own. And so, Philippians 2:6 might better be translated: "Who, because He was existing in the very nature of God, did not consider this equality with God the act of getting what was His, but rather in giving up that which was His."

He Made Himself Nothing ...

There are two immediate questions concerning this phrase: First, what does the verb *made himself nothing* (or *emptied himself)* mean? Second, how much of the immediate passage goes with this phrase?

The verb in this perplexing verse has given its name to a theory about the incarnation of Jesus Christ called the "kenotic" theory. (The verb is *kenoun* and is translated in most older versions as "emptied himself." Thus, the kenotic theory of the incarnation is the theory of Jesus' "emptying" himself.) While there are several variations of the basic theory, the proponents of this view generally try to answer the question, of what did Jesus "empty" himself? The usual answers are that He emptied himself of, or gave up, one of the following:

1. Equality with God (Philippians 2:6).
2. The very nature (form) of God (Philippians 2:6).
3. The attributes of God, namely omnipotence, omniscience, and omnipresence.
4. Possession of the glory and prerogatives of God.

While each of these suggestions presents intriguing answers and each has its proponents, the text itself does not explicitly include any one of them as the clear and exclusive meaning. It is more helpful to consider how the phrase fits into the movement of the hymn. In typical poetic form for much of ancient poetry, Paul is here stating in a positive form what he had just affirmed in a negative form. The movement is from He "did *not* consider ..." but rather He "made himself nothing" (literally, "poured himself out").

This movement is possible especially when the object of the verb here does not go beyond the primary thrust of the text itself. There is no reason, from the text, to impose any of the suggested meanings above. The object of the verb is *himself*. The positive form of not considering equality, the act of getting what was rightfully His, is this very act—pouring himself out in behalf of mankind. The idea here is not that He divested himself of some quality or attribute of Deity (at least from this text), but rather that He gave himself completely to His mission. The same idea is stated in 2 Corinthians 8:9: "For you know the grace of our Lord Jesus Christ, that though he was rich, yet for your sakes he became poor, so that you through his poverty might become rich" (see also Ephesians 1:23; 4:10).

The second question is how much of the immediate passage goes with this phrase. By now, it should not be surprising that there is little agreement about the answer. Most modern English translations of this part of the text have been influenced by the versification of the text (which, of course, was not the way that Paul wrote and which may be subject to error). Therefore, they take two phrases as modifying the verb, "made himself nothing," namely, (1) "taking the very nature of a servant," and (2) "being made in human likeness." The following phrase, "and being found in appearance as a man" is really seen as modifying the next clause, "he humbled himself." The grammatical structure of this passage does allow for such division. There are, however, other possibilities. Following are at least three possible divisions of this passage:

	A	B

1.	But [He] made himself nothing
	taking the very nature of a
	   servant
	being made in human likeness
		He humbled himself
		being found in
		   appearance as a man
		[becoming] obedient to
		   death

2.	But [He] made himself nothing
	taking the very nature of a
	   servant
	being made in human likeness
	and being found in appearance
	   as a man
		He humbled himself
		[becoming] obedient to
		   death

3.	But [He] made himself nothing
	taking the very nature of a
	   servant
		He humbled himself
		being made in human
		   likeness
		being found in
		   appearance as a man
		[becoming] obedient to
		   death

While any degree of certainty escapes careful study here, the third of these options seems to fit the overall structure of the text. The primary reason is not so clear in any English translation, but does appear in the Greek. A diagram of a literalistic translation of verses 6-8 may clarify the point:

Who
   in the form of God existing
      did not consider something to be grasped [as]
         equality with God
            but
      poured out himself
         taking the form of a slave

   in human likeness becoming
         and being found in appearance as a man
      humbled himself
         becoming obedient unto death
            even death on a cross.

As is evident from this rather crude diagram, *in the form of God* is parallel with *in human likeness*. Although this point is based upon technicalities, the understanding of the text is influenced by the conclusions about the matter. Having concluded that the phrase *taking the very nature of a servant* alone modifies the verb phrase *made himself nothing,* a brief comment needs to be made about it.

The word *nature* here ("nature of a servant") is the same one as earlier ("nature of God"; Philippians 2:6), namely, *morphe.* There, *nature* means both inward nature and outward form. That meaning fits here as well. The image of the Messiah as servant is well-known in the Old Testament. In Isaiah, the Messiah was to come in the form of a servant; He "poured out his life unto death" (Isaiah 53:12); finally, "He will be raised and lifted up and highly exalted" (Isaiah 52:13). The parallels here in Isaiah are apparent with this Philippian passage. Furthermore, Jesus demonstrated this servanthood spirit throughout His ministry, both in the upper room with towel and basin, and with frequent teachings. (See John 13:1-17; 15:20; Matthew 10:24; Luke 6:40; 22:27.)

The third action Jesus did was an act of humbling himself (Philippians 2:8). As explained above, there appear to be three ways in which He humbled himself, although most English translations put some of these modifiers with other phrases. First of all, He was "made in human likeness" (Philippians 2:7; literally, "in the likeness of man was born"). The verbal form translated "made" or "born" is in contrast to the parallel phrase of Philippians 2:6, "Being in very nature God." There, the emphasis was that He always had existed in the very nature of God. Here the emphasis is that His likeness to human beings did have a beginning; thus, the word is frequently translated as "born." The word *likeness* sometimes merely means similar to, without duplicating the reality (e.g. Revelation 9:7); but it is sometimes used to mean the essence of that with which it is compared (e.g., Romans 5:14; 6:5). It is used interchangeably throughout the Greek Old Testament with *nature (morphe), image (eikon),* and *appearance (schema).* The question, of course, is which of the possible meanings applies here? Did Jesus merely *seem* to be in human form, or was His "human likeness" a true representation of His real essence? The question, of course, is at the very heart of who Jesus was. It cannot be concluded here that Paul is trying to say that Jesus was not completely human by his use of the word *likeness.* He has made it clear in other places that Jesus *was* human (e.g. Romans 8:3ff; Galatians 4:4; Colossians 1:22; see also Hebrews 4:14—5:8), and possible meanings of this word do not contradict those assertions or ones made elsewhere in this letter. Furthermore, when the literary structure is taken into consideration, the focus is on His humility rather than an exhaustive definition of His nature. He demonstrated a humility "being in very nature God"; He also exhibited humility "being made in human likeness."

A second way in which Jesus humbled himself was that He was "found in appearance as a man" (Philippians 2:8). This is the third description focusing upon the humanity of Jesus: "the very nature of a servant" (Philippians 2:7), "in human likeness" (Philippians 2:7), and "appearance as a man" (Philippians 2:8). This third description reiterates the thrust of the other two. Jesus Christ was fully man; in this status, He demonstrated the same kind of humility that He had in His preincarnate state. The word *appearance (schema)* generally refers to what is perceptible by the senses. It was that human dimension of Jesus that was affirmed by the apostles: "That . . . which we have heard, which we have seen with our eyes, which we have looked at and our hands have touched—this we proclaim concerning the Word of life" (1 John 1:1).

The third and final way in which Jesus demonstrated humility was when He "became obedient unto death—even death on a cross" (Philippians 2:8). One of the obvious questions here is to whom or what was He obedient? It seems obvious that He was obedient to God; His obedience was ultimately to His Heavenly Father. Since it was an obedience "to death" or "even as far as death," it could be argued that, in a sense, He even became obedient to the principalities and powers of this world. (See the later discussion in this volume on Colossians 2:9; see also Colossians 2:15; Ephesians 6:12.) Death was the final power of these "elemental spirits." His victory over them was His humility and obedience—even in face of their greatest power. It was in that humility and obedience, however, where He was victorious, for by submitting to death, their greatest weapon, and conquering it, He made this great power of theirs of no effect. (See Matthew 12:29; Luke 10:18; Romans 16:20.) There is yet another sense in which He was obedient to the people. Jesus said that He had come "to seek and to save what was lost" (Luke 19:10). Jesus was willing to submit himself for the benefit of others; He did that even to the point of death, and death on a cross at that.

To sum up this part of the hymn, let us say that the purpose is to exhort the Philippian Christians to be and to act out who and what they are by virtue of being in Jesus. Because He is a part of their lives, they are able to demonstrate characteristics of humility that He demonstrated. There are actions Jesus did in demonstrating this humility: He (1) "did not consider equality with God something to be grasped," (2) "made himself nothing," and (3) "humbled himself." There are five descriptions of Jesus imbedded in this part of the hymn: (1) "being in very nature God," (2) "taking the very nature of a servant," (3) "being made in human likeness," (4) "[being] found in appearance as a man," and (5) "became obedient to death."

God Exalted Him to the Highest Place ...

The whole tense of this magnificent passage noticeably changes at Philippians 2:9. For one thing, "God" is now the subject, the actor, rather than an implicit Jesus. Before, it was Jesus who acted and whose nature was described; now it is God who responds to that same Jesus. Furthermore, the previous section focused upon Jesus' humiliation; this section focuses upon His exaltation by God.

The theme of the exaltation of the Messiah is a common one in the Bible. Isaiah described the suffering servant who would "be raised and lifted up and highly exalted" (Isaiah 52:13). Daniel pictured "one like a son of man" who was "given authority, glory and sovereign power; all peoples, nations and men of every language worshiped him" (Daniel 7:13, 14). This theme became a characteristic part of the preaching of the early church. On the day of Pentecost, Peter said of Jesus, "Exalted to the right hand of God, he has received from the Father the promised Holy Spirit and has poured out what you now see and hear" (Acts 2:33). Paul wrote the Ephesians that Jesus was "seated . . . at his right hand in the heavenly realms, far above all rule and authority, power and dominion, and every title that can be given, not only in the present age but also in the one to come. And God placed all things under his feet and appointed him to head over everything . . ." (Ephesians 1:20-22). The writer of Hebrews explained that "we see Jesus, who was made a little lower than the angels, now crowned with glory and honor because he suffered death, so that by the grace of God he might taste death for everyone" (Hebrews 2:9; see also Acts 3:13; 5:31; Ephesians 4:8-10; Hebrews 1:3, 13; 4:14; 7:26; 12:2; 1 Peter 1:10-11; 3:22).

The reason for His exaltation may not be quite so apparent as is its place in apostolic preaching. The New International translation begins with *therefore,* which might suggest a cause-effect relationship—because of Jesus' humility and obedience, He was rewarded by God with this exaltation. However, the word here translated "therefore" *(dio)* does not usually demonstrate cause and effect (as does *therefore* in Romans 12:1). The word might better be translated here "through which" (corresponding to its etymological meaning), that is, through which events (His actions and His status) God exalted Him. There is a sense in which this part of the hymn is just the obverse of the first part. Humility, "pouring out" himself—these are characteristics of the very nature of God. The exaltation is also part of His character. He is exalted not just *because* of His obedience, but, moreover, *through* His humility and self-giving. The act of self-giving is the place of

41

exaltation. That is the whole anomaly of God's kingdom; it is all askew. There is strength in weakness (1 Corinthians 1:25); there is wisdom in "foolishness" (1 Corinthians 1:20ff); the last shall be first (Mark 10:31); the servant shall be master (John 13). And here, the one who poured himself out on behalf of His creation will be exalted above it. The ascension of Jesus is an important doctrine of Christian faith and is often implied along with the resurrection (e.g., 1 Peter 3:18ff). The exaltation is not to be seen as different from His pre-existent state; rather, the focus is upon the ratification of God's order for His world. In spite of all of the forces of evil culminating in the cross, God's order holds true.

He Gave Him the Name That Is Above Every Name

The matter of His exaltation is restated in Philippians 2:9b-11 in the bestowal of a "name that is above every name." Some may suppose that the reading of Philippians 2:10, "at the name of Jesus," may indicate that the superior name spoken of here is *Jesus*. The text means, however, the name that belongs to Jesus, that is possessed by Jesus. It seems from Philippians 2:11 that this name is *Lord,* though some hold that *Lord* is not a name but a title, and the name is not yet revealed. Since a name was seen as indicative of its bearer's character, however, *Lord* seems to fit here. The Psalmist wrote of this event: "The Lord says to my Lord: 'Sit at my right hand until I make your enemies a footstool for your feet'" (Psalm 110:1). One of the earliest confessions of the church was the simple one, "Jesus is Lord" (Romans 10:9; Acts 2:36; see also Matthew 28:18; Ephesians 1:20, 21).

The grand consequence of Jesus' status and work is for the purpose that "every knee should bow" and "every tongue confess that Jesus Christ is Lord." In Isaiah 45:22 and 23, the language of this passage is echoed:

> Turn to me and be saved, all you ends of the earth; for I am God, and there is no other. By myself I have sworn, my mouth has uttered in all integrity a word that will not be revoked: Before me every knee will bow; by me every tongue will swear.

That Jesus becomes the focus of such worship is yet more proof that He is seen as equal with God. This praise and recognition will be universal, and is poetically described as "in heaven and on earth and under the earth" (Philippians 2:10).

A concluding word concerning this magnificent passage seems appropriate. If the point of this passage is to illustrate the previous admonitions (be of one mind, and act in humility toward others), it may seem a bit strange to find one of the most beautiful Christological statements in all of Scripture. It does not appear that the point of this passage is to correct a misunderstanding about the nature or work of Jesus. Their Christology is apparently all right. Neither is the point of the passage to correct any immoral behavior. Rather, the point is that they are not acting (or thinking) with proper humility; this deficiency, as with all others, is ultimately connected to theology, in Paul's mind. If they will only remember what kind of people they are in Christ Jesus, if they remember that they are *His* kind of people, then and only then can they follow these lofty admonitions. They cannot be of one mind or act in humility toward one another because of their own righteousness; it is only because of who *He* was and because they are *in Him* that makes it possible. "Thanks be to God for his indescribable gift" (2 Corinthians 9:15).

Admonitions Repeated (2:12-18)

Paul now returns to the restatement of admonitions made early in this chapter, focusing again upon both actions and thinking. The first restated admonition is one of action: "Work out your salvation with fear and trembling" (Philippians 2:12). This command must not be taken out of its context. Paul is not reverting to a theology of works here. He earlier exhorted them to be "likeminded" and to look "to the interests of others" (Philippians 2:2-4). He then explained that they had this power because they were in Christ Jesus and because of who He was. Therefore, it is the natural working out of the nature of Jesus to achieve this "salvation." There are times when the word means "wholeness" or "health" (Mark 5:34; Acts 4:9), and this meaning seems to be implied here. He addresses the entire church (the command is plural and not directed to individuals). They are to be and to act in ways consistent with their motives as formed in, and demonstrated by, Jesus Christ.

They are to do this good work whether Paul is absent or present, "not only in my presence, but now much more in my absence" (Philippians 2:12). The possibility of his absence from them seems of great concern to Paul. Earlier, he said, "Whether I come and see you or only hear about you in my absence," he wanted to hear of their faithfulness and harmony (Philippians 1:27). Here he says the same; they are to be quite serious about this work, "with fear and trembling," as he puts it. He is not really pessimistic about this prospect of unity, however. Because they have always obeyed his teachings previously, he believes they will continue to do so (Philippians 2:12).

A second restated admonition to them is that they are to "do everything without complaining or arguing" (Philippians 2:14). These negative traits characterized God's people in the wilderness after the Exodus; they did not demonstrate that character of the Rock (viz., Jesus) who guided them (1 Corinthians 10:4). They did not bring joy to Moses because of this dissension. (See Moses' speech in Deuteronomy 31:24ff.) Paul, however, is more optimistic; they "shine like stars in the universe," they are cause for his boasting, they make his labors worthwhile (Philippians 2:15-17).

He ends this restatement of the admonitions with one that focuses upon how they think: "Be glad and rejoice with me" (Philippians 2:18). This letter, as has been noted, is the epistle of joy. The burdens that they face and the uncertainty of his own future do not prevent the Philippians from the experience of a real joy or from sharing that joy with Paul. Once again, he affirms that real joy is not dependent upon circumstances from without, but rather upon the nature within the individual. It is this assurance that leads Paul to make this admonition to rejoice.

Example of Timothy and Epaphroditus (2:19-30)

There are no two persons any more representative of these principles (i.e., being like-minded, of one spirit, acting toward others with humility, and working out salvation without complaining) than Timothy and Epaphroditus. Paul now turns to them in the closing part of this chapter. Both of them illustrate in human terms what it means to carry out the theme of the hymn (Philippians 2:5-11).

Timothy's life is not too well-known; what is known comes primarily from Acts 16—18 and 1 Corinthians 4:17; 16:10, 11. He is also mentioned in Paul's company in Colossians, Philemon, 2 Corinthians, Romans, and Acts 20. In Paul's mind, he was unique. He says of him, "I have no one else like him" (Philippians 2:20). The word used in this description is literally "of equal spirit" *(isopsychon)*. What Timothy does when he comes to them is what Paul would do. The most outstanding characteristic of

Timothy mentioned at this point is that he does not look out for his own interests but rather is concerned about their welfare (Philippians 2:20). That characteristic, of course, was the very point Paul exhorted earlier in this chapter. Paul does not reveal just how Timothy illustrated this trait. What is known about him, however, is consistent with it. Timothy first met Paul in Lystra during the *(Acts 16)* second missionary journey. He was already a believer and wanted to accompany Paul. He had not been circumcised, however, as the son of a Jewish mother and Gentile father. He and Paul agreed that he should be so as not to present unnecessary barriers to their preaching of the gospel. From the very first, then, Timothy demonstrates a willingness to forego his own rights in consideration for others. (It should be noted that Paul did not insist that Titus be circumcised lest the practice become equated with the gospel; see Galatians 2:3.) And so Timothy plans to go to visit the Philippians to see how they are and to bring Paul news about them. As he does so, they will have a servant who demonstrates the very theme of this chapter.

Although only slightly acquainted with Timothy, the Philippians knew Epaphroditus well. He was their minister whom they had sent to help Paul in his need in prison. He had brought along the latest gift from them to Paul. Nothing is known of Epaphroditus beyond this letter. He probably came from a pagan family; his name comes from the goddess Aphrodite (Epaphroditus should not be confused with the "Epaphras" of Colossians and Philemon). Paul has the highest respect for him. He, too, demonstrates quite effectively the theme of service found in this chapter. To Paul, he is a "brother, fellow worker and fellow soldier" who has helped him at a critical time (Philippians 2:25). This service almost cost him his life (Philippians 2:27, 30), although how is not known. He is their minister; the word used to describe him thus is an unusual one *(leitourgos),* meaning one who performs a sacred service. He was their minister to Paul and had performed a sacred service by attending to his physical needs. Once again, Paul does not recognize the sacred-secular dichotomy that becomes so characteristic of the ministry of the church later. He had been their messenger to Paul; he now becomes Paul's messenger to them as the carrier for this very letter. He, like Timothy, is to be received and listened to; they both demonstrate the joy of service with the mind of Christ.

CHAPTER THREE

Joy in Persevering Faith

Philippians 3:1-21

As noted in the Introduction, there are many questions about whether or not this chapter really fits in this letter. The problems that lead to this conclusion are several.

1. The tone is more harsh than the rest of the letter.
2. It sounds (on the surface) as if Paul is drawing to a conclusion (*"Finally,* my brothers . . .").
3. The tone in 4:10 becomes rather irenic again.
4. Some translate the word *rejoice* (NIV, Philippians 3:1) as "farewell," which is a possible rendering of *chairete.*

These objections to the place of Philippians 3:2—4:9 in the letter are not ultimately convincing, however. For one thing, while it is true that the tone of the letter changes, it does not always follow that there is no unity. In other letters, Paul's topics are numerous and sometimes abruptly introduced (e.g. Romans 12; Galatians 5:13; Ephesians 4:25). Each of the four chapters of this letter has the word *joy* or *rejoice* early in the chapter (Philippians 1:4; 2:2; 3:1; 4:1). Here in chapter 3, Paul begins the third series of admonitions: "Rejoice in the Lord" (Philippians 3:1). In chapter 1, he described a joy that sustains in suffering. In chapter 2, he described a joy that is realized in service. Now he turns to a joy that is gained in persevering faith. He will strike yet another dimension of the "rejoicing" theme in Philippians 4:1, 4. So there is no real reason to see this shift of tone as mandating a lack of unity for this part of the letter.

Furthermore, the word translated as "finally" *(to loipon)* is not always used for conclusions, but sometimes as a transitional word (as in 1 Thessalonians 4:1, 2; 2 Thessalonians 3:1). In this sense, the word can be translated "in addition," or "and now," or "well then." Of course, many preachers are famous for saying "In conclusion" and then continuing to preach without concluding!

47

That 4:10 becomes irenic again is no ultimate problem either. As noted above, the change of tone is not absent in other of Paul's letters.

The New international Version correctly translates *chairete* as "rejoice" rather than "farewell." It is, of course, a common word in this "epistle of joy" (Philippians 1:18; 2:17, 28; 4:4, 10). There is no good reason to insist that it be taken as "farewell" here in the middle of the letter. Paul does not use this word to mean farewell at the end of a letter except perhaps in 2 Corinthians 13:11.

Third Series of Admonitions (3:1, 2)

After encouraging the Philippians to harmonious service, and drawing attention to the self-giving service of Jesus, Timothy, and Epaphroditus in chapter 2, Paul begins this third series of admonitions with the theme of the letter—"Rejoice." Though he fears that it may seem that he is too repetitive, it is not laborious for him: "It is no trouble for me to write the same things to you again" (Philippians 3:1). They need to know the breadth and depth of this joy of his. In spite of suffering abandonment, even in the face of possible execution, he can continue to say, "Rejoice." There is even some "safeguard" in such repetition of important material.

The second in this third series of admonitions begins with quite a rhetorical flourish: "Watch out for those dogs, [watch out for] those men who do evil, [watch out for] those mutilators of the flesh" (Philippians 3:2). The figure of speech here is an anaphora, that is, one in which successive clauses begin with the same word or sound. The intensity with which Paul approaches this topic is all the more apparent in this demonstration of oratorical style. The English translation could capture some of that emotion by such a translation as follows: "Consider those mutts! Consider those malevolent migrants! Consider those mutilators of the flesh!"

This word, translated "Watch out for," might also be taken as "consider" in this grammatical construction. If so, the thrust of the command would suggest that these persons are not so much a threat to the Philippian Christians as they are an example of faithless and joyless people. It does not appear that they endanger this congregation, unlike the situation described in Galatians. The point is that once faith in Jesus is substituted for by anything else, it is not possible to know the kind of joy of which Paul speaks.

Just whom Paul means by these vivid descriptions is not clear. *Dogs* is a term of disrepute; they are considered unclean and disreputable. Jesus described those who reject God's truth as "dogs," and it was a favorite Jewish epithet for Gentiles. (See 1 Samuel 17:43; 24:14; Proverbs 26:11; Isaiah 56:10, 11; and the NIV footnote at Deuteronomy 23:18). If indeed these persons are insisting upon some measure of the Jewish law or custom, as seems to be the case, Paul is turning their own word onto them—they are the real disreputable ones. They may be workers, busy with the show of religion, but it is ultimately *evil* work they do. It is not some holy sign of covenant they keep, but merely the practice of mutilation of the flesh (an obvious reference to the practice of insisting on circumcision). Their actions and attitudes are not evidences of a faith that occasions a real joy.

The Example of Paul (3:3-21)

Having given these two admonitions, Paul then follows the pattern for this letter; he now offers an example of what he means. In this instance, he is the sole case. He compares and contrasts himself first of all to the legalists (Philippians 3:3-16), then to the libertines (Philippians 3:17-21).

Contrast to the Legalists (3-16)

Real joy comes through a persevering faith. This fact is seen no more clearly than in its contrast to the legalists with whom the Philippians are acquainted. If there is any rejoicing to be done, it is "in the Lord" (Philippians 3:1). Those who are in Him are the true "circumcision" (Philippians 3:3), these "who put no confidence in the flesh." The joy of which Paul speaks does not come from, nor depend upon, outward circumstances. If that were the case, Paul would have every reason to have joy. He enumerates his own benefits from a human perspective:

1. *Circumcised on the eighth day.* Not only did Paul have the mark of the covenant, but he had received that sign on the eighth day, as prescribed by the Law and strictly observed in the tradition of the Pharisees (Genesis 17:12; Leviticus 12:3). The timing of this act had become so important that it was one of the few tasks that could legally be performed on the Sabbath (John 7:22, 23). Unlike the proselytes to Judaism who were circumcised as adult converts, Paul was a man of the covenant from his infancy.

2. *Of the people of Israel.* Once again, Paul stresses that he was not a Jewish proselyte, but rather was born a Jew.
3. *Of the tribe of Benjamin.* This tribe descended from the youngest son of Jacob (i.e., Israel) and Rachel. From this tribe came Paul's namesake, King Saul. Along with the tribe of Judah, Benjamin helped to reform the kingdom after the Exile. It was in this territory that the holy city, Jerusalem, with its mighty temple were located.
4. *A Hebrew of Hebrews.* This phrase probably means that although Paul was born outside of Palestine and lived among the Jews of the Diaspora, he had not abandoned the Hebrew dialect as many had done (Acts 6:1; 22:2, 3).
5. *In regard to the law, a Pharisee.* This characteristic is the first in the list that represents a definite choice. The Pharisees were the strictest of all of the Jewish groups. They studied and observed the oral tradition of the fathers as well as the written Law of Moses. They came under severe criticism during the ministry of Jesus, but are mentioned only here outside of the Gospels and the book of Acts. Paul was taught by one of the outstanding Pharisees of his day, Gamaliel (Acts 5:34; 9:1; 22:3).
6. *As for zeal, persecuting the church.* Not content just to study the laws and traditions, Paul demonstrated his commitment to these principles as he understood them by actively persecuting those who had strayed away from orthodox Judaism into this new Messianic sect. The persecutor of the church was to become a persecuted part of the church.
7. *As for legalistic righteousness, faultless.* Paul lists as his final characteristic of his pre-Christian days a faultless observation of all the regulations. From a human perspective, Paul had done all that could possibly be imagined; he was faultless. He never says, however, that this kind of "faultlessness" ever brought him joy. The problem was that this "faultlessness" was not an unqualified righteousness. It was rather a righteousness the parameters of which were determined by the law (Philippians 3:6) as over against that righteousness that is through faith in Jesus Christ (Philippians 3:9).

Paul expands this very point about his faith in Christ in the next section (Philippians 3:7-11). There are three significant and revealing words or phrases in the passage. The first is the title of *Christ* himself. Before Paul's conversion, the law was all consuming; now it is Jesus Christ who is his focus. In the space of a few short verses, His name punctuates the writing: "for the sake of Christ" (Philippians 3:7); "greatness of knowing Christ Jesus" (Philippians 3:8); "gain Christ" (Philippians 3:8); "found in him" (Philippians 3:9); "faith in Christ" (Philippians 3:9); "know Christ and the power of his resurrection . . ." (Philippians 3:10). Jesus Christ was Paul's goal, his impetus, his source, and his hope. Before, the focus was on principle; now, it is on a person.

The second significant word or phrase in this passage is the word *loss* (or the verb form *have lost*). "Whatever was to my profit I now consider *loss*" *(zemian)*. In fact, "Everything [has become] *loss*" compared with his relationship in Christ Jesus. Furthermore, he can say, "I have *lost* all things" for the sake of Jesus. The gain from being in Jesus Christ is so striking that all else pales to insignificance.

The third significant word is the verb *consider* (Philippians 3:7, 8). One of the important changes for Paul was his thinking, i.e., his perspective or world view of all reality. What he formerly considered of value, "I now *consider* loss"; in contrast to his knowledge of Jesus, he now "*consider[s]* everything a loss"; "all things," he says, "I now *consider* them rubbish." All of reality is seen from a totally different perspective. The joy of a persevering faith is discovering in Jesus Christ a whole new way of understanding what is valuable and real in personal experience; it is discovering that real righteousness is only found in Jesus Christ and not through personal merit.

Another dimension of this joy in persevering faith is the difference there is when one can say, "Enough. I have arrived. I have done what I must in order to be acceptable." Paul makes it clear in this next section (Philippians 3:12-16) that such a time does not occur in this lifetime. It is not exactly clear what specific practice or doctrine Paul is addressing here that is characteristic of the legalist types encountered by the Philippians. Some understand that some Jewish teachers taught that it was possible to reach a state of perfection before God by being circumcised and following all of the precepts of the law. If indeed this teaching is in the background of Paul's writing here, he is flatly denying the possibility of such perfection. While it is possible to "know Christ" and to "gain Christ" (Philippians 3:7-11), none of these actions is done exhaustively.

51

Paul can claim, then, that he has not "already obtained all this," or "already been made perfect"—that he does not consider himself "yet to have taken hold of it" (Philippians 3:12, 13). What does he mean by "all this" and by "it"? The answer to this question is not so clear. Actually, neither word is found in the Greek text. The objects of the verbs *have obtained* and *taken hold of* are missing and must be supplied by the readers. Paul could be talking about the "resurrection from the dead" (3:11), or "knowing Christ Jesus" (3:8) or "gain[ing] Christ" (Philippians 3:8) or "righteousness that comes from God and is by faith" (Philippians 3:9). There is a sense in which none of these has been fully realized by Paul in his earthly life; he strives for the completion, the "perfection" (i.e., making complete or whole) of each one of these.

Paul's vagueness of language here might very well be due to his attempt to include them all in his meaning. It is also possible that Paul is using language from these teachers who taught about an attainable perfection; "obtaining," "made perfect," and "taking hold," may have been the very language of these teachers. Paul claims that these tenets of their teaching are not characteristic of his life.

It seems ironic that in Philippians 3:12 he says that he is not "perfect" *(teteleiomai),* but then three verses later lists himself among the "mature" *(teleioi,* the same word as found in 3:12). Some resolve this puzzle by translating the second instance as "mature," which is certainly a possibility. One signifies absolute perfection while the other a relative perfection. But there is another plausible, and even more compelling, possibility. Paul is fond of using irony throughout his writing and may very well be doing so here. He has stated the principle of possible perfectionism (Philippians 3:12-14). He now applies the issue specifically to his readers. There are some there who believe they are "perfect" *(teleios).* With slight tongue in cheek, he says that all of us who *are* "perfect" *(teleios)* or "mature" (NIV) will "think about" or "be so minded" (as I have just explained previously). Some of them, however, are not like-minded, but rather "on some point ... think differently" (Philippians 3:15). The point seems to be that Paul acknowledges that some in Philippi think differently about this matter of perfectionism. He disagrees with them, and his life is a testimony of the difference of that understanding (i.e., he has not reached perfection as they have so claimed). But, in the end, God will have to deal with this difference—"that too God will make clear to you" (Philippians 3:15). The difference exists, is admitted, but left up to God to deal with. It will not become an occasion for division. The last word on the matter is this: "Only let us live up to what we have already obtained" (Philippians 3:16). In spite of our differences with regard to perfectionism, we each should live according to our own understanding of God's truth.

The implication of this passage is significant for the contemporary church. So many churches struggle with regard to just how much diversity it can allow without harming its witness and vitality. The problem is one of doctrinal purity versus visible unity. On the one hand, the stress is put upon the visible unity of the church to be realized organizationally through an ecumenical structure. On the other hand, there are those who favor a separatist movement, who feel that unity on any other basis is a shallow sham. These relegate unity to the invisible church and to spiritual relationships. Doctrinal purity is of greater value then visible unity.

Given the emphatic position of the New Testament on the unity of the church, the salient question is, "Does this unity refer to the visible or the invisible church?" It certainly would apply to the invisible church; no one can deny that. But it must also affect the life and work of the visible church as well; it is to be the means of bringing the world to belief (John 17:21). It is true that this unity cannot *create* unity; it is created by the Holy Spirit. One can, however, demonstrate this unity in the life and work of the visible church. One cannot create unity through human agency; it must, however, be kept in "the unity of the Spirit through the bond of peace" (Ephesians 4:3).

Even the command to maintain unity does not get at the heart of this doctrinal purity versus visible unity issue. Is there a word from the Lord? In an oft neglected text, there are normative directions given for this problem. The situation Timothy faced in the church is described in 2 Timothy 2:16-18.

> Avoid godless chatter, because those who indulge in it will become more and more ungodly. Their teaching will spread like gangrene. Among them are Hymenaeus and Philetus, who have wandered away from the truth. They say that the resurrection has already taken place, and they destroy the faith of some.

53

Two teachers, Hymenaeus and Philetus, were teaching false doctrine—that the resurrection was not in the future, but rather had already happened. They were "modernizing" the gospel; they were liberals "demythologizing" the message to fit Greek philosophy. Paul is clear that they are wrong—badly wrong. He had spoken out strongly against the teaching before (in 1 Timothy) and had even "handed [them] over to Satan" (1 Timothy 1:20). But they were in the church again, somehow, and teaching impure doctrine. If Paul had excommunicated them, somehow they were back in the church and with liberal theology. How was Timothy to handle this situation? Can you read Paul's instructions and step out of the cultural context for a brief time?

> Nevertheless, God's solid foundation stands firm, sealed with this inscription: "The Lord knows those who are his," and, "Everyone who confesses the name of the Lord must turn away from wickedness" (2 Timothy 2:19).

Paul first told Timothy that the matter was entirely in God's hands. No false teacher can ultimately succeed at shaking the foundation of the church. Other leaders are to know that God sees the wrong; they, therefore, are to stay away from error. They must not imitate those whose doctrine is wrong.

Then there follows one of the most remarkable statements concerning the relationship between doctrinal purity and visible unity in all of the New Testament: "In a large house there are articles not only of gold and silver, but also of wood and clay; some are for noble purposes and some for ignoble" (2 Timothy 2:20).

A revealing passage, indeed! This metaphor can only mean that in the church, one can always find truth and error. Thank goodness, God does allow error! He doesn't "zap" it every time it occurs. Perfect doctrinal purity is an ideal never realized in this human world. This does not mean indifference to doctrinal truth. On the contrary, in the next verse, Paul says: "If a man cleanses himself from the latter [i.e., what is ignoble], he will be an instrument for noble purposes" (2 Timothy 2:21). The church is to strive for true doctrine and to be alerted to the false. The strength of the church, however, is in God's hands and not in man's. So Paul says Timothy "must not quarrel; instead, he must be kind to everyone, able to teach, not resentful. Those who oppose him he must gently instruct" (2 Timothy 2:24, 25). That's how God suggests dealing with those in error. And for what purpose? Paul says, "In the hope that God will grant them repentance leading them to a knowledge of the truth" (1 Timothy 2:25). The desire to recover those in error is greater in God's mind than to separate from them. That is a point worth hearing.

Contrast to the Libertines (17-21)

In contrast to the legalists, Paul now turns to the opposite end of the spectrum and addresses the problem of the libertines. The legalists are guilty of building the walls too high around the church. The libertines are tearing all the walls down and destroying the distinctiveness of the church from the world. Those who have come out of a pagan background are having difficulty in knowing what to think or how to act amidst such diversity. To them, Paul advises, "Join with others in following my example, brothers, and take note of those who live according to the pattern we gave you" (Philippians 3:17).

At first reading, this may sound a bit self-serving. Paul says, in essence, "Do as I do." While such words certainly could reveal such an attitude, one must remember what Paul has claimed. He is not perfect; he has not arrived; he struggles for the goal. In this way, then, he can say without fear of sounding egotistical, "Join me in this journey of faith." He includes here, as well, his associates who are like-minded; they, too, are to serve as models: "Take note of those who live according to the pattern we gave you."

It may seem on the surface that the libertines, those who allowed great freedom in terms of behavior and practice, would have the greatest joy. They could do whatever they wanted in the name of religion. Yet Paul has the harshest words for them. Their actions actually proved them to be "enemies of the cross of Christ" (Philippians 3:18). His punctuated description of these people hardly needs expansion: "Their destiny is destruction, their god is their stomach, and their glory is in their shame" (Philippians 3:19). In contrast to these, it is the one with the persevering faith who will experience the joy of which he speaks. He sums it up at the end of the chapter: "We eagerly await a Savior from [Heaven], the Lord Jesus Christ, who, by the power that enables him to bring everything under his control, will transform our lowly bodies so that they will be like his glorious body" (Philippians 3:20, 21).

CHAPTER FOUR

Joy in Loyal Friends

Philippians 4:1-23

Fourth Series of Admonitions (4:1)

Paul begins this last series of admonitions with an exhortation similar to one that occurred earlier in chapter 1: "Stand firm in the Lord" (Philippians 4:1; cf. 1:27). While there are those who understand that this verse (Philippians 4:1) is a conclusion to the previous section, there is also a sense in which it begins the final part. *Therefore* ties it with what has gone before. They are citizens of Heaven and wait for Jesus' return. *Therefore,* they ought to be able to "stand firm in the Lord" in light of that hope. Moreover, the admonition is tied to what follows as well. The New International Version translates it, "That is how you should stand firm," but the Revised Standard may make the connection clearer, "Stand firm thus *[outos]* in the Lord"; the "thus in the Lord" is expanded upon in the following verses. The two ladies mentioned in this chapter are to agree with one another "in the Lord" (Philippians 4:2). The church is to rejoice "in the Lord" (Philippians 4:4). Paul himself rejoices "in the Lord" (Philippians 4:10) because they show concern for him. It is clear, then, that this verse serves as a transition from chapter 3 to chapter 4; it sums up the former and previews the latter. The verse might be paraphrased as follows: "Therefore, since you are citizens of Heaven who await the return of Jesus from there to control all things and to give new, glorified bodies, continue to stand firm in the Lord thus. . . ."

The affection Paul has for those in this church just exudes from this passage. The extent of his feelings for them becomes apparent as the descriptions of them pile up. He describes them in the following ways:

1. *Brothers.* Six other times in this short letter he addresses them by this description (Philippians 1:12, 14; 3:1, 13, 17; 4:8). Even

those who preach Christ for the wrong reason are still called by this description. All of these so called are of the same family and therefore have the same rights and status.

2. *"You whom I love"* (literally, "beloved ones"). Over and again Paul expresses his love for these Philippians (e.g., Philippians 1:8; 2:1).

3. *"You whom I . . . long for."* This word occurs only here in the New Testament. In this concluding section, Paul reiterates his desire to be with them face to face (Philippians 1:8; cf. 1:22ff).

4. *"My joy and crown."* Of course, the importance of joy has been noted throughout. The Philippians, because of their faithfulness, are Paul's joy. He also calls them here his "crown." This word does not refer to the crown worn by royalty *(diadema),* but rather the type of laurel wreath worn by the winner at the Olympic games *(stephanos).* In the previous chapter, Paul used the metaphor of a race as symbolic of his life; here he affirms that the Philippians are symbolic of his victory in that race (cf. 1 Thessalonians 2:19; 1 Peter 5:4; Revelation 4:4). Because of their hope in the return of Jesus, because of the kind of people they are, Paul can confidently exhort them to "stand firm."

Example of Euodia and Syntyche (4:2, 3)

Following the pattern demonstrated throughout this letter, Paul follows a general admonition with specific example. The way that the Philippians can "stand firm in the Lord" is for Euodia and Syntyche to "agree with each other [literally, to "think the same thing"] in the Lord." Paul had been more general earlier in this letter; they were to be "like-minded" *(to auto phronete,* Philippians 2:2), and to have "this mind" of humility, which they naturally had by virtue of being "in Christ Jesus" *(touto phroneite,* Philippians 2:5, RSV). This word, *think* or *have an attitude* or *mind (phronein)* is certainly a key idea in this letter, used at least once in each chapter. (See Philippians 1:27; 2:2, 5; 3:15, 19; 4:2, 10). As discussed earlier (see the discussion of Philippians 2:2 and following), the idea of this term is more than holding the same opinions; it includes the harmony of mind and heart and purpose. It is a mind-set that comes from being in Christ Jesus (see Philippians 2:5). Paul then tells these two to stand firm and be of a common mind "in the Lord" (Philippians 4:2). Since they are in Christ Jesus (Philippians 2:5), and since it is His "mind" that demonstrates humility and sacrifice, they, then, can have this harmony, too.

The exact identity of these women and of their problem is not too clear. (Efforts to argue that Euodia is a male, i.e., Euodias, is not at all persuasive; most modern translations rightly take both of these as women.) There have been all sorts of suggestions as to their identity. For example, "Lydia," instrumental in the Philippian church (Acts 16) may be an adjective, i.e., "the Lydian" rather than a proper name. Some have conjectured, then, that one of these may be "the Lydian" of Acts 16. There is simply no way to substantiate this guess. Others have supposed that these names may be metaphors for fighting groups within the church and not refer to specific people at all. Again, however, there is no strong support for such conjecture. The names are common enough in inscriptions from this period; there is no reason to think that they are not real people.

It may be safer to conclude that they have some leadership function in the church. Women in Macedonia had greater roles in the life of the community than in many places in the Near East, especially when compared to Jewish congregations. The first convert of record on European soil was Lydia, a woman, in whose house it appears is the meeting place of the church (Acts 16; see also Acts 17:4, 12 for other places in Macedonia where women are mentioned as having a significant place in the church). Paul praises these women for their labor in the gospel ("contended at my side in the cause of the gospel"; Philippians 4:3). The problem is not role but attitude. It is no doubt unfortunate that all that is really known of these women, who had been of great help to Paul and the gospel in Philippi, is that they quarrelled. The example they are to follow is the example of Jesus Christ himself.

Paul asks his "loyal yokefellow" to help them. As in so many disputes, the intervention of a third party may prove to be helpful. Just who this person is remains as mysterious as the identities of the two women. The suggestions are plentiful: Paul's wife, Epaphroditus, Timothy, Silas, Luke, or the husband or a brother of one of the women, to name a few. An intriguing suggestion is that the Greek word here that means yokefellow is a proper noun and that Paul is addressing a man named *Syzygus* (NIV footnote). Another option is that this "loyal yokefellow" is not a specific individual, in which case Paul may mean to include the whole congregation in this metaphor—"you, the church, my true yokefellow, help these women." The precise definition remains uncertain.

The same problem exists with regard to the identification of Clement, a fellow-worker of Paul who, along with others, now has his name in the "book of life" (Philippians 4:3). They, along with the women, had labored side by side with Paul for the sake of the gospel. The problem of identification rests only with contemporary readers; Paul and the Philippians knew well who they were. All of the persons mentioned here have their names included in the "book of life," that is, God's record of His people. It is clear that the problem here is a spat in the family, not an attack from without.

Admonitions Repeated (4:4-9)

Paul completes this cycle of admonitions-example-admonitions with a series that returns to a refocus upon how one thinks. There are actually four imperatives in this section, all of which focus upon the reform of a way of thinking.

First, he encourages them: "Rejoice in the Lord always. I will say it again: Rejoice!" (Philippians 4:4). There are many reasons for joy, and Paul has dealt with several of them in this book. Fourteen times he uses the word *rejoice* or *joy*. In chapter 1, he described a joy that triumphs even in suffering. In chapter 2, there was a joy that comes through service. In chapter 3, he discussed a joy that results from a persevering faith. Now, in chapter 4, he turns to the joy of loyal friends. It is as if he anticipates a positive response to his appeal from Euodia and Syntyche and the loyal yokefellow. He can say with great confidence, then, "Rejoice." It is significant that so many of these admonitions that focus on a way of thinking are connected to the phrase *"in the Lord."* In Philippians 3:1, they are to rejoice "in the Lord." In Philippians 4:1, they stand firm "in the Lord." In Philippians 4:2, the two ladies are to agree "in the Lord." In Philippians 4:10, Paul claims that he rejoices "in the Lord." He has talked about working for the sake of Christ, of knowing Christ, of gaining Christ, and of faith in Christ (Philippians 3:7-9). It seems clear that these all go back to the passage in which they are admonished to have the mind of unselfishness and humility which they have by virtue of being in Christ Jesus (Philippians 2:5-11). Since they are in Christ Jesus, their whole way of thinking is affected. They can now see all of life from a different perspective, a Heavenly perspective.

With this perspective, with this mind that comes from being in Christ Jesus, they can rejoice and do so "always," (or more specifically, "in all situations" *(pantote)*. As he described in the first chapter, there is even joy in suffering if one has this perspective of Jesus.

Second, he exhorts, "Let your gentleness be evident to all" (Philippians 4:5). The word translated "gentleness" *(epieikes)* is a significant term in the New Testament. It describes the characteristic of a person who does not demand his/her own rights in relationships. Aristotle contrasted this characteristic to that one that expects exact and precise judgment. This "gentleness" goes beyond strict judgment. It is used to describe Jesus, "the meekness and gentleness *(epieikes)* of Christ" (2 Corinthians 10:1). The overseers of the church should demonstrate this quality (1 Timothy 3:3). In fact, all in the church should demonstrate it (Titus 3:2). Furthermore, this characteristic, Paul tells the Philippians, should be "evident to all" (Philippians 4:5), and not exclusively to the church. The world ought to see in the life of the church the willingness to go beyond the demands of strict justice to a point of acting with a giving, considerate, gentle spirit.

No one has caught this very characteristic more poetically than William Shakespeare:

> The quality of mercy is not strain'd,
> It droppeth as the gentle rain from heaven
> Upon the place beneath. It is twice bless'd:
> It blesseth him that gives and him that takes.
> 'Tis mightiest in the mightiest: it becomes
> The throned monarch better than his crown;
> His sceptre shows the force of temporal power,
> The attribute to awe and majesty,
> Wherein doth sit the dread and fear of kings;
> But mercy is above this sceptred sway,
> It is enthroned in the hearts of kings,
> It is an attribute to God himself;
> And earthly power doth then show likest God's,
> When mercy seasons justice.
>
> Merchant of Venice, Act IV, Scene 1.

Paul includes a puzzling phrase in this admonition to exercise gentleness: "The Lord is near" (Philippians 4:5). Does he mean that the Lord's presence is close at hand; so act in this way? Or perhaps he is proclaiming that Jesus' second coming is soon to happen. It is even possible that he means that Jesus' becoming flesh, that is, coming "near" to man, is near (recent). His ambiguity could even be intentional, suggesting more than one specific meaning.

Third, Paul continues this series of exhortations by saying, "Do not be anxious about anything" (Philippians 4:6). Earlier, Paul used the same word in reference to Timothy, but in a positive sense, "I have no one else like him who takes a genuine interest in [*merimnesei;* "will be genuinely anxious for," RSV] your welfare" (Philippians 2:20). Here (Philippians 4:6), the meaning is clearly negative.

This section sounds some of the themes from Jesus' Sermon on the Mount (Matthew 5—7), and especially on this point. Jesus taught, "Do not worry *(merimnate)* about your life, what you will eat or drink . . ." (Matthew 6:25ff). One might be tempted to plug in to this Scripture any number of contemporary self-help, positive-thinking philosophies. To do so, however, ignores the context of the passage. Paul is not just whistling in the dark with regard to worry. He is not just trying to remove it as a psychological cause of a lack of progress, health, and adjustment. There are real, concrete, and specific reasons for not worrying. They are "in the Lord" (see above); "the Lord is near" (Philippians 4:5).

The specific alternative to this bothersome worrying is "by prayer and petition, with thanksgiving, present your requests to God" (Philippians 4:6). Once again, Paul strikes one of the themes from the Sermon on the Mount: "Ask and it will be given to you; seek and you will find; knock and the door will be opened to you" (Matthew 7:7). The point of Jesus' teaching here is that since God is good and capable of responding to the petitions of His people, He will do so. Not to ask is a demonstration of a lack of faith that God is really in control. The word for "anxious" *(merimnate)* literally means divided mind. For those who are "in the Lord," those who have the mind of Christ, therefore, are ones who do not have such a "divided mind." Rather, their "mind" is focused upon the God who is in control.

The result of this praying is the acquisition of "the peace of God, which transcends all understanding" (Philippians 4:7). When God's people are able to see all reality from His perspective, when they are "in the Lord" to that extent, then they can begin to respond in a similar way, a God-like way, to their world. They can "stand firm" and "agree with each other" and "rejoice in the Lord" and "not be anxious about anything." That is what God's peace does for His people.

Paul concludes this section, in which he repeats the admonitions, with quite a rhetorical flourish (Philippians 4:8, 9). In so doing, he sums up themes he has emphasized throughout the letter. He began by stating his desire for them to "abound more and more in knowledge and depth of insight . . . to discern what is best" (Philippians 1:9, 10). He wanted their *thinking* to be affected by their Christianity. He also focused upon their actions; he wanted them to be "pure and blameless" (Philippians 1:10). He now concludes with these same emphases.

The sentence, though rhetorically attractive in the Greek, is complex in English translation. A modified diagram of the sentence is as follows:

> If anything is excellent
> or [if anything is] praiseworthy
>
>   Think about such things: whatever is true
>   whatever is noble
>   whatever is right
>   whatever is pure
>   whatever is lovely
>   whatever is admirable
>   Put it into practice: whatever you have learned
>   and you have received
>   and you have heard
>   and you have seen in me
> And the God of peace will be with you.

The diagram makes obvious the focus upon thinking and acting that Paul has made in the admonitions of this letter. Again, he knows that actions follow from thoughts; how one thinks about things determines how he or she acts. He expands, then, this summary with this sentence.

It was the custom for philosophers of Paul's day to include a register of vices and virtues in their teaching. Their followers would memorize the list and concentrate upon incorporating the virtues and avoiding the vices in their daily lives. Many of the terms Paul uses here were included in some of those lists of the philosophers. It should not be thought, however, that Paul is merely copying their teaching. He frequently uses terminology common to other religious or philosophical traditions, but with new meaning (e.g., Colossians 2:9). While on the one hand, he may very well show by this list that there are some good features to this moral philosophy, he goes far beyond it as well. As pointed out above, these people are "in the Lord" (Philippians 4:1, 2, 4, 10; cf. 4:7). It is from that position that they are able so to think and act. They have this "mind of Christ" by virtue of being "in Christ" (cf. Philippians 2:5). So the whole impetus for this moral living is different from that of the moral philosophers contemporary with Paul.

This background, then, provides a basis for examining the various parts of this list as presented in the diagram above.

1. If anything is *excellent (arete)*. Both this and the conditional sentence that follows anticipate a positive response to the condition—"Yes, there is something excellent." This word was used by Plato, Aristotle, and the Stoic philosophers to refer to the main body of teaching about virtue. As over against some who argued that there was no objective or identifiable quality such as virtue, the moral philosophers contended that there was and tried to identify its extent. Plato, for example, popularized the four cardinal virtues: (1) wisdom, (2) courage, (3) moderation, and (4) justice. To this extent, then, the New Testament agrees with the moral philosophers; virtue does exist. The difference, of course, is the *source* of that virtue. For the Christian, the source is Jesus Christ; to the Greek philosopher, the source is in the human will.

2. If there is any *praise (epainos)*. In Greek philosophy, the word was often used to refer to that which was worthy of praise by men. The Biblical use of the term, however, usually focuses upon the praise of God by men (e.g., Philippians 1:11). Paul takes a typically philosophical word from Greek culture and once again gives to it a distinctively Christian meaning. The condition anticipates a positive response; so the meaning is "since there is something (or Someone) worthy of praise, then we should think and act thus." Paul sees God's character as the grounding for moral behavior.

3. Whatever is *true (alethe)*. The first of the six objects of thinking is the *true*. The word in Greek philosophy generally referred to that which was timeless as opposed to that which was

known by the senses. The Jewish understanding, however, reflects more of a concept of "faithfulness." Jesus is true because His words and His actions correspond with reality. The Greek idea of separating the physical and the spiritual, the temporal and the "true," is not part of the Biblical use of the term. The true, rather, potentially encompasses every component of human experience. Jesus discussed the truth both explicitly ("I am the way and the truth . . ."; John 14:6; "I tell you the truth, no one can enter the kingdom of God unless he is born of water and the Spirit"; John 3:5) and implicitly ("The kingdom of heaven is like . . ."; e.g., Matthew 20:1ff), and He demonstrated the truth by His actions. Paul, therefore, exhorts the Philippian Christians to think on those things that are true.

4. Whatever is *noble (semna)*. The word is used elsewhere in the New Testament only in the Pastorals to refer to a quality of the leaders of the church (1 Timothy 3:8, 11; Titus 2:2). In classical Greek, it was used as an epithet for the gods. The word is also translated "honest" (KJV), "honorable" (NASB), "reverend" (ASV footnote), and "venerable" (Ellicott). The verb form of the word means "to worship." Paul means, therefore, that they are to focus their minds on the high and noble rather than the base and tawdry.

5. Whatever is *right (dikaia)*. The word is also translated "just" or "righteous." It is largely used in the New Testament to describe God, Jesus, and men and women who were just in God's sight. (See John 17:25; Acts 3:13ff; 1 Peter 2:23, 24; 1 John 3:12; Revelation 16:5.) There is a righteousness of the law, but mankind has not attained it. "There is no one righteous, not even one" (Romans 3:10). The point here is not that one can attain the state of righteousness by merely thinking about it. Rather, being "in Christ," that is, having the "mind of Christ," one is therefore enabled to think on things God has declared as just.

6. Whatever is *pure (hagna)*. The word is often used of moral purity or chasteness (2 Corinthians 11:2). As with other words in this list, it is characteristic of the leaders of the church (1 Timothy 5:22). Here it seems to carry the basic meaning of unmixed or pure actions. In this sense, Paul again reflects upon the opening of the letter. There he described those who preached Christ "out of selfish ambition, not sincerely" *(ouk hagnos,* Philippians 1:17). The meaning here, then, is that the Philippian Christians are to reflect upon pure unmixed actions.

7. Whatever is lovely *(prosphile)*. The word is not used elsewhere in the New Testament or in any of the list of virtues composed by the philosophers. It is used in Esther 5:1 (Septuagint) and has this same sense of making attractive or lovely. The Philippian Christians are to think about those things that bring out from others an awareness of the lovely.

8. Whatever is *admirable (euphema)*. The word is also translated "of good report" (KJV) and "gracious" (RSV). The most recent understanding of this word (used only here in the New Testament) discounts any passive meaning (e.g., "of good report") in favor of an active meaning, such as that which is "well-spoken," that which will be heard as gracious speech.

Paul moves from this list of eight objects of their thinking to focus upon their actions (Philippians 4:9). The competent teacher of Paul's day not only taught a body of material, but served as a model to his students. This pattern was particularly true in the early church. Without the Bible in its present form, the church needed to look to the teachings and examples of its leaders, especially the apostles. The first two verbs of this passage focus upon the teaching of Paul. First, they are to practice whatever they "have learned" from him and "received" from him. The first one describes the normal result of his teaching. In the previous section, the object of their thinking is described as "whatever is . . ." *(hosa)*. The object is rather indefinite. In this section, however, the object is definite *(ha)*. Although the New International Version translates them both as "whatever," the Revised Standard makes an appropriate distinction—"whatever" for verse 8 and "what" for verse 9. The second verb of this first pair, *received,* designates a specific body of material that was to be passed on to others. That is exactly what Paul himself had done earlier, "For what I received I passed on to you as of first importance: that Christ died for our sins according to the Scriptures, that he was buried, that he was raised on the third day according to the Scriptures . . ." (1 Corinthians 15:3, 4). The Philippians were to "receive" his teaching in order to communicate it to others.

The second two verbs of the passage (Philippians 4:9) focus upon the ways that Paul himself is to be an important source for their behavior. They are to do what they "heard" from him. The distinction between this verb and the one previous to it is probably that this one refers to what they heard from Paul in informal speaking situations in contrast to the more formal teaching and preaching occasions. Much of Christian behavior would have been the topic of casual conversations between Paul and many of the Philippian Christians. These topics, too, serve as motivation for the Christian life.

Finally, they are to do what they saw him do. Perhaps the most confident message a Christian can proclaim is "do as I do." While the old shibboleths, "Actions speak louder than words," "I'd rather see a sermon that hear one," and "What you do speaks so loud I can't hear what you say," may not be completely true, Christian testimony and Christian conduct must be consistent. It is for Paul, and he wants it to be for the Philippians. When words and actions are consistent, then "the God of peace" will be with them (Philippians 4:9).

Conclusion (4:10-20)

The conclusion of the letter reveals much about the love and generosity of the Philippians as well as the fierce independence of Paul. The passage is a bit unexpected. Although it is entitled in the New International Version, "Thanks for Their Gifts," Paul never once says thank you in this passage. Perhaps the easiest way to get at the meaning of the passage is to look first of all at the giving of gifts by the Philippians followed by an examination of Paul's uneasiness with the gifts, his independent contentment, and his praise for their concern.

The Philippians had begun to support Paul about ten years before the writing of this letter. Not long after they received the gospel from Paul, they began to support him as he left Macedonia: "In the early days of your acquaintance with the gospel, when I set out from Macedonia, not one church shared . . . except only you" (Philippians 4:15; see Acts 16). Furthermore, during his stay in Thessalonica after leaving Philippi, they sent him aid more than once: "You sent me aid again and again" (Philippians 4:16). Their giving to him was known by other churches and proved a point of Paul's boasting about them: "And when I was with you and needed something, I was not a burden to anyone, for the brothers who came from Macedonia supplied what I needed" (2 Corinthians 11:9). Most recently, of course, they had sent their latest gift with their own leader Epaphroditus, gifts that were "a fragrant offering . . . to God" (Philippians 4:10, 18).

Over against this generosity of the Philippians stands a great uneasiness on the part of Paul to accept this kind of generosity when directed toward him. He repeatedly made it clear that he preferred to be financially independent from the churches. "We work hard with our own hands" (1 Corinthians 4:12), he wrote, and later said to this same church, "We did not use this right [to take money from you]. On the contrary, we put up with anything rather than hinder the gospel of Christ" (1 Corinthians 9:12; cf. 9:15; 1 Thessalonians 2:5-12; 2 Thessalonians 3:7-12). He makes it clear to the Philippians that although he accepted their gift, he had no real need of it (Philippians 4:11). He really has never had a need from them: "Not that I am looking for a gift, but I am looking for what may be credited to your account. I have received full payment and even more; I am amply supplied" (Philippians 4:17, 18). The word he uses here for "received full payment" *(apecho)* is often used in business transactions to mean "paid in full." He is telling them, and not too subtly, that they need not send him any more. He already has more than enough.

The reasons for this uneasiness are complex and not so explicit. This text sheds some light. He uses four verbs that explain his independence in the matter: "For I *have learned* to be content whatever the circumstances. I *know* what it is to be in need, and I *know* what it is to have plenty. I *have learned the secret* of being content in any and every situation" (Philippians 4:11, 12). Paul has come to know such a dependence on God that he does not want any circumstances to threaten that dependence. He believes that God will work His will through whatever circumstances Paul finds himself in. It is a part of the "mind of Christ" to understand that contentment, like joy, does not come from outward circumstances; it can be realized even when in need or missed when having plenty. The phrase *have learned the secret of being content* (Philippians 4:12) comes from a word that literally means to be initiated. Through good times and bad, Paul has gone through the initiatory process to learn what it means to have real contentment, real joy. And so he can say, "I can do everything through him who gives me strength" (Philippians 4:13). The source of joy and contentment is Jesus Christ, and not in what mankind can or cannot do for him.

Finally, in spite of his strong statement of independence, he does praise the Philippians for their gifts. He begins this section with the characteristic "Rejoice ... in the Lord" (Philippians 4:10). He notes that often, no opportunity has been present for them to help: "At last you have renewed your concern for me.

Indeed, you have been concerned, but you had no opportunity to show it" (Philippians 4:10). Furthermore, even though he really did not need their help, he said to them, "Yet it was good of you to share in my troubles" (Philippians 4:14). The phrase he uses here is an idiomatic one, something akin to, "You did good!" Their gift, so generously given, has become a "fragrant offering, an acceptable sacrifice, pleasing to God" (Philippians 4:18). They have acted out of love for him and have given generously. Paul recognizes that motive and commends them for it, while at the same time upholding his own commitment to the independence of the ministry of the gospel. He is moved enough by their love to break into a doxology: "To our God and Father be glory for ever and ever. Amen" (Philippians 4:20).

Final Greetings (4:21-23)

Paul concludes this letter in a rather typical pattern for him, and one that conforms fairly well to the structure of ancient letters. The following diagram demonstrates this structure and compares it to several letters:

	Phil.	1 Cor.	2 Cor.	Gal.	2 Tim.
1. Personal relationships	4:10-19	16:5-18	13:1-10	6:11-15	4:9-18
2. Formal doxology	4:20		13:11b	6:16	4:18b
3. Concluding remarks	4:21, 22	16:19-22	13:12, 13	6:17	4:19-21
4. Benediction	4:23	16:23, 24	13:14	6:18	4:22

That this structure is repeated in several Pauline letters is one more evidence for the unity of this letter.

It appears that Paul particularly directs these remarks to the church leaders. He exhorts that they are to give greetings to "all the saints in Christ Jesus" (Philippians 4:21; literally, "each one of the saints in Christ Jesus"). It is not clear who "the brothers" are who also send greetings, but they probably would include Timothy (Philippians 1:1; 2:19), Epaphroditus (Philippians 2:25), and Luke (Acts 27:1). While it has been argued that the word *saints* often has a restrictive use referring to Jewish Christians (see chapter 1), Paul uses the term here in a more exclusive sense. In the same way that all in the church have become the new Israel, those who are in Christ Jesus might be spoken of as "saints."

Paul begins and ends this letter with "grace." It is because of the grace of God and Christ Jesus that there can be joy in suffering, joy in serving, joy through persevering faith, and the joy of loyal friends.

Part Two

Colossians

INTRODUCTION TO COLOSSIANS

Purpose of Colossians

The immediate purpose for Paul's letter to Colosse was to address a problem of false teaching and practice that had arisen in the church or the community. The basic issue dealt with the relationship of culture (i.e., the beliefs, traditions, and values of a people) and Christianity. This letter has great relevance, then, for anyone who has wrestled with such questions. To what extent does our cultural heritage mold our understanding of Christianity?

Traveling to foreign lands and worshiping with Christians of other cultures make this question all the more relevant. While leading a number of tours to Western Europe, I have enjoyed watching a transformation in the attitude of college students as they were exposed to unfamiliar practices of Christians. Their first reaction is, "Why do they do those dumb things?" But after a time, they begin to see through strange practices to the rich and significant meanings behind them. The practices, then, take on meaning and become useful expressions of praise or of faith.

The problem remains to ensure that any cultural practice by its very nature does not violate the heart of the Christian gospel. Paul wanted the Colossians to understand that certain practices and beliefs must be consistent with the person and work of Jesus. It is not that he wanted a particular cultural expression of Christian faith to be absolute. He merely did not want the expressions of faith to be inconsistent with the person and teaching of Jesus. The purpose of Colossians, then, is to present the person and work of Jesus as a refutation of the doctrinal and practical errors of false teachers in Colosse.

Christianity and Culture: the Historical Problem

The controversy over the relationship between Christianity and culture is a fundamental one. Many subsidiary issues that so often consume great time in the Christian community are answered when the problem of Christianity and culture is solved. What is the relationship of the created to the Creator? What is the relationship of the creation to itself? These questions are particularly important in light of the estrangement that exists between the righteous Creator and the fallen creation. They are important because of the popular interpretations of such texts as Colossians 2:21—"Do not handle! Do not taste! Do not touch!"—and 1 John 2:15—"Do not love the world or anything in the world. If anyone loves the world, the love of the Father is not in him." And they are important, too, because the way they are answered causes further disunity in this fallen creation and, more tragically, even in the redeemed creation of the church. These are the questions Paul answers in Colossians.

Before examining Paul's answer, it might be helpful to remember that this problem of Christianity and culture has been a perennial one in the history of the church. In each age, the church faced the problem anew. New answers, or at least new extensions of old answers, were given in the succeeding periods of church history. In his classic work on this topic, H. Richard Niebuhr *(Christ and Culture,* New York: Harper, 1951) draws five basic reactions to this question.

1. *Christ Against Culture.* Those who hold this position believe that there is nothing in the world that is good. All of creation is completely fallen. Original sin taints everything. Even the body at birth consists of an evil nature. The call of Christ is to separate from the world and to reject the culture of it. This view in early Christianity is best demonstrated by several anti-culture second-century Christians who actually spoke of Christians as a "third race" living above the culture of both Jew and Gentile. During medieval times, this view was extended to the monastic extremes. The desire was to subject the worldly life to the extent that the spiritual life could rise to perfection and control. To this end, Simeon Stylites lived buried up to his neck for several months. Then he constructed a pole sixty feet high upon which he sat for the next thirty years. To this end, people called the Bosci lived and grazed like cattle. Another man wandered naked around the foot of Mt. Sinai for fifty years (surely a record for streaking). Contemporary examples of this position include such groups and individuals as the Mennonites and Amish, Leo Tolstoy, some missionary enterprises that try to destroy or radically change the culture

of a foreign people, and even the hippies of the 1960s, who rejected the culture of middle-class America as *essentially* anti-Christian. Of course, in each case, the attempt to *reject* culture fails. The very rejection becomes an exclusive culture itself. One's orthodoxy is directly related to how closely he/she conforms to the "cultural" rejection of the cultural evil.

2. *Christ of Culture.* This position finds no tension in Christ and the world. Christ is seen through the world. Whatever is the most important in His teaching or His person and corresponds positively with culture is underscored. He becomes the great teacher, the great philosopher, the great reformer, or the great superstar. The Judaizers of the New Testament did this. They saw Jesus as the new prophet with the new law. The Gnostics of the second century did this (as well as their predecessors of the first century) when they saw Jesus as the one who brought that special knowledge necessary to attain spiritual heights. Abelard did it in the middle ages when he saw Jesus and His death (viz., Abelard's moral theory of the atonement) "doing in a higher degree what Socrates and Plato had done before him." Thomas Jefferson did this when he accepted of Jesus only that which fit Jefferson's concept of culture (viz., Jefferson's Bible without miracles). Jesus was a Jeffersonian Democrat! The classic liberalism of the nineteenth century is another example of the Christ-of-culture view. Like the Christ-against-culture group, there is the belief that the basic evil of the world is in culture. But rather than reject it and live beyond it, Jesus as the great teacher, great philosopher, et al., comes teaching the Fatherhood of God and the brotherhood of man. He shows us how to live in harmony in the context of our culture and does nothing beyond that.

3. *Christ Above Culture.* Like the Christ-of-culture group, this group believes that there is more to Christianity than the cultural expression of it. Christ is in culture, but not all of Him. Furthermore, since Jesus is Lord of all, the church becomes the supervisor of culture. It oversees it and directs it. Consequently, the same monastic system that demonstrated such a radical Christ against culture in the early stages becomes the preserver and protector of culture in later years (viz., Thomas Acquinas). Roger Williams is one of the foremost examples of this attitude in America.

4. *Christ and Culture.* Like the Christ-against-culture group, this group does not see Christ's work and influence in the daily living of the individual. But rather than try to live beyond the

normal boundaries of the culture, one lives in two worlds. He obeys God *and* Caesar. In one sphere of his existence, his life is based on faith. In the other sphere, it is based on reason. There can be no contradiction in the areas of these two spheres because they each are governed by a different basis. One cannot talk about science versus the Bible; they are in different realms. Those who fall in this group do not see work, study, leisure time, or any of the parts of normal living as related to Christianity.

5. *Christ the Transformer of Culture.* Although more time will be spent on this concept later, basically the view is that mankind is converted *in* his culture. His conversion, partly at least, is establishing a proper relationship between mankind and his culture. And then, as the name suggests, the world itself is changed by redeemed man.

The City of Colosse

The ancient city of Colosse (also spelled Colossae) was located 100 miles almost due east of Ephesus in the Lycus valley and along the Lycus river, a tributary of the larger Menander. By Paul's day, it had become a Roman province and was associated with two other cities not much more than ten miles apart, Laodicea and Hierapolis. Centuries earlier, Colosse was a significant city situated as it was on a major trade route from the west to the Euphrates river. Both Herodotus *(Histories* vii, 30) and Xenophon *(Anabasis* i, 2, 6) attest to its greatness. By Paul's day, however, its importance had declined as its two sister-cities had grown in comparison. Strabo described it as a "small town" (xii, 8, 13). J. B. Lightfoot observes that "Colossae was the least important church to which any epistle of St. Paul is addressed" *(Commentary,* p. 16). In addition to the native Phrygian population and the Romans who settled there during its provincial days, several thousand Jews settled in the area over 100 years before Paul arrived there. And so, a once-great city now small, populated by a cosmopolitan conglomeration of peoples including Jews, was the setting for this important letter. By the twelfth century, Colosse was uninhabited; its site was not rediscovered until 1835.

The Church at Colosse

It is by no means certain that Paul founded the church in Colosse or was, in fact, ever there. Some see his reference in

Colossians 2:1 to those "who have not met me personally" as evidence of his unfamiliarity to the church. The question, however, cannot be determined with certainty. At any rate, he was familiar with the church. During his two-year-plus ministry in Ephesus, many Jews and Greeks in the province of Asia (which included Colosse) were converted by his preaching. Some of the persons in the church are known, however. There was Epaphras, most probably the founder of the church, who at the time this letter was written was with Paul in his imprisonment. Paul affirms that they had learned the gospel from him (Colossians 1:7). He was a "dear fellow servant" and "faithful minister of Christ" (Colossians 1:7) who reported to Paul of the conditions in the church. At the end of the letter, he sent greetings, and was described as "wrestling in prayer" for them and working on their behalf as well as those at Laodicea and Hierapolis. Possibly he ministered to churches in those cities as well as Colosse.

Other members of the congregation include Onesimus, the escaped slave who was at this time "our faithful and dear brother" (Colossians 4:9). He was returning to them to be received "no longer as a slave, but ... as a dear brother" (Philemon 16). He had been Philemon's slave, but Paul himself would pay all that he owed (Philemon 19). Philemon, Apphia, and Archippus (perhaps father, mother, and son) were all members of the church there and opened their home for its meeting place. Beyond these observations are the allusions in the letter itself to what is often called the "Colossian heresy."

The Problem in Colosse

The Christians in Colosse faced this same problem of the relationship of the created to the Creator. In fact, the main reason Paul wrote this letter was to correct a problem that had arisen in the church over this very issue. Unfortunately, since Paul never had the course, "Introduction to Research Writing 101," he did not practice the useful but bothersome practice of including explanatory footnotes. Therefore, we do not exactly know what this Colossian heresy was. But we can get some good ideas about it just from the letter itself.

At least three outstanding characteristics of this problem in Colosse are apparent from the letter.

1. *Intellectual Exclusiveness.* Before, Paul had argued against a nationalistic exclusiveness (Galatians). Here it is against an

intellectual exclusiveness. Apparently this heretical group took pride in that they possessed some spiritual message *(logos)* or wisdom *(sophia)* that was exclusively theirs and the possession of which made them special. Paul took up their language. They had a "philosophy," but it was empty reasoning (Colossians 2:8). They merely had the appearance of wisdom (Colossians 2:23). Against this intellectual exclusiveness, Paul preached a wisdom available for all (Colossians 3:16; 1:28).

2. *Speculative Theology.* A second characteristic of the heresy is that they had a great tendency toward speculation in regard to a theology of creation. Apparently, there was some belief in the role of intermediate spirits in the act of creation. Perhaps they were predecessors of the Gnostics of the second century, who believed that the supreme God could not have created the world since all matter was evil. The purpose was, then, with the aid of these intermediate beings, to rise from the physical and the evil to the spiritual and the good. This could be done by the special knowledge of the system or structure of these intermediate beings (Colossians 2:18).

3. *Rigid Asceticism.* This was the ethical conclusion to this speculative philosophy. Its adherents enforced several rules designed to subordinate the physical—"Do not handle! Do not taste! Do not touch!" (Colossians 2:21).

The concern at this point is not with what name is attached to this heresy. It has certain features that resemble an incipient gnosticism and other features that resemble the Judaizers. Lightfoot demonstrates that there is a striking resemblance in the Essenes of Palestine and this group in Colosse. Here, the concern is more with the nature of the problem itself than with the name for it.

The issue here is not merely one of practical daily living, although that is involved and will be discussed in later chapters. But more basic is the nature of the Creator and His relationship to the created. Particular, too, is the place of Christ in this Creator-created relationship.

The Letter to the Colossians

The Authorship of the Letter

Three times in the letter, the author claims to be Paul the apostle (Colossians 1:1, 23; 4:18). His authorship is attested by several church fathers. It was not until about 1838 when the first serious question was raised about the Pauline authorship, focusing upon certain differences in language usage and doctrinal emphases when compared to other Pauline letters. Another issue pointed out by some is the comparison Colossians has with Ephesians. When the particular circumstances, however, which gave rise to the epistle are considered, such objections to Paul's authorship do not carry much weight.

There is not sufficient evidence, either from the letter itself or from external sources, to doubt that the apostle Paul wrote this letter.

The Occasion of the Letter

It appears that Epaphras joined Paul in his imprisonment (whether voluntarily or not is uncertain, see Philemon 23) and reported to him the conditions of the church in Colosse and the Lycus valley. In response to his visit and the new information he brought, Paul wrote this letter. At about the same time, he wrote Philemon and Ephesians, which were to be delivered by Tychichus and Onesimus, presumably during the same trip. Philippians was probably written later from the same place of Paul's imprisonment. The place of Paul's imprisonment and the writing of this letter is a matter of conjecture, though his Roman imprisonment seems the most plausible site. (See the discussion of the place of the writing of Philippians for further treatment of this question.)

The Structure of the Letter

As with many of Paul's letters, the structure of Colossians is normally divided into two broad areas: a doctrinal section (chapters 1 and 2) and a practical section (chapters 3 and 4). There are, however, other helpful ways to think about the structure. After a rather typical introduction (Colossians 1:1-14), there follows a beautiful, poetic description of Jesus as Creator and as Reconciler (Colossians 1:15-20). This poetic hymn is followed by a discussion of the immediate results of Jesus' reconciling work in the lives of the Colossians and in Paul's own life (Colossians 1:21—2:5). Most of the rest of the letter, then, centers around Paul's commands to the Colossians, which are constantly based on the person of Jesus as revealed in the hymn. Such an outline would look like this:

PART ONE: HYMN OF JESUS (Colossians 1:1-2:5)
I. Introduction (Colossians 1:1-14)
   A. Salutation (Colossians 1:1, 2)
   B. Prayer of Thanksgiving (Colossians 1:3-8)
   C. Prayer of Petition (Colossians 1:9-14)

II. The Supremacy of Jesus in Creation and Reconciliation (Colossians 1:15-20)

III. The Result of Jesus' Reconciliation (Colossians 1:21—2:5)
   A. For the Colossians (Colossians 1:21-23)
   B. For Paul (Colossians 1:24-29)
   C. Paul's work for the Colossians (Colossians 2:1-5)

PART TWO: WARNINGS AGAINST FALSE TEACHINGS (Colossians 2:6-23)
I. "Live in Him" (Colossians 2:6-8)
   A. "Rooted" (Colossians 2:7)
   B. "Built up" (Colossians 2:7)
   C. "Strengthened in the faith" (Colossians 2:7)
   D. "Overflowing with thanksgiving" (Colossians 2:8)

II. Watch Out for False Teaching (Colossians 2:8-15)
   A. Its shortcomings (Colossians 2:8)
   B. Possible aspects of Jesus' character and headship (Colossians 2:9-15)
      1. Fullness of the Deity (Colossians 2:9)
      2. Fullness of His body, the church (Colossians 2:10)
      3. "Circumcision" of sinful nature (Colossians 2:11)
      4. Baptized in His death, raised in His power (Colossians 2:12)
      5. Made alive when dead (Colossians 2:13)
      6. Forgiven with cancelled debts (Colossians 2:13, 14)
      7. Spiritual powers disarmed (Colossians 2:15)

III. Do Not Be Judged by Rules (Colossians 2:16, 17)
   A. Either food or festival (Colossians 2:16)
   B. They are shadows; reality in Christ (Colossians 2:17)

IV. Do Not Be Disqualified for the Prize (Colossians 2:18, 19)
   A. By one who delights in false humility (Colossians 2:18)

B. By one who worships angels (Colossians 2:18)

C. By one who depends upon visions (Colossians 2:18)

D. By one who has lost contact with Jesus (Colossians 2:19)

V. Do Not Obey Rules of the World (Colossians 2:20-23)
   A. You died to the "basic principles" of this world (Colossians 2:20)
   B. Examples of these rules (Colossians 2:21)
   C. They will perish (Colossians 2:22)
   D. Though having appearance of wisdom, they're useless (Colossians 2:23)

VI. Set Your Hearts on Things Above (Colossians 3:1)
   A. Because you have been raised with Christ (Colossians 3:1)
   B. Christ is above, at the right hand of God (Colossians 3:1)

VII. Set Your Minds on Things Above (Colossians 3:2-4)
   A. Your life is hidden with Christ in God (Colossians 3:3)
   B. You will appear with him (Colossians 3:4)

VIII. Put to Death the Earthly Nature (Colossians 3:5-8)
   A. Sexual immorality (Colossians 3:5)
   B. Impurity (Colossians 3:5)
   C. Lust (Colossians 3:5)
   D. Evil desire (Colossians 3:5)
   E. Greed (Colossians 3:5)
   F. Anger (Colossians 3:8)
   G. Rage (Colossians 3:8)
   H. Malice (Colossians 3:8)
   I. Slander (Colossians 3:8)
   J. Filthy language (Colossians 3:8)

IX. Do Not Lie to Each Other (Colossians 3:9-11)
   A. You have taken off the old (Colossians 3:9)
   B. You have put on the new (Colossians 3:10, 11)

X. Clothe Yourselves (Colossians 3:12-14)
   A. As God's chosen people (Colossians 3:12)
   B. With compassion, kindness, etc. (Colossians 3:12)

C. Bearing with each other (Colossians 3:13)
D. Forgiving each other (Colossians 3:13)
E. Ultimately in love (Colossians 3:14)

XI. Let the Peace of Christ Rule in Your Hearts (Colossians 3:15)
   A. You were called to peace (Colossians 3:15)
   B. Be thankful (Colossians 3:15)

XII. Let the Word of Christ Dwell in You (Colossians 3:16, 17)
   A. As you teach (Colossians 3:16)
   B. As you sing (Colossians 3:16)
   C. Do all in name of Jesus (Colossians 3:17)

PART THREE: HOUSEHOLD RULES (Colossians 3:18—4:1)
   I. Wives and Husbands (Colossians 3:18, 19)

   II. Children and Fathers (Colossians 3:20, 21)

   III. Slaves and Masters (Colossians 3:22—4:1)

PART FOUR: CLOSING (Colossians 4:2-18)
   I. Final Commands (Colossians 4:2-6)
   A. Pray (Colossians 4:2-4)
   B. Be hospitable to outsiders (Colossians 4:5, 6)

   II. Final Greetings (Colossians 4:7-18)
   A. Tychicus (Colossians 4:7, 8)
   B. Onesimus (Colossians 4:9)
   C. Aristarchus (Colossians 4:10)
   D. Mark and Barnabas (Colossians 4:10)
   E. Jesus Justus (Colossians 4:11)
   F. Epaphras (Colossians 4:12, 13)
   G. Luke (Colossians 4:14)
   H. Demas (Colossians 4:14)
   I. Brothers at Laodicea, and Nympha (Colossians 4:15, 16)
   J. Archippus (Colossians 4:17)
   K. Paul (Colossians 4:18)

CHAPTER FIVE

Opening Greetings

Colossians 1:1-14

Salutations (1:1, 2)

There are some respects in which Paul's greetings are quite ordinary; they follow the typical form of letter writing for Paul's day. Actually, they combine the Greek style with the Oriental. The difference in these two styles is as follows:

Greek	Oriental
Name of sender	Name of sender
Name of addressee	Name of addressee
"Greetings" (literally, "Grace")	"Peace"

There are some Biblical examples of a purely Greek salutation:

"James, a servant of God and of the Lord Jesus Christ, To the twelve tribes scattered among the nations: Greetings" (James 1:1).

"The apostles and elders, your brothers, To the Gentile believers in Antioch, Syria and Cilicia: Greetings" (Acts 15:23).

"Claudius, Lysias, To his Excellency, Governor Felix: Greetings" (Acts 23:26).

There are also a few examples of a purely Oriental greeting:

"King Nebuchadnezzar, To the peoples, nations and men of every language, who live all in the world: May you prosper greatly" (literally, "peace be multiplied to you"; Daniel 4:1).

Thus, Paul's "grace and peace" is a combination of these two styles.

It was also common to make the introductions of these letters more extensive by adding explanatory words to the basic structure. Paul does this in an informative way. The descriptions he includes are not accidental or examples of mere wordiness. They, rather, reveal some of the emphases he will make in the context of the letter. And so here he is "an apostle of Christ Jesus by the will of God" (Colossians 1:1). He used the same description in 2 Corinthians 1:1, where he spent a greater part of that letter defending his authority to preach and teach. Though that is not the case here in Colossians, he does want to establish his authority with a church that does not know him intimately. Since he will address serious doctrinal issues in this letter, they need to understand the position from which he writes. He is an "apostle of Christ Jesus," so designated by God himself. His position has nothing to do with his own virtue (Galatians 1:11ff; Ephesians 3:2ff), but was rather by God's own decision. His authority is not grounded in his own knowledge, but in God's revelation of himself to Paul.

There are times when Paul uses the term *apostle* in a nondistinctive sense, such as describing Silvanus, Timothy, and himself as "apostles of Christ" (1 Thessalonians 2:6, 7). Here, however, he alone is described as an apostle. The restrictive use of the title underscores his authority even though he has not had an intimate relationship with the church. He does not speak as a disinterested observer, but as one commissioned by God himself for this task.

Timothy is identified as Paul's companion—not an apostle, but "our brother." He is similarly mentioned as a companion in the salutations of 2 Corinthians, Philippians, 1 and 2 Thessalonians, and Philemon. There is no indication here or elsewhere that those listed with Paul in these salutations were co-authors, but rather co-workers who preached and taught the same thing. Timothy does not appear again in this letter and apparently did not have a close relationship to the congregation in Colosse. He had become Paul's companion during the first missionary journey and had worked with him from then on (Acts 16:1), especially spending considerable time on the road on Paul's behalf (see Acts 20:4; 1 Corinthians 4:17; 16:10; 2 Corinthians 1:19; Philippians 2:19; 1 Thessalonians 3:2-6). He is described elsewhere as a "brother" (2 Corinthians 1:1), a "minister/servant" (2 Corinthians 3:6; 6:4), a "fellow worker" (Romans 16:21), a "good soldier of Christ

Jesus" (2 Timothy 2:3), Paul's "true son in the faith" (1 T\
1:2), and his "dear son" (2 Timothy 1:2).

It is not clear whether there are two groups who are recipients of this letter or just one. The New International Version takes it to be one, "the holy and faithful brothers in Christ." However, Paul seldom uses the word *holy* as an adjective; so there may be two sub-groups who are addressed here: the "saints" *(hagioi),* or Jewish Christians, and the "faithful brothers in Christ," the Gentile believers.

Paul subtly combines the Greek and the Oriental forms of greetings here. Rather than the normal Greek form *(charein),* "Greetings!" he uses the noun form of the word *(charis),* "grace." This word has taken on for all Christians a rich new meaning. It is through God's deliberate action on behalf of all men that they are able to have fellowship with Him. That action is described as "grace" and serves as the ground for Christian theology (especially Acts 4:33; 6:8; Romans 1:5; 3:24; 4:4; 5:2, 15ff; 6:1ff; 12:6; Ephesians 1:6, 7; 2:5, 8; 3:2; 4:7). This change in the Greek salutation is slight but significant. The Oriental form also carries theological significance. A characteristic form of greeting yet today in the Near East is "Shalom" (peace). The word used in the Greek language for *shalom* is the word that Paul characteristically uses in his greetings *(eirene).* As with *shalom,* it means more than just the absence of war, but rather includes a well-being of the entire community.

Thanksgiving and Prayer (1:3-14)

The six verses of Colossians 1:3-8 are all one sentence in the Greek, one that is hard to follow or to translate smoothly. The basic structure of the thanksgiving sections of letters include (1) a statement of thanksgiving, (2) an indication of the time or frequency of the thanksgiving, (3) a statement of the reasons for thanksgiving, and (4) the goals of the thanksgiving prayer. Paul follows this normal pattern with quite some elaboration.

Although Paul begins the prayer with *we,* he uses it in almost an editorial way. There are several who send greetings at the close of the letter (Colossians 4:10ff), but here Paul is merely using the formal *we.* The object of his thanksgiving is God, "the Father of our Lord Jesus Christ" (Colossians 1:3). The God to whom he prays, Paul affirms, is the very One whom Jesus revealed.

The reason for his thanksgiving falls into a familiar triad: faith, love, and hope. This pattern occurs in other thanksgiving sections of Paul's letters with one of the triad occasionally missing. For example, in 1 Thessalonians 1:3, Paul offers thanks for their faith, love, and hope. In 2 Thessalonians, however, he omits any mention of hope, and thus offers a clue early on to their problem. (See the Introduction to 1 and 2 Thessalonians later in this work.) Other places in Paul's writings where the triad occurs include Romans 5:1-5; 1 Corinthians 13:13; Galatians 5:5, 6; Ephesians 4:2-5. We also find it in Hebrews 6:10-12; 10:22-24; 1 Peter 1:3-8, 21, 22. Generally there is a temporal dimension to this triad. Faith looks to the past, toward the work of Jesus on the cross and the power of God in His resurrection. Love has a present dimension as it is carried out in concrete action in behalf of the saints of God. Hope has a future dimension in the expectation of the fulfillment of all of God's promises.

Here, however, this temporal element seems not so predominant. Faith is also a present reality; it is described as "in Christ Jesus" (Colossians 1:4). Not that Jesus is the object of faith, as elsewhere in Scripture, but here faith is in the realm of Christ Jesus. Those who are "in" Jesus exercise a faith, therefore. Hope is also a present reality; it is already "stored up for you in heaven" (Colossians 1:5). Hope here, then, is the content of that which is anticipated. Paul uses the word *hope* to describe both the act of hoping and also the content of the hope. In this passage, he uses it in the latter sense. While it is a present reality, its fulfillment will be in the future. It serves, then, as the wellspring of faith and love (Colossians 1:5).

The first glimpse of the problem facing the Colossian Christians may emerge in Colossians 1:5-8. In contrast to the new and false teaching to which the Colossians were exposed, Paul reminds them of the truth they had already heard from their own faithful minister, Epaphras. It was a truth that had been heard and received "all over the world" (Colossians 1:6). That is to say, unlike the false teachings, which are local and parochial, the true gospel has universal recognition. By implication, then, there is no reason for the Colossians to abandon the universal gospel that they already hold for a less authentic and generally unrecognized one.

In the next section (Colossians 1:9-14), Paul brings the focus back to the prayer he began in Colossians 1:3. Before (Colossians

1:4-8), Paul discussed the *reasons* for his prayer; now, he discusses the *content* and *result* of the prayer. It is that they might have the "knowledge of his will" (Colossians 1:9)—in contrast to the "special" knowledge imparted through the false teachers. When they have this knowledge in answer to the prayer, the result is simply that they "live a life worthy of the Lord" and "please him in every way" (Colossians 1:10). Paul then expands that result with four descriptions of what it means to live a worthy life and please Him. First, it means "bearing fruit in every good work" (Colossians 1:10). The classic passage of Galatians 5:22ff comes to mind here. Both to the Galatians and the Colossians, Paul makes it clear that "bearing fruit" (those ones mentioned in Galatians 5:22ff) can only be done when one is in conformity to the will of God; it is the Spirit's fruit and not mere human production. Second, he says that this result is "growing in the knowledge of God" (Colossians 1:10). He takes up this theme again in Colossians 2:2. The extent to which one "knows" God and His will is directly correlated to living in harmony with Him. Third, there is a strengthening that leads to "great endurance and patience" (Colossians 1:11). Patience is one of those fruits of the Spirit (Galatians 5:22). Paul's use of the terms *great endurance* and *patience* includes more than mere personality traits; he particularly means that in face of great trial at the end of the ages and in light of the apparent absence of Jesus then, the Spirit will aid the Christian with these characteristics. Finally, there is joyful thanksgiving to the Father (Colossians 1:12), who gives an inheritance in His kingdom. The ultimate result of the "knowledge of his will" is the privilege to share as inheritors a part of His very own kingdom. One of the earliest promises of God was given to Abram (Genesis 13:14-17), and renewed a number of times later, that he and his descendants (the "saints" or set-apart ones) would receive a great inheritance. That promise is now fulfilled (filled full; made complete and perfect) through Jesus and is available to all who "have redemption, the forgiveness of sins" (Colossians 1:14) in Him. It is part of the "mystery" revealed to "the saints" to include Gentiles in that inheritance (Colossians 1:26).

CHAPTER SIX

The Supremacy of Jesus

Colossians 1:15-20

Along with Philippians 2:5-11, this passage is certainly one of the most beautiful, exalted, and poetic descriptions of Jesus in all of the New Testament. The passage has generated voluminous books and articles. Many scholars believe that this passage was used as a creedal statement or hymn at baptismal services. Jesus is pictured here as unique and all-inclusive. He is seen in relationship to creation and to the church, themes quite foreign to contemporary ears and emphases of a "personal" Lord who "comes into your heart." This Jesus is greater than such a contemporary view of Him.

There is no more significant passage for today's world or today's church than this one.

It also forms the basis of Paul's arguments throughout this letter. Whatever heresy threatened the Colossian church, it severely diminished the person of Jesus and, thus, tore away at the very core of Christianity. Paul sets out here the supremacy of Jesus over creation and over the church. In reality, the rest of the letter merely expands upon these assertions. Because the passage is so crucial to the letter, it deserves a more thorough treatment. The relationship of Jesus to creation is considered first, followed by some implications of that supremacy to the contemporary world. Then, the relationship of Jesus to the church is considered, followed by implications of that relationship for the contemporary world.

Relationship to Creation (15-17)

"He is the image of the invisible God" (Colossians 1:15). The word here is *eikon.* Jesus is the *eikon* of God. How does one know what God is really like? Who can say? In one sense, it is possible to know what God is like through His creation. Paul wrote that

"since the creation of the world God's invisible qualities—his eternal power and divine nature—have been clearly seen, being understood from what has been made, so that men are without excuse" (Romans 1:20). This truth has been generally recognized. Plato claimed that the whole world was the *eikon* of God. Plutarch and Philo described the sun as God's image. But this gives only an incomplete image of God.

Another image of God is man himself, the final act of the first creation. "Then God said, 'Let us make man in our image, in our likeness.' ... So God created man in his own image, in the image of God he created him; male and female he created them" (Genesis 1:26, 27). James's restrictions on the cursings of men by the tongue is because men "have been made in God's likeness" of God" (James 3:9).

And yet even man is an imperfect image of God—an unreliable index of God's true character. A further image of God in the Old Testament is Israel. God had intended for Israel to show forth His character to all the world.

Arise, shine, for your light has come,
    and the glory of the Lord rises upon you.
See, darkness covers the earth
    and thick darkness is over the peoples,
but the Lord rises upon you
    and his glory appears over you.
Nations will come to your light,
    and kings to the brightness of your dawn (Isaiah 60:1-3).

But, of course, again Israel did it in an imperfect way. It was not until Christ became flesh that He demonstrated the perfect character of God. "The Word became flesh and made his dwelling among us. We have seen his glory, the glory of the One and Only, who came from the Father, full of grace and truth" (John 1:14). Jesus, and He alone, was the perfect image of God's character. He alone revealed what God really had in mind for mankind all along. It was just this unique status of Jesus that Paul wanted to stress to the Colossians who had apparently not recognized what Jesus really showed about God's character.

"He is ... the firstborn over all creation" (Colossians 1:15). It's difficult to translate the Greek word accurately. The idea of an actual *birth* in this word is remote indeed. Adam is described in

Rabbinic Judaism as the "firstborn of the world"[1] even though he was not born at all, but created. There are two prominent ideas contained in this word: priority and sovereignty. Both fit the context.

The point of "priority" is not that Christ is the earliest of created beings (although the English translation is unclear). There is a different Greek term that means first of all created beings, *protoktistoi.* Clement of Alexandria used this term to refer to the highest order of angelic beings. So the point is not that Christ was the earliest of all created beings, but that He existed before *all* creation. That is the absolute preexistence of the Son. "In the beginning was the Word, and the Word was with God, and the Word was God" (John 1:1). The first part of the next two verses in Colossians makes it clear that Christ's own beginning is not a part of creation proper. "For by him all things were created.... He is before all things" (Colossians 1:16, 17). So He existed prior to, and independent of, creation.

Even more than priority, however, this word translated "firstborn" means *sovereignty.* The rights of the firstborn males in the ancient world are well-known, especially in ancient Israel. The word *firstborn* became a symbol for the power and status enjoyed by this position. It was in such a way that the title was given to the Messiah himself in Psalm 89:27: "I will also appoint him my firstborn, the most exalted of the kings of the earth." So strong did this word have the connotation of sovereignty by right of preexistence that even God is called the "firstborn" in some ancient Jewish writings. Christ as the firstborn of all creation means that He is sovereign of that creation by right of His preexistence to it.

But why? Why did Jesus have this title of sovereignty? "For by him all things were created . . . all things were created by him and for him" (Colossians 1:16).

"By him all things were created" (Colossians 1:16). Notice the succession of prepositions—"*by* him," "*by* him," "*for* him." The first phrase could better be translated "*in* him all things

---

[1]Midrash on Numbers, 4 (141c), cited by Wilhelm Michaelis, "πρωτότο-κος," *Theological Dictionary of the New Testament,* Vol. 6 (Grand Rapids: Eerdmans, 1968), pp. 875, 876.

were created." What does that mean? It is not so difficult to understand all things are made *by* or *for* Him. But how are they made *in* Him? Remember the context. Paul is explaining why Christ is sovereign over all creation. Remember that all creation was made to show God's glory (character). But because of sin, all creation was "subjected to futility." All of creation and even man, the height of God's first creation, were fragmented from what God wanted them to be. Now nature gave one small glimpse of God's character. Man gave another glimpse of God's character. Each part of creation, that is, all of the combined witnesses of God's character, came together in Him. Although a little out of order, Paul expands this idea in Colossians 1:19, "For God was pleased to have all his fullness dwell in him." And later, in Colossians 2:3, he described Christ as the one "in whom are hidden all the treasures of wisdom and knowledge." Before, the world, Adam, the Law, and wisdom had all been described as the firstborn of God. But now, Christ becomes the firstborn because He demonstrates in himself the completeness of God's character.

"All things were created by him" (Colossians 1:16). But not only is Christ that composite of all of creation, He is the agent of it as well. To the Gnostic belief that the material world had been created by an inferior being, Paul responds with a resounding, "No!" This material world was created by One who was the very image of God and who has sovereignty over it. Because it was created by Him, it could be described at the end of that creation as "very good" (Genesis 1:31). He had sovereignty over creation because He was the agent of its existence.

"All things were created . . . for him" (Colossians 1:16). Furthermore, He is the purpose for its existence. He is not only the beginning of creation, but the end as well, the Alpha and the Omega. The purpose of all of creation is to give glory and honor to the Creator. This is the end of creation.

> And every created thing which is in heaven and on the earth and under the earth and on the sea, and all things in them, I heard saying, "To Him who sits on the throne, and to the Lamb, be blessing and honor and glory and dominion forever and ever" (Revelation 5:13, NASB).

In another great hymn, Paul states this same theme of creation's end, "that at the name of Jesus every knee should bow, in heaven and on earth and under the earth, and every tongue confess that Jesus Christ is Lord, to the glory of God the Father" (Philippians 2:10, 11).

"In him all things hold together" (Colossians 1:17). Christ is not only the beginning and end of creation. He also maintains it in the interim period. It is Christ who makes the universe a cosmos instead of a chaos. The early Christians saw in Jesus' work this very principle. Six hundred years before Jesus lived, a philosopher named Heraclitus saw two complementary principles of the universe. The first was that everything was in a state of flux. One cannot step into the same river twice. The second was that in spite of this principle of change, there was a constant factor that held it all together. This principle he called the *Logos,* the Divine Reason, the Divine Mind. Of course, it is this very title that Scripture and the early Christians ascribed to Jesus. "In the beginning was the Word *[Logos],* and the Word was with God, and the Word was God" (John 1:1). "The Word *[Logos]* became flesh and made his dwelling among us. We have seen his glory . . ." (John 1:14). Jesus was that "Divine Logos" who gave order and structure and predictability to the world.

These, then, are the descriptions of Christ's relationship to creation. Paul includes them to correct the mistaken view that creation is evil and that salvation may be only by those who have the secret to escape creation through a series of intermediate and created personages, one of whom may have been Christ. In contrast, Paul emphasizes the following:

1. Jesus Christ is the image of God, therefore the unique and complete representation of God.
2. Jesus is the firstborn of all creation and, by right of priority and primogeniture, has sovereignty over it.
3. Jesus is the epitome of creation—all things were created in Him—He is the combination of witnesses of God's character from all His creation.
4. Jesus is the agent of creation, therefore beyond it himself.
5. Jesus is even the very purpose for which creation exists.
6. Finally, Jesus is the *Logos,* the power that makes a cosmos instead of a chaos.

Implications of the Lordship of Christ Over Creation

Although some implications of Jesus' relationship to creation have already been mentioned, they need to be considered in an extended and orderly fashion. What are the results of Christ's lordship over His creation?

(1) Purposive history. Even before he was a Christian, Paul was convinced that God was somehow in control of history. There was the Jewish concept of the two ages: this present evil age, and the glorious age to come when Israel's promises would be completely fulfilled. This is how Paul had pictured history. Think of this view of history as two circles tangent to one another. Each circle represents one of the two ages. When Paul was converted to Christ, he had his view of history changed as well. He now saw that the glorious age of God's people, rather than being tangent to this present evil age, had, in fact, intersected it at Christ's coming and God's people were living in both worlds. They were *in* this age, but not *of* it. They did not experience God's kingdom in its absolute completeness, but they had received a down payment of that glorious age that was and was yet to come. One has only to read the many kingdom parables of Jesus in the Synoptics and the emphasis that John's Gospel and Paul's several epistles make on the *now* of salvation to support this view.

Paul is so struck by God's work in history and what all it includes that he, time after time, calls it a "mystery." It had been hidden from all past generations, but "is now disclosed to the saints. To them God has chosen to make known among the Gentiles the glorious riches of this mystery, which is Christ in you, the hope of glory" (Colossians 1:26, 27; cf. also Ephesians 3:3-6). "The mystery" includes the Gentiles in God's new people.

Paul also asks them to pray for him so "that God may open a door for our message, so that we may proclaim the mystery of Christ, for which I am in chains" (Colossians 4:3). This idea of "mystery" was critically important to Paul. It was his prayer for them (who, remember, used this very same word to mean that special knowledge of the intermediate spirits) "that they may be encouraged in heart and united in love, so that they may have the full riches of complete understanding, in order that [for the final purpose] they may know the mystery of God, namely, Christ" (Colossians 2:2).

Paul was so convinced that God was in ultimate control of history that he could even see some good in the Roman government. That is, God could use such parts of history for His own purposes. There is even some irony here. Paul had looked forward to going to Rome to be vindicated of his charges. Yet, look what happened: Paul finally arrived in Rome less than a year after Nero's reign of terror had begun. He was still in prison and deserted by many Jewish friends. The scene itself is worthy of Kafka! But in this situation, Paul writes one of the strongest accounts of his undying faith in God's control. And he writes to those who are better off than he, yet who are beginning to doubt God's hand in their lives. What a scene of faith this is.

There is much in contemporary culture that resembles some of the attitudes and practices of the Colossians. Many believe that someone or something else is in control of their destiny. Horoscopes are in vogue, even with some people in high places. Others, who might claim a bit more sophistication, believe that Freud was correct and that who we are and what we do are determined by the conflict of the *id* and the *superego*. Yet others see behavior and attitudes determined by inborn instincts. Others believe that actions and attitudes are all determined by no more than the sum of one's environment. It is a radical position, for contemporary people and for Paul, to come to understand that none of these philosophies has the ultimate explanation of reality.

None of these theories holds up under scrutiny. None of them provides a basis upon which to form a philosophy of life, whether it is political, economic, sociological, or whatever. None can work because they have all evaluated history wrongly. Without the Biblical position of creation, secular history is hopeless, for as far back as secular history can go, man still sees himself as unique among all else in creation. And yet he is flawed. Secular history cannot explain that fundamental problem of human history and cannot affirm that God is working on that very problem. Christ's relationship to creation emphasizes that He is in control of our history.

(2) The importance of the physical. A second result is that creation is *worth* saving—all of creation is. The physical is important, too. God made it for a purpose. He declared upon its completion that it was "very good" (Genesis 1:31). But when sin came, it disrupted not only the harmony between man and God, but also the harmony in all of creation. It was cursed and was no longer the beneficient gift intended for man (Genesis 3:17-19). Paul says that "the creation was subjected to frustration *[mataiotes]*, not by its own choice" (Romans 8:20). And yet, fallen though it is, God decided "through him to reconcile to himself all things, whether things on earth or things in heaven, by making

peace through his blood, shed on the cross" (Colossians 1:20). Jesus Christ proved that creation is worth something by dying for it! That is exactly what Paul has said. In one sense, the incarnation affirms the same truth. God came in a *physical* form to save man and creation. He came not only with a body *(soma),* but He came in flesh *(sarx)* (John 1:14). But He was able to conquer the flesh (and not just the sexual connotation, either). His body was free from the penalty of the flesh. He arose with a body that could be seen with the eye, heard with the ear, and touched with the hands. No wonder Paul said without the resurrection of the body, faith is empty (1 Corinthians 15:14). Jesus reconciles *all things.* How? By the blood of His cross (i.e., by a physical act in space and time). "But creation is not reconciled!" one might say. No, but it is in the process of being reconciled with the aid of you and me as ministers of reconciliation.

> The creation waits in eager expectation for the sons of God to be revealed. For the creation was subjected to frustration, not by its own choice, but by the will of the one who subjected it, in hope that the creation itself will be liberated from its bondage to decay and brought into the glorious freedom of the children of God. We know that the whole creation has been groaning as in the pains of childbirth right up to the present time (Romans 8:19-22).

All Christians, then, are helping in this reconciliation of all things. That is Christian ecology that will last.

(3) The reality and locus of evil. The third result is that the existence of evil in the world is emphasized. Evil is not centered in man. That is not to say that man does not *do* evil or give himself over to it. It simply means that when Jesus destroyed evil, He did not destroy man.

> When you were dead in your sins and in the uncircumcision of your sinful nature, God made you alive with Christ. He forgave us all our sins, having canceled the written code, with its regulations, that was against us and that stood opposed to us; he took it away, nailing it to the cross (Colossians 2:13, 14).

How did he do this? The next verse tells: "Having disarmed the powers and authorities, he made a public spectacle of them, triumphing over them by the cross" (Colossians 2:15).

The cosmic battle between Satan and Christ has been fought already. John said "that the light [Christ] shines in the darkness, and the darkness [Satan] has not overcome it" (John 1:5, RSV). The battle has already been won.

How important it is to know who the enemy really is. Many act as if it were the system. If they could just find the proper economic theory, or social theory, or political theory, or educational theory, the world would run smoothly. Or in the church, if we could get the right technique, find the right program, or learn the right response to the particular question, our problems would be solved. The first step to solving any problem is to define it.

> For our struggle is not against flesh and blood, but against the rulers, against the authorities, against the powers of this dark world and against the spiritual forces of evil in the heavenly realms (Ephesians 6:12).

The tendency to confuse just who our enemy really is has led to what Eutychus has called the "Beelzebub Principle." In football, it is easy to spot the enemy. He has a different-colored jersey. In war, it is a little more difficult. General Patton, according to the movie, often took unnecessary risks just to beat Field Marshall Montgomery. In Christianity, so claims Eutychus, we have all but lost the ability to see the real enemy. For some, it may be those who refuse to subscribe to a human definition of the nature of Scripture. For others it may be members of different religious bodies. For someone else, it may be those who define "the ministry" differently. This tendency has led to the Beelzebub Principle, which he states thus: "A person's ability to recognize his enemy is in inverse proportion to the importance of that recognition." Eutychus closes with this cogent challenge:

> The enemy, dear friends, is the prince of darkness grim, the prince of this world, the first murderer, the father of lies who masquerades as an angel of light. And his cleverest victory is the successful promulgation of the Beelzebub Principle.
>
> Now try to keep that straight in the future, will you?[2]

---

[2] *Christianity Today,* (December 22, 1972), p. 300.

(4) The present indicative nature of our message. Another implication of Christ's relationship to creation concerns the tense and mood of our verbal message to the world. Notice those features in the hymn:

> He is the image of the invisible God, the firstborn over all creation (Colossians 1:15).

> He is before all things, and in him all things hold together (Colossians 1:17).

> For in him all things were created [past tense] ... all things have been created [perfect tense, a present-time quality] through Him and for Him (Colossians 1:16, author's translation).

Paul is telling what is, in fact, true (the indicative mood), and what he says is true right now (the present tense). These passages typify what is a common characteristic of the preaching in the New Testament. John preached in the indicative mood and the present tense. "The kingdom of heaven is at hand." Jesus preached in the same mood and tense. At Nazareth he preached, "Today is this Scripture fulfilled in your hearing." Peter preached in the same way. On Pentecost his sermon was "that God has made him both Lord and Christ—this Jesus whom you crucified." Peter took this magnificent Scripture and proclaimed the mighty acts of God.

What would contemporary preachers have preached that day? Perhaps, "You ought to make Jesus Lord and Christ." Peter preached that He is already Lord and Christ. Or maybe we would have said, "If you make Jesus Lord and Christ, then such and such will happen to you." Peter said, regardless of what you do, under no conditions save by the will of God, Jesus is Lord and Christ. It is a much stronger message to say what is than to say what ought to be or what may be under certain conditions. The gospel is *news;* and *news* is what is happening in the world. So the gospel is the account of the good things God has done and is doing in the world on our behalf.

Yes, there is a proper place for the imperative and conditional. Both can be found in the New Testament. But each time such an instance is found, it is clearly based on the indicative that has gone before it.

The problem is a tendency to stay in the past tense. Remember Harry Emerson Fosdick's advice that people do not come to church on Sunday just panting to hear the history of the Amalekites. And second, little attention is given to the indicative; the tendency is to hurry on prematurely to the imperative and the conditional. The factual and contemporary feature of Christ's role in creation speaks to our own witness today.

Thus, the Christ of Creation; the very image of the invisible God; the firstborn of all creation; the very epitome of creation; the agent, end and sustainer of creation gives purpose to our history; shows that all of life, even the physical, is important; reveals who the true enemy really is; and provides a message that is real and is present.

Apparently, the Colossians would make no lasting response to this letter. About thirty years later, John wrote this to a sister church in the Lycus Valley about twelve miles away from Colosse—a church with the same problems:

> To the angel of the church in Laodicea write: These are the words of the Amen, the faithful and true witness, the ruler of God's creation. I know your deeds, that you are neither cold or hot. I wish you were either one or the other! So, because you are lukewarm—neither hot nor cold—I am about to spit you out of my mouth. You say, "I am rich; I have acquired wealth and do not need a thing." But you do not realize that you are wretched, pitiful, poor, blind and naked. . . .
>
> He who has an ear, let him hear what the Spirit says to the churches (Revelation 3:14-17, 22).

May the world hear what the Spirit says about the Christ of creation.

Relationship to the Church (18-20)

The second part of the hymn (Colossians 1:18-20) deals with Jesus' relationship to the *new* creation, the church, and some implications of that relationship. This correspondence between the first creation and the new creation is not peculiar to Colossians or even to Paul, but is implicit in most of the New Testament books. Matthew's Gospel begins with the same title as the book of Genesis in the Greek Old Testament, "The Book of Genesis" (i.e., the book of beginning). Mark and John both begin their Gospels with the word *beginning,* reflecting the "In the beginning" of Genesis 1:1 and the first creation (Mark 1:1, John 1:1, NASB).

The word *church* comes from the Greek word *ekklesia.* This word has both a Greek and a Jewish background that give meaning to the word as used in the New Testament.

In nearly every Greek city, as for example, in Athens, there was a body of citizens who were called the *demos,* the full citizens of the city. At periodic intervals (at Athens, at least ten times a year) a herald would go all throughout the city calling the citizens to the *ekklesia,* the assembly, where the affairs of government were discussed. The *ekklesia,* then, was actually that group of persons who responded to the call of the herald to become a part of the group. In this sense, the *ekklesia* of the New Testament is that group the members of which have responded to the call of the herald. That's the only way to become part of the *ekklesia.*

The second background for this word translated "church" is the Jewish background. When the Septuagint was translated from Hebrew, the translators used the Greek word *ekklesia* for a Hebrew word that is often translated into English as "the congregation of the assembly of Israel." And so, for Greek-speaking Hebrews, this became the meaning of *ekklesia.* When used in such a way as this, the assembly was the group that met together to hear the word from Jehovah. So it is in Deuteronomy 9:10, "The Lord gave me two stone tablets inscribed by the finger of God. On them were all the commandments the Lord proclaimed to you on the mountain out of the fire, on the day of the assembly." And in David's address to Israel about the temple, he said, "So now I charge you in the sight of all Israel and of the assembly of the Lord, and in the hearing of our God: Be careful to follow all the commands of the Lord your God, that you may possess this good land and pass it on as an inheritance to your descendants forever" (1 Chronicles 28:8). Their use of the term, then, describes the first church of God, a group of people gathered together to hear a word from the Lord. This idea most certainly carried forward into the church of the New Testament.

Consequently, to put these two background uses of the word together, the church in its worship constitutes a gathering to hear a word from the Lord. The church in its composition constitutes all of those who have responded to the call of the herald to come to the assembly (cf. Barclay, *The All-Sufficient Christ).*

But what of the function of the church? It is here that Paul uses one of the most striking metaphors to describe the relationship that Christ has to the church, that the church has to itself, and that the church has to the world. The church, he says, is the "body" of Christ. In light of this metaphor, what are those relationships?

First for consideration is Jesus' headship over the church. "He is the head of the body, the church" (Colossians 1:18). Paul still has the problem fresh in mind that gave occasion for this letter in the first place. One of the primary problems is that the Colossian heresy is lowering the place of Christ. Paul has dealt with that issue in the first stanza. Another problem arising out of the Colossian problem is the impairment of the unity of the church caused largely by the exclusiveness that they are practicing. Paul deals with that issue here in the second stanza of the hymn—the problem of unity.

One of the primary consequences of Christ's headship over the church is, of course, that He is the one who is in control. As the head controls the body, so Christ controls the church. It is He alone who determines the actions of the parts of this body. He alone gives life to the body. One can live without many other parts of the body, but certainly not without the head. That is not dispensable. Although there is much debate over the definition of death, it is pretty well accepted that death occurs when the brain stops functioning. It is the head that gives life. It also gives protection. It is the brain that tells the body to keep a hand out of the fire. It tells the body something is wrong—the safety of the body is being endangered. Of course, Christ does the same thing to His body, the church. He has a warning system for danger to the church. He warns that there are some things that are harmful for the health of the body, the church. Some of these are dealt with later in this volume. He also warns that there are certain needs of the body for good health.

Another consequence of Christ's headship over the church is that He is superior to all else in the church. He is not just another prophet or wise Rabbi or demiurge who has emanated from God. He is unique, and as so, superior. There are at least five subordinate ideas to Christ's superiority over the church here in this text.
1. "He is the beginning" (Colossians 1:18). The word translated "beginning" *(arche)* is difficult to translate because it has more than a temporal meaning. It means more than just

"first in succession of things." It can have reference to rank as well as time. In such cases, it means "the primary source from which all else has evolved." In this way, the philosophers of Paul's day use this word. Most probably, the Christians in Colosse have argued over the source of the cosmos and the source of the church. Paul proclaims to them that it is Jesus who is the source of the church and is therefore superior to it.

2. "The firstborn from among the dead" (Colossians 1:18). Again, the term *firstborn* also has more than merely a temporal significance. There is a sense in which the temporal is true here, of course. Earlier, Paul wrote that Christ has "been raised from the dead, the firstfruits of those who have fallen asleep" (1 Corinthians 15:20). Jesus was raised to die no more. In this sense, His resurrection was first. But beyond the temporal meaning, there are the prerogatives of primogeniture. He is superior in the church because He has the rights of the eldest brother. He is described as the firstborn of the dead. This term, then, could also mean that He has the power by right of primogeniture to rule the dead. Even death cannot separate those who are a part of His body, the church.

3. "In everything he might have the supremacy" (Colossians 1:18). These honors, the beginning and firstborn from the dead, were given to Him so that He might have first place in all things in creation, in resurrection, and in the church.

4. "All his fullness dwell in him" (Colossians 1:19). The word *fullness (pleroma)* was a technical word used by the Gnostics to refer to the total of all the attributes of God. Parts of these attributes were held by different divine beings who were considered to be intermediaries between God and the world. Any communication between man and God had to pass through them. So they had to be treated with respect. But Paul passes them by and says that one man—Jesus Christ—has all the fullness of God, the totality of His attributes. Therefore, He can be the one and only intermediary between man and God. There is another interesting sidelight here. In the Rabbinic writings, there are similar formulations as Colossians 1:19. The Hebrew word *shekinah* is used instead of *pleroma*. The *shekinah* was God's presence in the Temple, the fullness of God in the Temple. And so, not only does Christ become the fullness of God over against the Gnostic belief of

intermediate spirits, but He is the fullness of God that replaces the Temple. The Temple was the center of worship for old Israel. Jesus Christ has become the center of worship for the new Israel.

5. "Reconcile to himself all things . . . by making peace through his blood, shed on the cross" (Colossians 1:20). Jesus Christ is superior because He alone is able to reconcile all things, in Heaven and on earth, to himself. The word *reconcile* here could be translated "unite." He unites all things to himself. The implications of the restoration of all things to himself have already been discussed. The implication here is simply this: the very same act that brings harmony and peace to all the universe is the act that brings the church into realization—His death on the cross. The church of God (i.e., Israel) had tried for centuries to be the redeemed society. It had tried to live in a righteous relationship with God. It had tried to be the people of God. But all had been in vain. But then Jesus Christ came. He redeemed the church. He made the church the people of God, the *laos*. He empowered the church to live righteously by the power of His Spirit. He did all of these things as a part of His reconciliation of all things. He is superior to the church because He was able to do what no one else could do—redeem the church as He redeemed the cosmos, doing both by the blood of His cross.

A third consequence of Christ's headship over the church is His closeness to it. As the head, He is intimately and vitally united with the church. In describing this vital relationship between Christ and the church, Paul uses a figure that is obscure to the modern world. Perhaps he is implying a biological concept no longer familiar. At any rate, he says in Ephesians 4:15, "Speaking the truth in love, we will in all things grow up into him who is the Head, that is, Christ." Connection to the head in this vital union is necessary for growth. The same figure is used in Colossians 2:18, 19:

> Do not let anyone who delights in false humility and the worship of angels disqualify you for the prize. Such a person goes into great detail about what he has seen, and his unspiritual mind puffs him up with idle notions. He has lost connection with the Head, from whom the whole body, supported and held together by its ligaments and sinews, grows as God causes it to grow.

103

But how does the growth originating in the head take place? The context of these two passages helps to explain. In Ephesians, the context is one in which the greatest threat to the church was disunity. How can the church have unity? It achieves unity by first of all recognizing the vocation of witness to the mystery of God (cf. Ephesians 3). God's people are to discern their gifts, their *charismata,* for helping one another to be able to witness of God's mystery. They exercise these gifts in love and so attain a "unity of faith" and unity of "knowledge," growing up into perfection (completeness, unity) into Christ, the Head.

In Colossians, the context is slightly different. (Ephesians focuses on the church of the Christ; Colossians, on the Christ of the church.) Here Paul is warning the Christians of the systems of religions that compete with the lordship of Christ. He tells them in Colossians 2 that they have been liberated from the law, and from those demonic forces that condemned them by the use of the law:

> Having canceled the written code, with its regulations, that was against us and that stood opposed to us; he took it away, nailing it to the cross. And having disarmed the powers and authorities, he made a public spectacle of them, triumphing over them by the cross (Colossians 2:14, 15).

The only reason, then, that the church could be lured into a false religious discipline was if it removed itself too far from the Head who had done these acts. Just as in some way in Paul's analogy, the body's vitality and life is related to its closeness to the head, so the church begins to die as it separates itself from the Head to unite with others.

In one case, then (Ephesus), the close relationship to the head is stressed for the sake of unity. In another case (Colosse), the close relationship to the Head is stressed for the sake of fidelity and the avoidance of heresy and death.

In these ways, then, Christ is Head of the church.
1. *He is in control* by directing its actions, generating its life, and offering it protection.
2. *He is superior* as its source (the beginning, firstborn, preeminent one), as the fullness of God is in Him, and as reconciler of all things.
3. *He is vitally linked to it.* As the body retains its connection to Him, it is able to avoid such pitfalls as disunity and heresy.

Implications of the Church as Body

The church needs a clearly defined authority. Jesus is the head, the controller, the one who is superior, the source *(arche)*. The body cannot function properly without recognizing this. The Bible becomes the nerve center from the head to the body. Thomas and Alexander Campbell recognized this and urged a return to the sole authority of Scripture. For the Bible to be authoritative, then, it must have objective meaning. It cannot mean whatever one sees in it on a mere devotional level, disregarding the total communicative aspect of speaker, audience, occasion, and other relevant facts. True, it can speak on an existential level of living, but it still speaks objective truths.

The center of the church is a person; not rules, not law. The "fullness" of God was moved from the temple (i.e., law) to Jesus. It is *Christ* who is the head, not a system. Christ is the source of life for the church—not a reward for keeping rules and regulations.

The unity of the body must be affirmed. Through participation in baptism and the Lord's Supper, the essential unity of the participant with all other Christians is demonstrated. Unity is not just an agreement to be accommodating—it is not unity by compromise. Rather, it is a unity of dependence on God's grace regardless of intellectual status. Whatever potential division there might be in the church, each side needs to consider this oneness dramatized by baptism and the Lord's Supper.

Criticism of the church is dangerous. Some criticism may be valid. But there is a never-ending responsibility of every Christian to minister to other parts of the body to help them function, and then to be ministered to by other parts. It is easier to criticize than to minister to the church.

The church is the body of Christ. May we be healthy parts of that body. May we respond to the Head, Jesus Christ. May we work harmoniously with other parts of the body. May we help the body be a servant of God to the world.

CHAPTER SEVEN

The Results of Jesus' Reconciliation

Colossians 1:21—2:5

Results for the Colossians (1:21-23)

With Colossians 1:21, the tone changes significantly from the noble beauty of the Christological hymn to the specific application of Jesus' work to the Colossians. In Colossians 1:21, Paul describes their former state; in verse 22, their present state; and in verse 23, the condition of remaining in this present state. This section is reminiscent of Ephesians 2:1ff. In Ephesians 1, Paul described the privilege of being a part of Israel, God's chosen people, the original "saints." In Ephesians 2, he turned to the condition of the Gentiles in Ephesus, describing them as "dead in your transgressions and sins." Then, in Ephesians 2:13, he said, "But now in Christ. . . ." The same pattern is found here in Colossians. Most of the time when Paul uses the pronouns *we* and *us,* he is referring to Jewish believers. Most of the time when he uses the pronoun *you,* he is referring to Gentiles to whom he is writing.

The lofty themes from the hymn are here particularized. There, Jesus reconciled "all things" to himself (Colossians 1:20); here, He reconciles them (i.e., the Colossians Gentiles) to himself (Colossians 1:22). There, the reconciliation was effected "through his blood, shed on the cross" (Colossians 1:20); here, it occurs "by Christ's physical body through death" (Colossians 1:22). There, all of creation came by His power (Colossians 1:16); here, the gospel is preached "to every creature under heaven" (Colossians 1:23).

Paul describes the Colossians' former condition in three ways. First, he says that they were once "alienated" from God. The phrase, only used of Gentiles and never of Jews, is reminiscent of Isaiah 57:19. The prophet Isaiah speaks of a time to come when even the Gentiles, those "far off," will hear and receive a message of peace from God. Paul expands upon this point in Ephesians

2:12. Here he affirms that the estrangement of Gentiles not only is from Christ, but also is from Israel, from the covenant, and from any hope. That this alienation has been removed through Jesus Christ, Paul calls the "mystery" (Ephesians 3:6; Colossians 1:26, 27) that was revealed to the apostles and Jewish believers first of all (Ephesians 1:9ff). Until Jesus came, however, the Gentiles were in a continual state of alienation from God.

Paul also describes these Gentiles—before Jesus "reconciled" them—as "enemies in your minds" (Colossians 1:21). In Ephesians 4:18, he says that Gentiles "are darkened in their understanding." And in Romans, he describes these ones as having "thinking [that] became futile" (Romans 1:21) and a "depraved mind" (Romans 1:28). Paul surely believes that people who live without the knowledge of God cannot have their thinking in harmony with the world about them. There is much in history that would seem to bear out of this truth. Many attribute the rise of modern science in the western world to the Christian "mind" that existed there. That is not to say that all were Christians who were active in this development, but rather that they worked from a Christian understanding of the world about them. Without this Christian understanding, scientific advancement was limited.[3]

The third description of the Gentiles without Jesus is that they also demonstrate "evil behavior" (Colossians 1:21). The causal relationship is not exactly as the New International translation suggests, "enemies in your minds *because* of your evil behavior." Rather, the evil behavior results from the hostile mind. The principle is that actions follow thoughts. The relationship of actions-thoughts is well-known, both on a personal level as well as a corporate one.[4]

The *but now* of Colossians 1:22 is rhetorically striking. Paul draws a sharp contrast to their present condition in Jesus Christ. This great and cosmic reconciling work of Jesus is also personal

---

[3]For an extended treatment of the relationship of Christianity and the rise of modern science, see Reijer Hooykaas, *Religion and the Rise of Modern Science* (Grand Rapids: Eerdmans Publishing Company, 1972).

[4]See Francis Schaffer, *Escape From Reason* (Downers Grove: Intervarsity, 1960) for a discussion of the thoughts-actions relationship as demonstrated in the history of Western Europe and the United States.

and comes about through the death of His physical body. The Christian faith is not merely a system of religion or a collection of dogma, but rather a relationship with the Jesus who died and arose. The emphasis here upon the physical body is surely to underscore the error of the false teachers in Colosse of denying the importance of the physical. The purpose of this reconciliation is "to present you holy ... without blemish and free from accusation" (Colossians 1:22). The word *holy* here is the same word translated "saints" in Philippians 1:1. Because of Jesus' death, the Gentiles can now become "saints," that is to say, consecrated and dedicated to a particular service. The descriptions here of the reconciled ones do not refer to personal conduct, but rather their position in Jesus Christ. It is only "in Christ" that one may appear before God as described here.

Paul concludes this section with a condition. The Colossians can employ Jesus' reconciling work only so long as they "continue in [their] faith" and are "not moved from the hope held out in the gospel" (Colossians 1:23). As in the thanksgiving section, faith and hope are here linked. The language here is the same used to describe the foundation of a house. If the Colossian Christians are to withstand the threats of the false teachers, they must have this sure foundation of faith and hope. Paul affirms that the gospel is proclaimed to "every creature under heaven" (Colossians 1:23). Unlike the gospel of the false teachers, which was for a select few, the gospel of Jesus, which Paul preached, is for everyone. (See Colossians 1:28ff.)

Results for Paul (1:24-29)

This section focuses upon the results of Jesus' reconciling work for Paul himself. There are two broad consequences he mentions: (1) he has become a sufferer because of the reconciling work of Jesus (Colossians 1:24), and (2) he has become a servant-preacher because of that work (Colossians 1:25-29).

Upon first reading, Colossians 1:24 appears to present a real paradox. The question created here is this: How can there be anything "lacking" in Jesus' afflictions? Some have taken this statement to mean that Jesus' sacrifice on the cross was not sufficient for the reconciliation of *all* mankind, and so help is needed from the "treasury of merits" of the "saints." Some especially righteous people, so the view goes, had more merits than demerits at the end of their lives, and this excess can be used up, if properly appropriated, by those who have too few. But that can hardly be Paul's meaning in this passage. As much as any other New Testament book, Paul presents Jesus as unique and all-sufficient in this Colossian letter. That, as has been demonstrated, is the central thrust of the hymn (Colossians 1:15-20) and, thus, the whole letter. There must be another explanation.

The word translated "afflictions" in this passage is never used in the New Testament to refer to the work of Jesus on the cross, and it does not so refer here. The "afflictions" must be of a different sort.

There was a belief, revealed in Jewish apocalyptic literature, that in the "last days" before God's kingdom would be fully established, the faithful ones would go through a period of great hardship and persecution. Daniel prophesied of the end times that "there will be a time of distress such as has not happened from the beginning of nations until then. But at that time your people—everyone whose name is found written in the book—will be delivered" (Daniel 12:1). The same theme is found in the New Testament. After Paul and Barnabas had been stoned in Lystra, they explained to their disciples, "We must go through many hardships to enter the kingdom of God" (Acts 14:22). After discussing their sufferings as well as his, Paul writes to the Thessalonians these words: "You know quite well that we were destined for them [i.e., trials]. In fact, when we were with you, we kept telling you that we would be persecuted" (1 Thessalonians 3:3, 4). The classic passage dealing with this issue is in Romans, "I consider that our present sufferings are not worth comparing with the glory that will be revealed in us" (Romans 8:18; see also 8:38, 39). The most extended treatment of this dimension of suffering is in 2 Corinthians (see 2 Corinthians 1:3-8; 2:4; 4:17; 6:4; 7:4; 8:2, 13), where Paul makes it clear that "afflictions" (he uses the same word in all of the Corinthian passages as he does in Colossians 1:24) are to be the normal lot of the Christian. He is equally sure, however, that God will sustain them through these "afflictions" and that they will experience a great joy having borne them.

It is the lot of the church, then, to suffer. As Jesus suffered in His body on the cross, His present body, the church, will suffer—not to complete His reconciling work, but rather for the *joy* of the church. There are two truths imbedded here that sound strange to this modern world. First, there is the underlying understanding of the corporate nature of the church. The individual finds identity, not so much in *self*, as in his place in the body, the church. It is the body that suffers, and when one becomes part of that body, suffering is experienced. It is the body, the church, that experiences release and joy from that suffering. It is only by participation in the body that these experiences are gained.

Second, in an age bombarded with gospels of prosperity and of positive thinking, to affirm the central role of "afflictions" seems bizarre. Many religious leaders, especially some television evangelists, emphasize that a result of faithfulness is prosperity, usually meaning the freedom from want or trouble. The Biblical view here, however, is that those who are part of the body, the church, will suffer for the church. In the same way that a parent suffers for a child who is ill or in pain, any member of Christ's body suffers when any part of that body suffers. In this same way, then, Jesus also suffers. As the Head of this body, he feels the pain of afflictions most acutely. Paul, as well as anyone, understood this fact. When he encountered Jesus on the road to Damascus, Jesus asked him, "Saul, Saul, why do you persecute me?" (Acts 9:4). Of course, it was the church, the body of Christ, that Paul persecuted. It was the same as persecuting Jesus himself. Later, Jesus told Ananias, "I will show him how much he must suffer for my name" (Acts 9:16). Here, then, is one major consequence of Jesus' reconciling work for Paul: suffering was to be his lot.

A second major consequence was that Paul had become a servant to the church and a preacher of the word of God in its fullness (Colossians 1:25-29). He was a servant *(diakonos),* he said, by the "commission" of God. The word *commission (oikonomian)* has a rather specific use in the New Testament, which helps clarify Paul's understanding of this commission. In Ephesians 1:10, Paul uses the word to describe the "plan" or "administration" of God's will to bring all things together under the lordship of Jesus. He uses it again in Ephesians 3:2, 3, "Surely you have heard about the *administration* of God's grace that was given to me for you, that is, the mystery made known to me by revelation. . . ." In both of these passages the "commission" *(oikonomian,* also "administration" or "plan") is connected to the *mystery* that was revealed to Paul. It was his special "commission," given to him by God, to proclaim the word of God in its fullness. The awareness that he was participating in God's grand design for the world gave Paul the foundation he needed for this ministry and made it possible for him to endure the hardships that came in the course of service.

Paul describes the object of his ministry as presenting "the word of God in its fullness" (Colossians 1:25). As noted in chapter 6, *fullness* is an important concept in Paul's theological formulations for the Colossians. In Colossians 1:19, he affirms that all the fullness of God dwells in Jesus. In Colossians 2:9 and 10, he reasserts that fact and then adds that they, the church, are now the fullness of God. (See chapter 8.) Paul goes on to describe this "full" word of God as a "mystery" (Colossians 1:26). Here is one of the most important dimensions of Paul's teaching, both to the Colossians and to the Ephesians. (See the next section of this chapter for a further discussion of "mystery.") It is likely that the false teachers in Colosse were teaching a different kind of mystery, one that may have been similar to any one of the several pagan mystery religions that were contemporary to Paul. The mysteries in the pagan world were rites performed to depict the destiny of the god who was worshiped. This performance, or pageant, was designed to give the followers of the religion an opportunity to participate in the fate of this god and thereby obtain salvation.

The word *mystery* had also come into Jewish usage long before Paul's time, especially prominent in Daniel (2:18, 19, 27-37, 47). There it referred to future events, the knowledge of which was reserved for God alone. There are at least five dimensions to Paul's use of the term in the twenty-one times he uses it in his letters. While certain similarities may exist to the Greek and the Jewish usages, Paul employs the term in his own exclusive sense. First, he affirms that the mystery has been hidden for ages and generations (Colossians 1:26, 3:4, 9; Ephesians 3:5; Romans 16:25). That is not to say that there was never any indication of the content of this mystery before. Rather, it "was not made known to men in other generations as it has now been revealed" (Ephesians 3:5). It was through Jesus that God's plan for all things was made known and accomplished. Second, this mystery did not come to be through the efforts of man. It was not divined by some secret formula, ritual, or practice. It came about solely by the initiation of God. It was "not the wisdom of this age or of the rulers of this age" (1 Corinthians 2:6). It was made known particularly to Paul (Ephesians 3:3) and the "holy apostles and prophets" (Ephesians 3:5) and done so "through the prophetic writings by the command of the eternal God" (Romans 16:26). It was also revealed to "the saints" that the Gentiles were to be included in God's "glorious riches" (Colossians 1:26, 27). Third, a significant part of the content of this revelation was that "the Gentiles are heirs together with Israel, members together of one body, and sharers together in the promise in Christ Jesus" (Ephesians 3:6). The purpose of its proclamation was that "all nations might believe and obey him" (Romans 16:26) upon hearing of this mystery. Fourth, the content of the revelation went even further, however. Not only should Gentiles hear and profit from this mystery; rather, "the rulers and authorities in the heavenly realms" (Ephesians 3:10) should come to know of God's eternal plan effected through Jesus. As has been seen already (Colossians 1:20), the purpose of the "mystery" is ultimately "to bring all things in heaven and on earth together under one head, even Christ" (Ephesians 1:10). Fifth, Paul asks for prayer that he might be able to present this mystery "fearlessly," and "clearly" as God opens doors for this purpose (Colossians 4:3, 4; Ephesians 6:19).

In Colossians 1:28 and 29, Paul uses three words to describe his ministry, as well as that of his colleagues (for he has switched to the pronoun "we" here). First, he says that they "proclaim" Jesus. The word is almost exclusively used in the New Testament to refer to missionary preaching (i.e., preaching to non-believers). That which is said to be "proclaimed" includes the following: the Word of God (Acts 13:5; 17:13), the resurrection (Acts 4:2), forgiveness of sins (Acts 13:38), the mystery (Colossians 4:3), the testimony about God (1 Corinthians 2:1), the gospel (1 Corinthians 9:14), and Jesus (Philippians 1:17, 18; and here, Colossians 1:28). He expands upon this process by the use of two other terms to describe his ministry to them. He says that he "admonishes" and "teaches" them. The gospel message is not complete with the announcement of it alone. There is need for a more thorough application of it to the lives of people. This activity is done to "everyone," a word that Paul repeats three times in Colossians 1:28 (two times in NIV). In contrast to the exclusiveness of the false teachers in Colosse, the Christian gospel is for everyone. All have access to "all wisdom," not just the elite.

Paul's Work for the Colossians (2:1-5)

A third result of Jesus' reconciling work is Paul's specific work in behalf of the Colossians. This letter and Paul's efforts are not for the Colossians alone, but also include the nearby Laodiceans (see also Colossians 4:16). It is apparent from the language Paul uses here that he has in mind the metaphor of the church as the body of Christ, a theme he struck in the hymn (Colossians 1:18). Whereas there the force of the metaphor of the body was that it recognized the authority of the Head, Jesus Christ, here the point is that the church is a body that works together for its own health, strength, and mutual benefit. Using this metaphor in such a way, Paul is using a metaphor that is well known in ancient literature. Plato referred to the cosmos as the body of God whose parts worked in harmony. Seneca compared the world to a body in which "all the members agree among each other, for it is the function of each to serve the whole." It is no unusual metaphor that Paul picks to describe the relationship of the members of the church; the church functions together like a body.

There is a principle in physiology called "homeostasis." This principle illustrates the thrust of Paul's metaphor. Homeostasis is the tendency that the physical body (or any other living organism) has to maintain a state of optimum stability when other conditions threaten to disturb that condition. In other words, all parts of the body work together beneficially to keep all members of the body making their own contribution. The temperature regulation of the body is a simple example. Normally, a human being has a body temperature of 98.6 degrees Fahrenheit (or 37.5° C). That is just an average and any single person's normal temperature may deviate from that. However, when the temperature of the body begins to rise, the homeostasis—the state of optimum stability—is endangered. Then other members of the body come to the aid, because if the body temperature stays at, say, 108 degrees for any length of time, death will result. Several mechanisms work to correct the problem. (1) The sweat glands open to allow more water to get to the surface of the skin to evaporate and to carry off body heat. (Excess water goes from the kidneys to the skin where its evaporation has greater effect than as urine loss.) (2) Heat-producing activities of the muscles and abdomen slow down. (3) Blood flow to the skin may increase, aiding body cooling. (4) Convulsions may also occur, which also have the effect of lowering body temperature. There are many other examples of the body working together in unbelievable ways to preserve the homeostatic level.

One point that Paul is getting at with this body metaphor is that there must be a spiritual homeostasis. The body of Christ on earth must exercise these homeostatic principles to remain a healthy body and avoid spiritual death. The body of Christ in Colosse does not have a very good homeostasis. There are some parts of the body who are not making their necessary contribution to the rest of the body, particularly because of this intellectual exclusivism. Rather than an exclusivism, Paul proclaims "Him, admonishing *every* man and teaching *every* man with *all* wisdom, that we might present *every* man complete in Christ" (Colossians 1:28, RSV). He deliberately emphasizes that the gospel is for *every* man—he repeats the phrase three times—and that *every* man is taught with *all* wisdom as compared to the partial knowledge of the Colossian heresy. This particular verse (Colossians 1:28) reveals the lack of spiritual homeostasis that exists in Colosse.

Paul continues in Colossians 2:1-5 to state this principle of mutual interdependence. The key word in this passage is *united (sumbibasthintes)*. Paul's great struggle is that they might be encouraged, and this by being united or knit together (RSV). Paul uses this word elsewhere to mean instruct, but here and in Ephesians, he uses it in its more common meaning, united or knitted together or grows together. Luke uses the word twice. In Acts 9:22, "Yet Saul grew more and more powerful and baffled the Jews living in Damascus by proving [*sumbibazon;* literally, "putting all the parts together"] that Jesus is the Christ." In Acts 16:10, "After Paul had seen the vision, we got ready at once to leave for Macedonia, concluding [*sumbibazontes,* putting all the pieces together] that God had called us to preach the gospel to them." The idea is that all of the parts work together or fit together with a beneficial result.

Concept of Gifts

One of these results of working together beneficially is encouragement, "that they may be encouraged in heart and united in love" (Colossians 2:2). How seemingly insignificant it is to be merely a comforter in the body of Christ. Yet there is scarcely an activity of the body working together that Paul mentions more.

> ... [God] who comforts us in all our troubles, so that we can comfort those in any trouble with the comfort we ourselves have received from God (2 Corinthians 1:4).

But God, who comforts the downcast, comforted us by the coming of Titus, and not only by his coming but also by the comfort you had given him (2 Corinthians 7:6, 7).

Tychicus is described as one who was sent by Paul to comfort or to encourage the Ephesians and the Colossians (Ephesians 6:21, 22 and Colossians 4:7, 8). Paul admonishes the Thessalonians to "encourage [comfort] each other with these words" (1 Thessalonians 4:18), and prayed in their behalf for God to "encourage [comfort] your hearts and strengthen you in every good deed and word" (2 Thessalonians 2:17).

The word translated in these passages as "comfort" or "encourage" literally means to call alongside of. In the ancient Greek democracy, each citizen had to represent himself when called before the council in trial. He would often employ a *paraklete,* literally, "one who is called alongside," to go to the trial with him. This paraklete would stand by his side and tell him what to say—thus giving him comfort, encouragement, and assurance. This is exactly what the members of the church do to each other. They stand alongside of one another in times of trial. This becomes a *primary* function of the church.

A second result of working together beneficially is that it brings true knowledge of God's mystery (Colossians 2:2, 3). Here is an idea not often underscored. The problem is with the word *mystery.* It has not been translated, but rather transliterated from the Greek *mysterion.* The term is best understood by looking at the way Alexander the Great used it. Before a major battle, Alexander would gather his generals in his tent and explain precisely what he wanted each to do during the battle. Then, after the battle was over and they had won the victory (as they usually did), Alexander would reconvene his generals and explain how what each one of them had done fitted into a total plan for victory. This debriefing session was called *to mysterion,* the mystery session. That is exactly the sense in which Paul uses the term. It might better be translated as "strategy." Perception of God's working out His will to unite all things in Christ (i.e., "true mystery") is directly related to the working together ("being knit together") of the church.

Again, there is a parallel passage in Ephesians 3:17, 18: "Being rooted and established in love, [you] may have power, together with all the saints, to grasp how wide and long and high and deep is the love of Christ." Knowing God's mystery is not just a matter of intellectual superiority, as some in Colosse have thought, but it is, at least partially, dependent on the harmonious working of the whole body.

A third result of being knit together is that it provides safety from heresy. "I tell you this so that no one may deceive you by fine-sounding arguments" (Colossians 2:4). "Then we will no longer be infants, tossed back and forth by the waves, and blown here and there by every wind of teaching and by the cunning and craftiness of men in their deceitful scheming" (Ephesians 4:14). It is only by working together, resulting in encouraging, growth, and getting hold of the true knowledge of God's mystery, that the church can avoid the heretical attacks on its very foundation. If the church in Colosse is to resist the heresy that threatens it, it will have to be done through a concerted effort of all the members.

Before leaving this concept of the church as a body that works together for its own good, two areas in which this very function is dramatized deserve attention. One is the Lord's Supper, "For anyone who eats and drinks without recognizing the body of the Lord eats and drinks judgment on himself" (1 Corinthians 11:29). The King James also has "body of the Lord," but the better manuscripts of this text do not say, "of the Lord." Paul had begun to discuss the divisions of the church at Corinth. "I hear . . . there are divisions among you" (1 Corinthians 11:18). And so the point is this: they cannot authentically participate in the Lord's Supper, which act symbolizes the unity of the body, and at the same time be a part of factions within the church. The result is a kind of blasphemy. Whoever does such a thing is ignoring a certain truth (disunity) that exists, and is even affirming that the opposite (unity) exists by participating. Such a circumstance would be comparable to a man who had terminal cancer in a final stage denying that he was ill (i.e., denying the presence of disharmony in his body) and deciding to run the marathon in the Olympics. "That is why many among you are weak and sick, and a number of you have fallen asleep" (1 Corinthians 11:30).

There is another dramatization of the unity of the church, too: baptism. "For we were all baptized by one Spirit into one body— whether Jews or Greeks, slave or free—and we were all given the one Spirit to drink" (1 Corinthians 12:13). It is at the point of baptism that all become one. Otherwise, there may be distinctions in intelligence, in "spirituality," in prominence. But in baptism, no distinction is made in this matter. Everyone is treated the same. Everyone is immersed the same way. Everyone is raised the same way. Everyone becomes "one" with all others who have become members of the body in such a way. This act demonstrates oneness because it demonstrates absolute dependence on God for His grace. Apparently, baptism had become merely an initiation rite to the Colossians. From that point, they believed, the person must acquire the right "knowledge" to be a part of the body. For them, baptism did not have this symbol of unity, this message of oneness. Paul writes to them that "you have been given fullness in Christ.... having been buried with him in baptism and raised with him through your faith in the power of God, who raised him from the dead" (Colossians 2:10-12). What those Colossian disciples needed to know was not secret rites of a Christian mysticism. Rather, they needed to realize that the "fullness of God," the complete revelation of His character and will, is found in Jesus Christ, and subsequently in His body, the church. They all had encountered that fullness in the same way—first, by recognizing their own inability to achieve it; second, by being introduced by baptism into that body that contained it.

This then, is another relationship that is generated by the body metaphor—the church is a body that works together for its own health, strength, and mutual benefit. It is a body that has spiritual homeostasis. It is a body in which all the parts work together for the good of the whole. When such harmony of the body of the church is realized, the results are the encouragement of the members, true knowledge of God's mystery, and safety from heresy. The harmonious relationship is dramatized in the life of the church in the Lord's Supper and baptism, both of which point to the unity of the body.

CHAPTER EIGHT

Conduct Not Governed by Rules

Colossians 2:6-23

Up to this point, Paul has described the Christ of creation and the Christ of the church. He now turns to the Christ of conduct.

Paul's writings (as does the whole New Testament) demonstrate the proper relationship between doctrine and ethics, between what happens in the mind and what happens in actions. This emphasis is often missed today. The relationship between doctrine and daily living is not readily seen in the church. In some quarters, the emphasis is made on doctrine. What one believes is more important than what is done. Doctrine is the unifying factor. And it is often doctrine of a negative tone. Others emphasize the ethics of daily living and de-emphasize or ignore doctrine. "Christianity is not doctrinal, but relational," they say. There are some who stress both doctrine and ethics, but ethics comes first. The way one lives becomes the primary proof of his doctrine. Doctrine is true first and foremost due to the kind of life lived.

But Paul does not relate doctrine and ethics together in any of these ways. He does emphasize both. Depending on particular circumstances, at times he emphasizes doctrine more, at other times ethics more (in Colossians, roughly two fifths is doctrinal and three fifths ethical). Always, however, there is the relationship between them. The ethical living is not stressed as necessary to become a Christian; it is necessary (or natural) because one *is* a Christian. It is the logical extension into daily life of the regenerating work of Jesus. After writing for eleven chapters in Romans of the wonderful saving power of the gospel to make one righteous by faith, Paul says, "I urge you *therefore,*" and then continues to deal with the practical daily matters such as hospitality, citizenship, and opinionism. These matters are examples of how the one made righteous by faith shall live. This same pattern of doctrine and ethics is seen in other epistles.

And so it is with Colossians. After writing in magnificent prose about the Christ of creation and the Christ of the church, Paul turns in Colossians 2:6 to the practical aspects of what he has said before. Following, there are four obvious areas of daily conduct upon which he touches.

1. In Colossians 2:6, he begins to discuss the Christ-directed conduct and the fact that it is not governed by legalistic regulations.
2. In Colossians 3:1, he begins to discuss the Christ-directed conduct as it demonstrates in personal life the characteristics of the new life in Christ.
3. In Colossians 3:18, he begins to discuss how the Christ-directed conduct demonstrates in family relationships the characteristics of the new life in Christ.
4. In Colossians 4:7 and following, Paul does not discuss, but rather demonstrates, another area of daily conduct that is an extension of the new life in Christ: a Christ-directed conduct that shows great concern for individuals.

There is a remarkable parallelism in the first two of the areas of Christ-directed conduct. First of all, there is the general principle of conduct stated:

A. "So then, just as you received Christ Jesus as Lord, continue to live in him.... See to it that no one takes you captive through hollow and deceptive philosophy, which depends on human tradition and the basic principles of this world rather than on Christ" (Colossians 2:6, 8).
B. "Since, then, you have been raised with Christ, set your hearts on things above.... Set your minds on things above, not on earthly things" (Colossians 3:1, 2).

Then follows the reason for that principle of conduct:

A. "For in Christ all the fullness of the Deity lives in bodily form ..." (Colossians 2:9-15).
B. "For you died, and your life is now hidden with Christ in God" (Colossians 3:3).

Then there is an extension of the principle of conduct:

A. "Therefore do not let anyone judge you by what you eat or drink ..." (Colossians 2:16-23).
B. "Put to death, therefore, whatever belongs to your earthly nature ..." (Colossians 3:5-17).

The Principle Stated (2:6-8)

The primary consequence of this teaching about the nature and work of Jesus is that we are to "continue to live [literally, "to walk"] in him." Paul can command the Colossians to act accordingly because he knows that they "have received Christ Jesus as Lord." He is not commanding persons outside the fellowship of the church to live this way; only those who are in Christ can so walk. Their religious experience was never meant to have merely an intellectual dimension, but to include a behavioral one as well. To this simple and clear command, Paul adds a number of explanatory, though mixed, metaphors. He takes one from botany— "rooted" in Him. The word suggests permanent and long-lasting roots that give strength and life. He continues with a metaphor from construction—"built up"—suggesting a continuous process of growing. (See 1 Corinthians 3:9 for this same pattern of mixed metaphors.) The next description, "strengthened" (the KJV has "established"), comes from the legal world. It denotes a contract that is signed, sealed, and delivered. Finally, they are to overflow—as a river overflows its banks—with thankfulness to God for His mystery that has included them. If these Colossian Christians are to stand against the false teachings to which they are exposed, they must have this kind of grounding in faith.

In Colossians 2:8, Paul makes the first direct attack upon this false teaching by stating the principle negatively. He does not directly state just what the Colossian heresy is. But it is possible to extrapolate enough from his letter to determine certain of its characteristics. One of these was apparently some kind of extreme asceticism. Unlike the situation found in Galatians, this asceticism was one not stemming primarily from a desire to keep the Mosaic Law. Rather, it seems to stem from an incipient Gnostic dualism—a belief that all matter, all things physical, are evil and therefore to be avoided. The logical consequence was that by certain ascetic practices, one could rise above the level of the physical world.

The warning, then, is that they beware ("see to it" in the NIV) lest they be captured (as by a pirate) by a philosophy described as "hollow and deceptive." This is the only place in the New Testament where the word *philosophy* occurs. Paul is not condemning all philosophy; only that which is "hollow and deceptive."

He makes three assertions about it. First, he says that it is dependent upon human *tradition*. In Mark 7:8, the same word is used to refer to the explanations of the Jewish law given by the Pharisees. It may be in this sense that Paul uses the term here. Apparently, these false teachers were passing off their teaching as a part of the tradition handed down from the ancestors. Paul's affirmation, though, is that it is *human* tradition, not divine.

Second, he says it depends on "basic principles of this world." There is no consistent agreement as to what Paul means by "basic principles," but it is clear that he focuses here on the cardinal error of the Colossians. Basically, there are two possibilities. The Greek word *(stoicheia)* was used early of objects standing in a row, and so was used of letters of the alphabet. The word in this sense would mean then, the elemental teachings, the A, B, C's, the tradition of men over against the teaching of Christ. This meaning fits the context—they were troubled by a body of teaching that included ascetic rules.

There is another possibility, however. The word *stoicheia* came to mean the elemental constituents of the cosmos, namely earth, water, air, and fire. Later, the word was used specifically for the stars, especially the twelve signs of the zodiac, to which were attributed personality and power over the lives of men and the course of nature. If Paul is using the word in such a way as this, then it should be translated "elemental spirits" (as RSV, NEB). There are two compelling facts that support this latter translation. For one thing, they (the spirits) are contrasted with Christ, a natural antithesis. Moreover, there is the problem of angel-worship (Colossians 2:18), which gives support to this translation. Consequently, the conduct of these Colossians is being governed by the alleged astrological spiritual powers. By certain ascetic practices, they believe, they are able to overcome those spirits hostile to them and gain the grace of those favorable to them. Conduct is governed by the spirits and not by Christ. Here again, a doctrinal issue, the status of Christ, manifests itself in practical daily living.

Third, the philosophy is not dependent upon Jesus. As noted, above, the Christian message is not merely a system, but a relationship with Jesus. He is both the originator and the focus of this religion.

The Reason for the Principle (2:9-15)

The reason for this principle, stated first positively and then negatively, now follows and is two-fold. Most basic is the very nature of Jesus: "in Christ all the fullness of the Deity lives in bodily form." (See Colossians 1:19.) Some believe that the elemental spirits of this world were referred to as "the fullness" when they were taken all together. If so, then Paul is saying that it is Jesus who is the fullness of God rather than these elemental spirits. He says, then, that the Colossians have been given this fullness *in Christ*. This status comes, not through some special kind of knowledge communicated through some mystical rite, but rather from being *in* Jesus, that is to say, from a personal relationship with Him.

Six times in this passage (Colossians 2:9-15), Paul emphasizes this intimate connection to Jesus. It is a theme he began in Colossians 2:7, "rooted and built up *in him*." First, he says that they have been given this "fullness" and that they received it "in Christ." It was necessary for Jesus to assume a physical body to demonstrate this full character of God. "The Word became *flesh* .... We have seen his glory ... *full* of grace and truth" (John 1:14, emphasis mine). Now it is His body on earth, the church, that demonstrates His "fullness," His glory. A parallel passage in Ephesians is even more explicit: "And God placed all things under his feet and appointed him to be the head over everything for the church, which is his body, the fullness of him ..." (Ephesians 1:22, 23).

As pointed out above, *fullness* is a technical term used by the Gnostics to mean all the attributes of God, which were held in part by several intermediary beings. This word *fullness* was used in ancient literature to describe a ship with a full complement of sailors. It was ready to function in an optimum way. Aristotle used this word to describe a city who had as its citizens those artisans, craftsmen, and educators who could make the city function effectively. And so *fullness* means that situation in which an institution or unit is prepared to operate in the most effective way because all the parts are there.

This characteristic of the church as the body, therefore, captures one more dimension of the body metaphor. Two characteristics have already been seen: (1) the body recognizes and responds to its head, and (2) the body has sufficient parts that work together for its common good. Now, the church is the body through which God's character is revealed to the world. The first characteristic of this metaphor focuses upon the vertical dimension, the head and the body. The second characteristic focuses upon the internal dimension, working harmoniously together for its own health. The third characteristic focuses upon the outward dimension, the benefits that come to the world because of this work.

The second and third times Paul says "in him" or "with him" are in Colossians 2:11 and 12: "*In him* you were also circumcised ... not with a circumcision done by the hands of men but ... by Christ, having been buried *with him* in baptism." Just what this circumcision "in him" means is not clear. The New International Version translates it "putting off of the sinful nature" (Colossians 2:11), but this rendering may be an interpretation more than a translation. At any rate, this view takes the "circumcision of Christ" (literal translation of Colossians 2:11) to mean "the circumcision that Christ gives," i.e. baptism. So (according to the meaning of the NIV translation) Jesus, at the baptism of an individual, removes that one's sinful nature in the same way that circumcision removed flesh from the physical body. The person so baptized was "raised with him" (the fourth time Paul has used the phrase) from the burial of baptism with the new nature to live in union with Jesus, who was raised from the dead.

There is another interpretation of this passage, though, that has merit, even though it is not in harmony with the New International Version's translation of it. Notice two other translations of Colossians 2:11.

Revised Standard Version	**New American Standard Bible**
In him also you were circumcised with a circumcision made without hands, by putting off the *body of flesh in the circumcision of Christ.*	And in Him you were also circumcised with a circumcision made without hands, *in the removal of the body of the flesh* by the *circumcision of Christ.*

In either the Revised Standard Version or the New American Standard Bible, the meaning of the New International is a possibility. *Body of flesh* could mean sinful nature. *Circumcision of Christ* could mean circumcision done by Christ. But there are other possibilities. The *circumcision of Christ* could very well refer to His death. Their "circumcision" (their purification), then, was due to "the putting off of the body of flesh" (i.e. the death of Jesus; see Colossians 1:22), a circumcision not of human origin. It

124

originated solely in Jesus. Circumcision is not, then, a figure for baptism, but rather for Jesus' death.

Three of the primary parts of the ancient gospel were the death, burial, and resurrection of Jesus (1 Corinthians 15:3, 4). These parts are evident here: "Putting off the body of flesh" (His death), "buried with him in baptism" (His burial), and "raised with him" (His resurrection). The emphasis is that salvation does not come by human office ("by the hands of men") but rather through contact with the death, burial, and resurrection of Jesus in baptism. One might even speculate that the false teachers in Colosse were trying to enforce circumcision on the church. To them, Paul says, that it is the death of Jesus ("the circumcision of Christ") that puts them in a right relationship to Jesus. His death was a mighty act of God ("not . . . done by the hands of men").

The fifth and sixth uses of "with him" or "in him" occur in Colossians 2:13 and 15 respectively: "made you alive *with Christ*" (Colossians 2:13), and, "He made a public spectacle of them, triumphing over them *in him*" (Colossians 2:15, RSV). The passage repeats the thrust of Colossians 2:9-12, although the figures are different. Now he describes this new relationship as "made alive" and as the forgiveness of sins. There is an interesting change in Colossians 2:13 and 14. For the past several verses, Paul has been addressing the Gentiles, always identified as "you." Now he includes the Jewish readers, the "us." Here, the figure is the canceling out of a written code of laws by nailing it to the cross. It no longer need condemn the Jews since its power has been nullified for those "in him."

The Extension of the Principle (2:16-23)

Having established the principle (Colossians 2:6-8) and pointed out several reasons for it (Colossians 2:9-15), Paul now returns to the principle and extends it to more specific actions. In this paragraph, Paul enumerates the specific kind of conduct they had demonstrated (Colossians 2:16-23). Their conduct demonstrated both Jewish and Greek elements. As an example of Jewish influence, Paul says, "Therefore do not let anyone judge you by what you eat or drink, or with regard to a religious festival, a New Moon celebration or a Sabbath day" (Colossians 2:16). While perhaps having a Jewish background, their conduct of abstinence of certain foods and drinks is not completely Jewish either in motivation or extent. They abstain, not to keep the law, but to

125

gain prestige in the eyes of the astrological spirits. Furthermore, they go beyond the Mosaic distinction of clean and unclean meats. Lightfoot conjectures that, like the Essenes, they also prohibit all meats and wine, and simply eat bread and a few vegetables. The regulations of special days, annual, monthly, and weekly (which is what the text means) sounds more Jewish on the surface. They did observe such holy days. But again the connection may only be tangential. The motive is merely to get the favor of the spirits. There may be, in fact, some astrological significance to the changing of the moon, seasons, and such. It may be a symbol of the power of these spirits.

The practice of one who "delights in false humility" (or "delighting in self-abasement," NASB; Colossians 2:18) and worship of angels seems to have primarily Gnostic origin (although the Essenes worshiped angels to some extent, too). The word translated "voluntary humility" (KJV), or "self-abasement" (NASB), could be translated as readiness for service. The Colossians were so devoted to these angels that they were eager to perform the cultic acts and carry out the regulations laid down by them. One part of the Colossians' conduct that is certainly of Greek origin is their instruction quoted by Paul in Colossians 2:21: "Do not handle! Do not taste! Do not touch!" (Although, again, there are some Jewish parallels in the Talmud.) This quotation apparently demonstrates the extent of their religious teaching. In fact, some believe that *do not handle* means sexual abstinence. The word is used in such a way in 1 Corinthians 7:1.

There are at least four shortcomings to the legalistic conduct of the Colossians:

1. They are engaged in what is a mere shadow of reality. "These are a shadow of the things that were to come; the reality, however, is found in Christ" (Colossians 2:17). These regulations that had Jewish connection were given to symbolize that which would succeed them and be the fulfillment of them. Thus, the writer of Hebrews develops his letter around this theme. When the Colossians focus on the external rites, they are focusing on the form rather than the substance that is available. Moreover, it is a form no longer an essential factor in God's scheme of salvation.
2. Such practices lead to a special kind of pride. The man whose whole life is wrapped up in celebrating special religious days, in keeping all the food laws and regulations, and in practicing

ascetic abstinence, even celebacy, is very prone to think highly of himself for his good works. The center focus of his attention becomes his own actions rather than the saving work of Christ.

3. Of great practical significance, these legalistic practices simply do not work. "Such regulations indeed have an appearance of wisdom, with their self-imposed worship, their false humility and their harsh treatment of the body, but they lack any value in restraining sensual indulgence" (Colossians 2:23). The one who hopes to achieve perfection by observing such a life-style is sorely disappointed. Unnecessary regulations of daily living actually are harmful because they have an appearance of controlling the evil nature, but in fact do no more than put a mask on it. Paul knew that a man had to admit he was unable to control his own life before Christ could do any good for him. That is exactly what the Colossians cannot do because of their legalistic conduct.

4. Finally, and perhaps most importantly, such legalistic conduct ignores the great work of Jesus in the life of the individual. His work in our lives, moreover, manifests itself in daily conduct. There is no need to be subservient to these "elemental spirits" because they have "died with Christ" (Colossians 2:20). The major thrust in the previous section (Colossians 2:9-15) was that their relationship to Jesus is the reason for their right relationship to God, and not their own efforts or their special status. It is because of who Christ is, and their being "in" or "with" Him that makes all the difference. The Christian life, Christian conduct, is not governed by rules. Rather, it is life and conduct governed by being in and with Christ (having "fullness" *in Him,* being *in His death* (circumcision), buried *with Him,* raised *with Him,* and made alive *with Him,* and since this world's powers are defeated *in Him.*

CHAPTER NINE

Conduct in Personal Relations

Colossians 3:1-17

The same three-part structure as was demonstrated in the previous section is apparent for this section:
1. The principle is stated (Colossians 3:1, 2).
2. The reason for the principle is given (Colossians 3:3, 4).
3. Then the extension of the principle is developed (Colossians 3:5-17).
Charles Spurgeon, a famous British preacher, said that this chapter begins in Heaven and ends in the kitchen, and so it does.

The Principle Stated (3:1, 2)

Paul continues the topic of baptism and the death and resurrection of Jesus. It is because these Colossians have been "buried with him in baptism" and also "raised with him through ... faith" (Colossians 2:12) that he is now able to give them these two commands. First, they are to set their "hearts on things above" (Colossians 3:1) and then set their "minds on things above" (Colossians 3:2). The first command focuses upon the direction of the will; the second focuses upon the object of the mind. In both cases, it is to be the "things above."

Apparently, the false teachers at Colosse were also emphasizing that their followers should strive for spiritual ends, too. In their case, however, they do so in order to abandon this world. The Christian, on the other hand, both desires and contemplates from a non-earthly perspective in order to live in the earthly realm in a consistent manner with that viewpoint. The following section, which gives significant attention to life on this earth, is evidence of this difference.

To view all of life from this Heavenly perspective is a primary characteristic of the Christian. To see life on this earth in the way that Jesus sees it is the goal. When God "exalted him to the highest place" (Philippians 2:9), at least part of the consequence was that He now has a perspective from eternity of all of His creation. While on earth, Jesus did have that perspective, but not fully. For example, He said of the last days for the earth, "No one knows about that day or hour, not even the angels in heaven, nor the Son, but only the Father" (Matthew 24:36). But since the ascension of Jesus to the right hand of God, He now has the perspective of God fully. He is able to impart this vision in substantial form to His body, the church. No one knew this better than Paul himself. Only after Paul encountered the exalted Jesus on the Damascus road did he come to some understanding of this perspective. He, as has been seen here and in Ephesians, calls his new understanding, a "mystery" (Ephesians 1:9; 3:3, 4, 9; 6:19; Colossians 1:26, 27; 2:2; 4:3).

The view from God's perspective is quite different from man's view from earth. Modern man sees a closed system in which events are caused solely by other events in that closed system. It is a world where human power, whether political, economic, social, or military, determine the course of things. Such a view, of course, gives occasion for decisions about values and relationships. If the perspective is all wrong, however, as Paul argues, then those values and relationships come under question. He wrote to the Corinthians, "God chose the foolish things of the world to shame the wise; God chose the weak things of the world to shame the strong. He chose the lowly things of this world and the despised things—and the things that are not—to nullify the things that are" (1 Corinthians 1:27, 28). When the body of Christ has the perspective of Heaven, it can understand that.

The Reason for the Principle (3:3, 4)

As in the previous section, Paul follows the commands with the reason for the commands. He repeats here what he has already affirmed, namely that the Colossians have "died" in Jesus and that they are hidden with Christ in God. That which "died," of course, was the old self with its human perspective. There is no other way to seek and to think about things "from above." It takes the perspective of Jesus himself.

There was an ancient belief that one's life could be protected if some image or token of it would be hidden away somewhere for protection. As long as this token was safe, it was believed that the person it represented would be safe as well. This kind of practice may be what Paul has in mind when he describes their lives as "hidden with Christ in God." They will be preserved because their present, new lives are with Christ. Furthermore, in Colossians 3:4, Paul continues this same thought by making the only clear reference in this letter to Jesus' second coming. Another reason for desiring and thinking of "things above" is that they will have their true character revealed for all to see at His coming. For now, what they really are, their true essence, is hidden from many. The world cannot understand this "desiring" and "thinking" on things above. When Jesus returns, however, He will reveal the truth about this world and expose the falsehood of seeing things only from a human perspective.

The Extension of the Principle (3:5-17)

Having established the principle of holy living and the basic reasons for it, Paul now extends this principle to specific areas of conduct. Here doctrine and behavior become inextricably bound together. Desiring and thinking about "the things above" do not mean that one lives an other-worldly life. The doctrine of union with Jesus has most specific implications for the here and now. The behavior described in this passage is not done in order to come into a right relationship with God; it is a result of that relationship with God that such behavior is demonstrated.

This extension falls into two broad sections. First Paul describes those behaviors to be avoided (Colossians 3:5-11). Then he describes the kind of behavior to be demonstrated (Colossians 3:12-17). Throughout the passage, he carries forward the figure of baptism. As Jesus cut off the flesh of His earthly life by His death, they who have contacted Him at that point are to do the same. They have died with Christ. As He rid himself of the human nature He had assumed, so are they to "put to death" the manifestation of their human nature, "whatever belongs to your earthly nature." Baptismal imagery is pervasive throughout: "put to death" (Colossians 3:5)—death in baptism; "rid yourselves of all such things" (Colossians 3:8)—putting off the old clothes at baptism; "put on the new self" (Colossians 3:10) and "clothe yourselves with . . ." (Colossians 3:12)—putting on the new clothes after baptism. The antithesis here is self-dividing. There are some characteristics that are "put off," or "put to death," not as a work of righteousness, but as a consequence of union with Christ's putting them to death. There are other characteristics that

131

are "put on" again, not as a work of righteousness, but because Christians have been raised with Christ in His new life and they are characteristic of Him.

First are the characteristics to be put off. This grim catalog easily falls into two categories: the sins of uncontrolled passion (Colossians 3:5), and the sins of mind and mouth against one's fellowman (Colossians 3:8).

"Put to death, therefore, whatever belongs to your earthly nature: [1] *sexual immorality,* [2] *impurity. . . .*" These first two mean about the same, but the latter term has a broader meaning. Sexual promiscuity was not considered so much of a vice in the Greek world, at least for the men. A married man could have extramarital intercourse as he pleased if he did not violate another civil marriage. Of course, the wife did not enjoy the same privilege, but was forbidden all extramarital sex. Paul makes it clear that the sexual ethics practiced by the church are in contrast to the world, and even to the way they also "once lived" themselves (Colossian 3:7). (3) *"Lust"* and (4) *"evil desires."* Again, in this context, these terms mean something very similar. Paul uses the word *lust* in Romans 1:26 to refer to homosexuality, and it is probably in such a sense that he uses it here. (5) *"Greed, which is idolatry."* This may be the most surprising in this list of sensual sins. And yet the desire to get and get, making gain the god that is worshiped, in many ways is fundamental to all sin. That is exactly why Paul links it with idolatry here.

In Colossians 2:6 and 7, Paul presents two circumstances surrounding this kind of behavior and pointing to its inconsistency with the Christian life. First of all, the "wrath of God" is coming upon those who practice such things. Several times when Paul describes such evil behavior, he affirms that God's judgment will result. In Romans 1:18-32, he catalogs a list of vices characteristic of the world without God and concludes that "the wrath of God is being revealed from heaven against all the godlessness" (Romans 1:18). Such people, he claims, "deserve death" (Romans 1:32). In 1 Thessalonians 4:6, after discussing some of these same practices, he declares that "the Lord will punish men for all such sins." Many see the phrase *wrath of God* referring either to a personification of this judgment to come upon the sinful or to a principle of recompense, and not to the result of God's direct will; the judgment, they say, comes as a consequence of actions in God's established order. Be that as it may, the fact of such judgment upon these unregenerated persons is most clearly affirmed throughout the Bible, both the Old and New Testaments.

A second circumstance surrounding this kind of immoral behavior is that it is characteristic of their pre-Christian lives (Colossians 3:7). Paul uses the past tense to describe these conditions. This pattern he used before: "Once you were alienated . . . now he has reconciled you" (Colossians 1:21, 22; see also 2:13). This time, the *but now* part of the pattern turns into a command rather than a description of their present state.

"You must rid yourselves of all such things as these" (Colossians 3:8). He continues with the sins of mouth and mind against one's fellowman. (1) *"Anger"* and (2) *"rage."* The first here refers to a deep-seated attitude; the other to a violent outburst of temper. Paul may not be emphasizing this technical difference, however, but listing synonymous words for cumulative effect. (3) *"Malice."* This term refers to that nature of man that actually seeks to do harm to others. This represents the disposition to harm; the other words represent actual attempts. (4) *"Slander"* and (5) *"filthy language."* The anger, rage, and malice are most often vented by slanderous talk about another or through abusive speech.

Once again, Paul repeats the figure of taking off the old and putting on the new, undoubtedly with the practice of baptism in mind. The results occasioned by baptism are striking, not only with regard to one's relationship to God, but also the relationship to others as well. There are some who still understand this radical act in this way. In Romania, it is the practice of baptismal candidates to sit together in white robes and sing a chorus together, a rough translation of which is "Clothed in Christ, clothed in Christ; we baptized ones are now clothed in Christ." They understand that their relationship to God and their actions before their ever-watching world are radically different because they have "put on Christ."

A significant consequence of being "clothed in Christ" is that all appear alike; differences are covered over in Him as well as reconciliation effected by Him. The list that Paul presents here (Colossians 3:11) cuts across many of the natural barriers of his day: national ("Greek or Jew"), ceremonial ("circumcised or uncircumcised"), cultural ("barbarian", i.e. a non-Greek speaking person, "Scythian," the lowest and crudest of the barbarians), or economic status ("slave or free"). It is not that these distinctions cease to exist absolutely; it is that they cease to matter for those who are in the body. Those who have put on Christ do not see such distinctions existing in others as significant or as barriers for fellowship since those others are clothed in like manner.

After the characteristics of the old man are taken off and put to death, the characteristics of the new man are put on and made alive (Colossians 3:12-14): (1) *"compassion,"* (2) *"kindness,"* (3) *"humility,"* (4) *"gentleness,"* (5) *"patience,"* (6) *"forbearance,"* (7) *"forgiveness,"* and (8) *"love."* These characteristics are assumed, not because by being this kind of person it is possible to become holy in God's sight. That attitude is absolutely antithetical to Paul's thesis in Colossians. He does not choose these characteristics as a composite of the ideals of other high ethical systems of his day. He does not choose these characteristics just because it seems like a good idea for people to behave in these ways. The context must be kept in mind.

What is it that makes some conduct evil and other conduct good? Is it that God does not want His people to have any fun, and so just arbitrarily sets up rules? Not at all. Some conduct is wrong because it is not typical of God's character. Other conduct is desirable because it is typical of God's character.

Paul concludes this section, which extends the principle of Colossians 3:1 and 2, with three all-encompassing imperatives (Colossians 3:15-17). First, he says that they are to "let the peace of Christ rule" in their hearts. Here, in contrast to other places in Paul's writings, this "peace" is not merely an inward calmness resulting from the presence of God's Spirit. Rather, he means here a peace that is characteristic of their relations together—"as members of one body you were called to peace" (Colossians 3:15). The peace of Christ manifests itself in the harmony of the body. This peace is to "rule" in their hearts. The word so translated primarily refers to the function of the umpire. In the face of any disturbance that might threaten the unity of the local body, the very "peace" that Jesus demonstrates is to referee that disturbance to the point of harmony.

Second, they are to "let the word of Christ dwell" in them (Colossians 3:16), and Paul gives them particular ways this is to be accomplished, although the translation of this passage is unclear. The two primary ways are illustrated at the top of page 135.

New American Standard Bible	**New International Version**
Let the word of Christ richly dwell within you, with all wisdom teaching and admonishing one another with psalms and hymns and spiritual songs, singing with thankfulness in your hearts to God.	Let the word of Christ dwell in you richly as you teach and admonish one another with all wisdom, and as you sing psalms, hymns and spiritual songs with gratitude in your hearts to God.

The problem is whether the psalms, hymns, and spiritual songs are examples of the teaching and admonishing that are done as expressions of the indwelling of the word of Christ (as the NASB takes it) or whether these forms of singing are parallel expressions of the indwelling word along with teaching and admonishing (as in the NIV). The word order, though by no means certain, slightly favors the former rendering. Furthermore, what is known about the nature of early singing in the church favors this understanding as well, for there were songs designed for both teaching and praise.

Probably there is no hard and fast distinction between "psalms," "hymns," and "spiritual songs." If there is any at all, *psalms* would refer to the Old Testament psalter while the other two to contemporary Christian compositions. An interesting side note to this passage is the kind of singing that seems to be implied here. They were to teach and admonish *one another* with these songs. Such a practice would not seem to occasion full congregational singing, but rather describe antiphonal singing (one part of the congregation singing a phrase and then another singing a phrase in response) or small groups singing to the entire congregation. Apparently, both of these styles characterized early Christian singing. Whether there are examples of full congregational singing in the New Testament is not at all clear.

Paul began the section with a command to desire and think about "things above." He ends this section with the admonition to "do it all in the name of the Lord Jesus" (Colossians 3:17). Every word and every deed is to be done in His name. The phrase *in the name of Jesus* is used in reference to Christian baptism, to salvation, to the giving of the Holy Spirit, and to the mission of Jesus (Acts 10:48; 4:12; John 14:26; 3:18). Here, however, it seems to be a more general meaning. In the ancient world, certain people had the authority to act on behalf of the king—in the name of the king. Paul affirms here that Christians are to be such for Jesus. What they do and what they say are to be done as Jesus himself would act or speak. Ultimately, there can be no comprehensive list of *do*s and *don't*s for the Christians. It is rather the awareness that Christians are here in Christ's stead that is the ultimate ethic.

CHAPTER TEN

Conduct in Family Relations

Colossians 3:18—4:1

Next, Paul turns to the Christ-directed conduct within the family, what Martin Luther called the *haustafeln,* the household rules. These principles are directed successively to wives and husbands, to children and fathers, and to slaves and masters. Similar sets of rules were common in the ancient world, both Greek and Jewish. Aristotle (384-322 B.C.), Seneca (55 B.C.-A.D. 41), and Polybius (c. 200-118 B.C.) are among the pagan writers who had such lists in their works. Philo and Josephus are two Jewish writers who include them.

There are two primary differences in the Greek approach to the household rules: (1) the chief focus was upon the rights of the free male and (2) the goal was the attainment of perfection or virtue through keeping such regulations. The Jewish treatment of these household rules were primarily consideration of the ethical behavior of Gentile converts to Judaism.

The example of the household rules in the New Testament serve another function. They demonstrate the new life in Jesus Christ. They follow as a natural result of being united with Jesus. The conduct is done "as is fitting in the Lord" (Colossians 3:18) and in a such way as "pleases the Lord" (Colossians 3:20). Furthermore, the conduct under concern is for *all* who are "in the Lord"— wives, children, and slaves as well as husbands, fathers, and masters. It seems that some in Colosse, with all of their concern over the worship of angels, observance of rituals, and practice of asceticism, were not careful about the day-to-day living in the home. To them, spirituality was escape from the material and mundane world. Paul can say to them "set your minds on things above" and at the same time admonish them to give attention to live out the spiritual life in the world of the here-and-now. These are not arbitrary rules given simply as the highest example of moral conduct of the age. Rather, Paul presents an extension into daily living of the implications of the Lordship of Jesus over all of life.

There are a number of parallel passages of such lists in the New Testament (e.g., Ephesians 5:21—6:9; 1 Timothy 2:8-15; 6:1, 2; Titus 2:1-10; 1 Peter 2:13—3:7), and a thorough understanding must include some consideration of them all. The most frequent order is that one found in Colossians: general guidelines, wives, husbands, children, fathers, slaves, masters.

While an examination of these parallel texts demonstrates that there are similarities, perhaps enough so as to suggest that there was a consistent and set teaching in the early church on these things, the occasion for each of these passages should be taken into consideration as well. The order in which the groups appear, the length of instruction given to each group, and which groups are omitted all may suggest particular problems of the recipients. While there appears to be a common body of teaching concerning these groups, the New Testament writers were free to apply and expand to the specific audiences as the need dictated. Space does not permit a full treatment of all the texts that consider these household groups. Following is a consideration of the pairs of groups dealt with in the Colossians text.

Wives and Husbands (3:18, 19)

The exposition of the Lordship of Christ in the marriage relationship is difficult because of some very hard-to-understand sayings about it. It is really impossible to resolve all of this tension in the course of this study, but the issue needs to be addressed. Paul begins by saying, "Wives, submit to your husbands, as is fitting in the Lord," and continues to the husbands, "Love your wives and do not be harsh with them." In Ephesians, where Paul gave a more extended treatment of this same principle, he began, "Submit to one another" (Ephesians 5:21). The verb *submit* means to decide voluntarily to serve one another. Jesus "submitted" to God, His Father: "Who, being in very nature God, did not consider equality with God something to be grasped, but made himself nothing, taking the very nature of a servant" (Philippians 2:6, 7). When a wife "submits" herself to her husband, she voluntarily decides to lay aside her privileges in order to serve him. When a husband "submits" himself to his wife, he does the same. This principle of *mutual* subjection is consistent with Paul's injunction to the Corinthians:

138

The husband should fulfill his marital duty to his wife, and likewise the wife to her husband. The wife's body does not belong to her alone but also to her husband. In the same way, the husband's body does not belong to him alone but also to his wife. Do not deprive each other except by mutual consent and for a time, so that you may devote yourselves to prayer. Then come together again so that Satan will not tempt you because of your lack of self-control (1 Corinthians 7:3-5).

The same note of equality is sounded by Paul in his letter to the Galatians: "There is neither Jew nor Greek, slave nor free, male nor female, for you are all one in Christ Jesus" (Galatians 3:28). Those who are "in Christ Jesus" have the *implications* of the traditional and cultural distinctions done away. The distinctions still exist, of course. There is obviously no loss of sexuality when people become Christians. The *implications* of those distinctions have changed, however.

Although it is not too clear exactly how Paul's teaching concerning this equality was always lived out, there are passages in the New Testament and in other early Christian literature to suggest that some had taken the matter of liberty and equality too far. It appears that some, indeed, understood Paul's teaching in Galatians 3:28 as a way to deny their sexuality altogether. In the apocryphal *Gospel of Thomas* is a strange saying that reveals an attitude, among other things, about male-female relationships in the middle of the second century, and one might suppose even back into the first century: "When you make male and female into a single one." This seems to suggest that a unisex movement, probably of some Gnostic origin, existed to some degree. The goal seems to be the denial of one's sexuality. There are hints of this attitude in the New Testament. The Corinthians wrote to Paul, "It is good for a man not to touch a woman" (1 Corinthians 7:1, NASB). The verb *to touch* means to have sexual relations. The Colossians also had a slogan, "Do not handle! Do not taste! Do not touch!" (Colossians 2:21; the verb *touch* is the same as in 1 Corinthians 7:1). The problem is the same—the denial of sexuality through avoiding sexual relations between husband and wife.

In summary, then, the issue of the relationship of men and women is a complex one, made all the more problematic by practices that are not too familiar to our world. On the one hand, Paul gives general principles that are grounded in Jesus' reconciling work (Galatians 3:28; Ephesians 5:21); on the other hand, he speaks to specific problems when the principle is misused or misapplied or is combined with non-Christian practices (1 Corinthians 11, 14; 1 Timothy 2, et al.). It is a true principle that husbands and wives are to submit to one another. It is a true principle that husbands are to love their wives. It is a true principle that the differences between males and females are to be affirmed, but those differences do not affect their standing in Jesus Christ.

Children and Parents (3:20, 21)

Notice that the children are directly addressed here. This fact presupposes that they are old enough to be responsible for their own actions and also that they would be in the assembly when the letter was read. The command to them is put quite strongly, *obey* rather than *submit* as to the wives. Paul uses this term in describing the obedience of a Christian to Jesus (Romans 6:17; 10:16; Philippians 2:12; 2 Thessalonians 1:8; 3:14; et al.). The command to them is strengthened all the more by the phrase *in everything*. The clarity of this command is reminiscent of the fifth commandment for children to honor their fathers and mothers and thereby have a long life (Exodus 20:12; Deuteronomy 5:16). In Exodus 21:15, the death penalty was the consequence of a child's striking his father or mother. Furthermore, there are examples of such injunctions to children in non-Christian writers such as Plutarch. But here the command has a Christian basis. They are to be obedient, "for this pleases the Lord." Literally, the phrase is "pleasing *in* the Lord." These children are not obedient merely out of social convention, but rather are acting out their Christian lives in this way.

While children are instructed to be obedient to their parents, it is the fathers who are singled out and told not to "embitter" their children. While there are times when the Greek word here translated "fathers" is used to refer to both parents (Hebrews 11:23), Paul may indeed have the fathers particularly in view here. In the Roman world, the *patria potestas* (the power of the head of the household) gave fathers almost unlimited power over their children. Instead of this model, Paul encourages that the greatest concern be shown toward the healthy development of the children. His tone sounds very modern; or perhaps to put it correctly, much of modern psychological theories of childhood development sounds very Pauline. Unfortunately, the practices of child rearing today do not always follow these principles advocated by Paul and many contemporary psychologists. On the one hand, there is the extreme in practice of extraordinary permissiveness, which leads to confusion and the failure to form values shared by the home and the Christian community. On the other hand, there is the extreme of a too rigid authoritarianism, which more and more leads to child abuse. Paul strikes a happy medium here. The phrase *become discouraged* is also translated "lose heart" or "be timid." The goal of fathers is to treat their children in such a way that they might develop a positive and confident attitude about themselves, their abilities, and their world. Of course, discipline is necessary for this to happen, but it must be a discipline tempered with love and respect for them as human beings and as gifts from God. There is no more noble and solemn responsibility in the world than that one.

Slaves and Masters (3:22—4:1)

Paul spends by far the greatest amount of space in this list of house rules with those pertaining to slaves and masters. Peter does also in his list (1 Peter 2:13-25). This fact is understandable here especially because the slave, Onesimus, is going back to his master in Colosse along with Tychicus, this letter, and the letter to Philemon, his master. Onesimus had run away from Philemon, but now, under Paul's influence, is returning to him, "no longer as a slave, but better than a slave, as a dear brother" (Philemon 16). This section, then, certainly is not merely an abstract code, but rather has immediate and practical implications for the Colossian church, for Onesimus, and for Philemon.

The whole issue of slavery in the ancient world is a complex one and goes beyond the purview of this study. It is a mistake, however, to think of this slavery as the slavery in the United States through the mid-nineteenth century. This slavery was not one based on race, but rather was more a part of the economic structure. Paul does not condemn slavery nor does he encourage revolt by slaves against their masters. Rather, he attempts to explain for those who are "in Christ" what it means to live out one's position as a slave or a master. He has already affirmed that there is neither slave nor free for those in Christ Jesus (Colossians 3:11). How, then is that freedom to be realized for those who are slaves and masters? Paul addressed the question in part in 1 Corinthians 7:21-24:

> Were you a slave when you were called? Don't let it trouble you—
> although if you can gain your freedom, do so. For he who was a
> slave when he was called by the Lord is the Lord's freedman; simi-
> larly, he who was a free man when he was called is Christ's slave.
> You were bought at a price; do not become slaves of men. Brothers,
> each man, as responsible to God, should remain in the situation
> God called him to.

Some have claimed that Paul's attitude of remaining "in the situation God called" them to can be attributed to his belief that Jesus was coming back to earth soon and so trying to obtain freedom was wasted effort. However, his treatment of slaves and masters in these house rules suggests something else. His point, both in 1 Corinthians 7 and in Colossians 3, is that one can serve Christ right where he is. The Christian life is not some utopian age, but is lived in the reality of the here-and-now. It is certainly not wrong for them to take their freedom if they can do so. However, the important issue is to demonstrate what it means to be "in Christ" in the present circumstances. Paul uniquely understands how this principle works in his own life. He wants to be freed from prison, yet he knows that he is able to live out the Christian life even in prison. He can say that "what has happened to me [imprisonment] has really served to advance the gospel" (Philippians 1:12). And so can slaves, too. The point is not that slavery is good; rather, God's power is sufficient to work through such conditions if the Christian ethic is demonstrated.

Paul answers four questions with regard to the service of the slaves.

1. What is the service? It is obedience "in everything" (Colossians 3:22). A few verses earlier, he had said "whatever you do ... do it all in the name of the Lord Jesus" (Colossians 3:17). He now particularizes that command for the slaves.
2. How are they to serve? He says not only when they are being watched, but rather with sincerity of purpose and reverence for the Lord (Colossians 3:22).
3. Why are they to serve this way? Because, he says, they are ultimately working for the Lord and not for men (Colossians 3:23). There is no other religion that values work in the way that Christianity does. Work, however menial it might seem, can be dedicated as service to the Lord—even attending to the church nursery!

4. What is the result of such service? They will receive an inheritance from the Lord (Colossians 3:24). According to Roman law, it was not legal for slaves to inherit property. These faithful slaves, however, already had an inheritance prepared for them by Jesus himself.

To the masters, Paul simply reminds them that they also have a Master; so they should treat their slaves justly and fairly. Probably not many Christian congregations have slave owners, and so Paul does not spend much time with this group. The word translated "fairly" here also means "equally." Though there is a human relationship determined to some extent by the conventions of society, the masters need to realize that "in Jesus" they are equal; they need to affirm Jesus' reconciling work by treating these slaves as their equals in the sight of God.

CHAPTER ELEVEN

Final Greetings

Colossians 4:2-18

After the section of household rules, with its directives to specified groups, Paul now turns to speaking to the entire congregation again. He first offers final admonitions to them (Colossians 4:2-6), then makes personal commendations and greetings (Colossians 4:7-15), and closes with final instructions and a benediction (Colossians 4:16-18).

Admonition to Prayer, Conduct, and Speech (4:2-6)

In this section, Paul makes three admonitions:
1. "Devote yourselves to prayer" (Colossians 4:2).
2. "Be wise in the way you act" (Colossians 4:5).
3. "Let your conversation be always full of grace" (Colossians 4:6).

While it is Paul's normal practice to open his letters with prayer for his readers, he frequently closes them by asking for their prayers for him. (See Ephesians 6:18; Philippians 4:6; 1 Thessalonians 5:17.) The word translated "prayer" most always means petition. There are two ways that they are to make these petitions: being watchful and being thankful. Watchfulness is frequently associated with prayer. Jesus, in the Olivet discourse, encouraged His disciples to watch (Mark 13:37). Again, He asked His disciples to "watch and pray" in the Garden of Gethsemane (Mark 14:38). In the former example, He certainly had His second coming in mind, and that may be Paul's meaning here. The object of these petitions would certainly be consistent with that understanding.

While being watchful focuses upon the future, thankfulness looks to the past. Paul has dealt explicitly in this letter with many reasons for their thankfulness. This inclusion serves primarily as a summary response they are to demonstrate.

There are also two objects for these petitions. The first is an open door (Colossians 4:3). Paul uses this expression to describe a condition that is just right for evangelism. "But I will stay on at Ephesus until Pentecost, because a great door for effective work has opened to me" (1 Corinthians 16:8, 9). "Now when I went to Troas to preach the gospel of Christ and found that the Lord had opened a door for me . . ." (2 Corinthians 2:12). Luke also used the phrase in the same way (Acts 14:27). Paul is ever the evangelist, always looking for strategic and receptive places to preach. His earnest desire is for those places to be made available for him.

Paul also asks them to pray that he will make a clear proclamation of the mystery (Colossians 4:3, 4). Taken as he is with "the mystery," Paul wants that mystery preached to the Gentiles. While the power of the gospel resides within the gospel, nonetheless Paul wants to preach it as clearly as he possibly can.

The second admonition in this section is to "be wise in the way you act toward outsiders" (Colossians 4:5). Ultimately, those who are not Christians should be moved by the life-styles of those who are. The church, as Jesus' body on earth, is to demonstrate the "fullness of God" in their individual and corporate lives. As Jesus was able to attract all sorts to himself, so the church, His present body, should do so as well. Furthermore, they are to do this by making the "most of every opportunity" (Colossians 4:5). Paul said the same thing to the Galatians, "As we have opportunity, let us do good" (Galatians 6:10). The Greek word *kairos* does not merely refer to a chronological time, but rather a critical epoch or opportunity that, if missed, may be gone forever.

The third admonition is to "let your conversation be always full of grace, seasoned with salt" (Colossians 3:6). The speech of Christians should always be gracious or charming. The *manner* of speaking to outsiders is important as well as the content of that speaking. Peter wrote that answers should be given "with gentleness and respect" (1 Peter 3:15). *Seasoned with salt* meant, in pagan writings, witty. Whether or not that is precisely what Paul means here, he does claim that Christian speech should not be dull or boring. In short, Paul says speak graciously and engagingly so an answer can be provided to everyone.

Personal Commendations and Greetings (4:7-15)

If, as Spurgeon said, chapter 3 begins in Heaven and ends in the kitchen, the whole letter begins with the cosmos and ends with the

146

individual. Paul apparently had never read modern ministerial ethics books and so made friends, close friends, in his ministry. Not that he showed favoritism; he simply felt especially close to some because of their relationship to his ministry. He mentions ten persons by name. In so doing, he opens his heart and shows that he is a man of great feeling and compassion for his friends.

1. Tychicus. This man was a frequent companion of Paul during the later years. Paul lovingly calls him "a dear brother, a faithful minister and fellow servant in the Lord."
2. Onesimus. Paul does not mention that he is Philemon's runaway slave, but "our faithful and dear brother, who is one of you" (Colossians 4:9). Along with Tychicus, he carries the letter to Colosse. "They will tell you everything that is happening here."
3. Aristarchus. Paul calls him, literally, "my fellow-prisoner of war" (Colossians 4:10). And so he was, as in Ephesus when he was captured by the mob. *See: Acts 19:29*
4. Mark. He is no longer the deserter, as on the first missionary trip, but Paul's companion in prison and one whom the Colossians could be sure to receive with welcome.
5. Jesus called Justus. He is a notable fellow-worker and one of a few Jews who has given Paul his loyalty.
6. Epaphras. This is the Colossians' own minister and founder, and one who "is always wrestling in prayer for you" or (literally) "agonizes" for their maturity (Colossians 4:12).
7. Luke. This is "the doctor" and frequent companion, who may be there to give medical attention.
8. Demas. This man, now faithful, will later desert "because he loved this world" (2 Timothy 4:10, 11).
9. Nympha. Because of her hospitality, the neighboring church of the Laodiceans had a meeting place in her house.
10. Archippus. As a member of Philemon's household, he was to be earnest with his ministry to the church there.

Final Instructions and Benediction (4:16-18)

There are three final instructions: (1) they are to read "this letter" (Colossians) in their church meeting; (2) they are to have it read to the Laodicean church; and (3) they are to get a letter from Laodicea.

It became the custom to read aloud the letters of the apostles in the church meetings, thus giving to them the authority of the Old

Testament Scriptures. Paul wrote in 1 Thessalonians 5:27, "I charge you before the Lord to have this letter read to all the brothers." The reference to a letter that the Colossians are to receive from the Laodiceans has generated much speculation. Obviously, there is no New Testament book entitled "Laodiceans." Some have thought this to be a letter from the Laodiceans to Paul. Others have speculated that it might be Ephesians or Philemon. Perhaps the most satisfactory hypothesis is that it is a letter written by Paul to the church at Laodicea that simply does not any longer exist. It is not possible to know, but the question is intriguing nonetheless.

Paul concludes the letter, after dictating most of it, in his own handwriting. He frequently ended or otherwise provided his signature in such manner. (See 1 Corinthians 16:21; Galatians 6:11; 2 Thessalonians 3:17; Philemon 19.) The brevity of his farewell is touching in its simplicity. *Remember* may mean "remember in prayer" as well as in their own mind. The final phrase, "Grace be with you," is the characteristic close of letters of the day.

Conclusion

And He is the image of the invisible God, the first-born of all creation. For by him all things were created, both in the heavens and on earth, visible and invisible, whether thrones or dominions or rulers or authorities—all things have been created by Him and for Him. And He is before all things, and in Him all things hold together. He is also the head of the body, the church; and He is the beginning, the first-born from the dead; so that He Himself might come to have first place in everything. For it was the Father's good pleasure for all the fulness to dwell in Him, and through Him to reconcile all things to Himself, having made peace through the blood of His cross; through Him, I say, whether things on earth or things in heaven (Colossians 1:15-20, NASB).

He is *Christ of Creation.* He is the image of God and the firstborn of all creation. He is the epitome, the agent, the end, and the sustainer of His creation. Because He is Creator, He gives purpose to the ongoing of the life of His creation. He shows us that the physical is important. It does have a rightful place in our lives on this earth. He shows us that evil really begins with Satan, and not with the material. And He also gives us a message that is true and is present.

He is *Christ of the Church*. He is the Head of the church; so He is in control, He is superior, and He is close to it. By His power, the church is a body that works together harmoniously, resulting in encouragement, growth, true knowledge of God's mystery, and protection from heresy. Also by His power, the church is a body that demonstrates the character of God as it proclaims the mystery of God to the world. Because the church is the body of Christ, we can see the need for a clearly defined authority, and that authority is the person of Christ himself. We also see the need to recognize the unity of the church, and in so doing, to check our criticism of it.

He is the *Christ of Conduct*. The fact that He is Christ of creation and Christ of the church means also that He governs our daily lives. We are not controlled by legalistic regulations or astrological powers. By His power, we have cut off the life of legalism and put on a new life that issues in characteristics that are His very own. He even is involved in the conduct of family relationships, urging mutual respect and service.

If our world does not know that Christ is Lord of creation, then it must hear the message of this letter. If our church does not know that Christ is Head of the body, then it needs to hear the message of this letter. If you and I do not know that Christ is Governor of our conduct, then we need to hear the message of this letter.

Christ of Creation! Christ of the Church! Christ of Conduct! I hope He is the Christ of your world, your church, and your life.

Part Three

1 and 2 Thessalonians

INTRODUCTION
TO 1 AND 2 THESSALONIANS

The City

The city known in Paul's day as Thessalonica is the modern city of Salonika. It lies about one hundred miles west of Philippi in the northeast of Greece and remains a flourishing city today. Although an ancient city named Therme ("hot springs") had been located on or near the site of Thessalonica, the city of Paul's day was founded in 315 B.C. by Cassander, the general of Alexander the Great. He named it "Thessalonica," after his wife and Alexander's half-sister. (*Thessalonica* etymologically means "victory on the sea.")

Since it was strategically located on the Egnatian Way, which ultimately connected Rome with the Danube River, it became a flourishing city with an estimated population of 200,000 in Paul's day. Under Roman rule, the importance of the city continued to increase when it became the capital of the province in 146 B.C. After 42 B.C., it was granted status as a "free" city, which meant that it could then be autonomous at the local governmental level. The local leaders under this system were called *politarchs,* a word found in Scripture only in Acts 17:6, 8, and confirmed in inscriptions. The population was basically Greek, with a smattering of Romans and at least enough Jews to have a fairly active synagogue (in contrast to the absence of one in Philippi).

The Church

After being disappointingly prevented from going into the southern province of Asia or into Bithynia to the north, Paul landed in Troas in the northwest of Asia Minor (Acts 16:6-8). There he saw in a vision a man (perhaps Luke himself) from Macedonia asking for his help (Acts 16:9). Paul, Silas, Timothy, and now, for the first time, Luke set sail for Neapolis, the seaport of Philippi and a two-day journey from Troas (Acts 16:10, 11). They met with some success there, but disturbed some of the citizenry and were beaten and imprisoned for a short time. After they were released, at least Paul and Silas made the journey to Thessalonica, a trip that would have taken the better part of a week (Acts 16:22—17:1).

As was his custom, Paul began preaching in the synagogues here and did so on three consecutive sabbaths (Acts 17:2). Some of the Jews heard and believed him, but many were opposed, especially because of his success with the "God-fearers," Gentiles who had accepted the ethical teachings of Judaism but had not become full proselytes. The Jewish opposition stirred up a mob, which went to Jason's house, where, apparently, Paul and his company had been staying. Not finding them there, they dragged Jason and the others before the politarchs, accusing them of "defying Caesar's decrees" (Acts 17:5-7). Subsequently, Paul and Silas left Thessalonica and went to Berea (Acts 17:10).

It is not clear from the account in Acts 17 just how long Paul was in Thessalonica. On first reading, it might appear that he was there around three weeks (having preached "three sabbaths"). However, there is some suggestion that he was there for a longer period. He did work at his trade while there (1 Thessalonians 2:9), which may mean he was there for a longer time. Furthermore, he received gifts from the Philippian church twice during his stay (Philippians 4:16), again suggesting a longer time. The solution to this dilemma may be that the three sabbaths' reference describes the period of time he spent among the Jews, and that he focused on the Gentile population after that. A significant number from the Gentiles constituted the congregation (1 Thessalonians 1:9).

The Letters

Authorship

Both 1 and 2 Thessalonians claim to have been written by Paul (1 Thessalonians 1:1; 2:18; 2 Thessalonians 1:1; 3:17). For the most part, not many question these claims. They were both accepted as Pauline by several authors as early as the middle of the second century. The internal evidence of Paul's authorship in 1 Thessalonians is strong as well. The language and style of writing are very much Pauline, even though he does not use a number of his characteristic terms. Furthermore, since Paul states his expectation to be alive at Jesus' second coming, it is unlikely that someone would have made such a claim after he had died (see 1 Thessalonians 4:15). Further questions of authorship of 2 Thessalonians is considered below along with the issue of the relationship of the two letters.

Date and Place of Writing

The book of Acts traces Paul's movement from Thessalonica to Berea to Athens and to Corinth (Acts 16—18). In 1 Thessalonians 2:17, Paul said that he had not been separated from the Thessalonians for a very long time; so the letter must have been written on this route. Timothy, who was sent from Athens back to Thessalonica (1 Thessalonians 3:1, 2), had returned to Paul with his news. He must have returned to Corinth, the next stop on the journey. Furthermore, Paul, Silas, and Timothy were not together anymore after Corinth, as far as is known.

The date for the writing can also be determined with a fair degree of certainty. When Paul arrived at Corinth, Gallio was proconsul of the area and Claudius was the emperor (Acts 18). Based on inscriptions at Delphi, Greece, most scholars believe that Gallio began his office in the summer of A.D. 51 or 52. It is likely, therefore, that Paul wrote two letters either in A.D. 50 or 51, since it appears that Gallio was rather new in his position (Acts 18:12ff). These two letters, then, represent what is generally considered to be the earliest Christian literature in all of the New Testament.

Relationship of 1 and 2 Thessalonians

For the most part, the unity of each of these letters is well accepted; the few questions raised concerning this issue are dealt with later in this work. What is more perplexing, however, is the relationship between the two letters. The questions usually fall into one or another of the following topics:

(1) *Similarity of the letters.* Even a cursory reading of the two letters reveals a similarity. Some, after careful study, have estimated that about one-third of 1 Thessalonians is covered in 2 Thessalonians. This similarity extends from words to phrases to ideas to an overall structure, which is different from the typical Pauline form. Why would two letters so similar as these two be sent to the same church and in such a relatively short period of time?

(2) *Different eschatological views.* The eschatological (study of the "last days") emphases of these two letters is seen to be different by some readers. A significant portion of both letters is spent dealing with the returning of Jesus and the accompanying events. In 1 Thessalonians, Paul assures them about those who have already died before Jesus' return (1 Thessalonians 4:13ff). Of that event, he says that he does not want to write about "times and dates"; that day will come like a "thief in the night" (1 Thessalonians 5:1, 2). In 2 Thessalonians, this emphasis of the imminence of the return seems to be silent. He says, rather, that certain things must happen before the return occurs (2 Thessalonians 2:3). Why would two letters sent to the same church within a relatively short time seem to take a different perspective concerning the second coming?

(3) *A different tone in the two letters.* Some have pointed out that there is a slightly more formal and detached tone in 2 Thessalonians compared to the first letter. For example, in 1 Thessalonians, Paul says, "We always thank God for all of you" (1 Thessalonians 1:2); in 2 Thessalonians, he states it in a more detached way, "We ought always to thank God for you, brothers" (2 Thessalonians 1:3; 2:13). Furthermore, in 2 Thessalonians, he gives them rather blunt commands: "We command you, brothers, to keep away from every brother who is idle," and, "Such people [who are idle] we command and urge in the Lord Jesus Christ to settle down and earn the bread they eat" (2 Thessalonians 3:6, 12).

While these issues certainly provide cause for consideration of the relationship of these two letters, they do not preclude the letters' being exactly what they purport to be, that is, letters written by Paul within a short period of time to the church at Thessalonica. There have been a number of suggested solutions and responses to problems raised by these issues.

(1) *Another author* for 2 Thessalonians who has remained pseudonymous. This solution is not widely accepted and is not supported by any substantial evidence within or outside of the letter itself. There are too many indications of the Pauline authorship. One variation of this view suggests that 2 Thessalonians was written to replace the eschatological teaching of 1 Thessalonians. Part of the basis for this view is that 2 Thessalonians refers to a prophecy or letter attributed to Paul and the others stating that the second coming had already occurred; they were to ignore

that letter (2 Thessalonians 2:2). Some see that letter as 1 Thessalonians. This view, however, leaves more questions unanswered than it answers. There is no substantial evidence that the letter of 2 Thessalonians 2:2 is 1 Thessalonians.

(2) *Co-authors.* Some suggest that Timothy and Silas served as co-authors to 2 Thessalonians. They are, of course, listed at the beginning, and furthermore, Paul adds his own handwritten signature and greeting at the end (2 Thessalonians 3:17). The solution is not really satisfactory, however. It is not likely that Paul would sign any letter to which he did not have major input. Such a suggestion does not appear to be viable for other letters in which Paul lists his companions.

(3) *Sent to other groups.* Some believe that 2 Thessalonians was sent to a different group than 1 Thessalonians. One version of this theory suggests that 1 Thessalonians was for a predominantly Gentile group and 2 Thessalonians was for a predominantly Jewish group. It appears from 1 Thessalonians that there was a large Gentile contingent, "You turned to God from idols to serve the living and true God" (1 Thessalonians 1:9). Furthermore, 2 Thessalonians makes much more use of the Old Testament, which may make it more adaptable to a Jewish audience. However, it should be noted that Paul's great concern is that there be no division between Jew and Gentile. It would be incongruous if Paul actually occasioned that disunity by a Gentile version and a Jewish version of essentially the same letter. An intriguing variation to the theory that these letters are directed to specific groups is that 1 Thessalonians is sent to the whole church and 2 Thessalonians largely addresses the leaders of the congregation. First Thessalonians 5:12ff encourages them to be responsive to the leaders of the church. First Thessalonians 5:14 briefly focuses upon the leaders, telling them to "warn those who are idle. . . ." In 2 Thessalonians, Paul expands upon the material explicitly directed to the leaders in 1 Thessalonians. This view has as its advantage a dependence upon textual evidence not characteristic of the other ones. However, it is by no means conclusive. The salutations in both letters are essentially identical. While the theory maintains the integrity of the text and accounts for some of the possible differences of focus, it is not established absolutely.

(4) *Second Thessalonians preceded 1 Thessalonians.* There are some who believe that the order of the epistles ought to be reversed. The traditional order of the epistles is due to the size of

each and not merely by internal evidence. Furthermore it appears that in 2 Thessalonians, the trials seem to be going on (2 Thessalonians 1:4, 5) while in 1 Thessalonians they are in the past (1 Thessalonians 4:10; 5:14). Another argument for the primacy of 2 Thessalonians is that in 1 Thessalonians 4:9 and 5:1, Paul began each section with the phrase "now about" *(peri de)*. In 1 Corinthians, where Paul used this phrase, he was answering previous correspondence (see 1 Corinthians 7:1; 8:1; 12:1 15:1; 16:1). Moreover, to say in 1 Thessalonians 5:1, "About times and dates we do not need to write to you," might suggest that he had already written concerning this topic (see 2 Thessalonians 2:1ff). These arguments for the priority of 2 Thessalonians are interesting and do not violate the authentic nature of either letter. It is theoretically possible that Timothy carried a letter (2 Thessalonians) from Athens to Thessalonica (1 Thessalonians 3:2). If this were the sequence, 1 Thessalonians would have then been written in response to the news Timothy brought back to Paul in Corinth.

While these arguments are plausible, they have not generally been persuasive, primarily because the case for the priority of 1 Thessalonians appears stronger. There is no explicit reference in 1 Thessalonians to a previous letter; there is, however, in 2 Thessalonians (2:2, 15). Furthermore, the sequence of teaching about the last days makes more sense with the traditional order. Some had stopped working, thinking the return was present; Paul tells them to keep on working. The problems that are dealt with in 1 Thessalonians appear to have worsened in 2 Thessalonians. There seems to be no compelling reason, then, to question the integrity or traditional order of these two letters.

Purpose

After some moderate success in the Macedonian ministry (Philippi, Thessalonica, and Berea), and having stirred up the Jews who had not accepted the Messiah, Paul was forced to leave for Athens. While waiting for Timothy and Silas, whom He had left behind in Macedonia, Paul engaged the Greek philosophers. Here again, he met with moderate success (Acts 17:16ff). Not too long, apparently, after Timothy and Silas arrived in Athens, Paul sent them back to Thessalonica because of his great concern for the welfare of the church (1 Thessalonians 3:1ff). He went on alone to Corinth, where Timothy and Silas joined him with a good report from Thessalonica (Acts 18:1, 5). It was this report that gave impetus and shape to 1 Thessalonians (1 Thessalonians 3:6ff). Timothy and Silas delivered 1 Thessalonians and then returned to Corinth, this time with a less favorable report. With great concern, Paul wrote 2 Thessalonians and dispatched Timothy and Silas once again with this second letter.

Each of these letters seems to have three primary purposes. The purposes for 1 Thessalonians are as follows:

1. To express Paul's pleasure at the healthy state of the church (1 Thessalonians 1:2-10).
2. To defend Paul and his colleagues against false charges (1 Thessalonians 2:1—3:13).
3. To exhort the Thessalonians to carry out Paul's teaching (1 Thessalonians 4:1—5:24).

The purposes for 2 Thessalonians are as follows:

1. To reassure the Thessalonians of God's justice and thereby encourage their continued hope (2 Thessalonians 1:3-12).
2. To refute that "the day" had come (2 Thessalonians 2:1-12).
3. To describe a proper response to idlers (2 Thessalonians 3:6-15).

Literary Structure

In some respects, the literary structure of 1 Thessalonians is quite similar to 1 Corinthians. In that letter, Paul followed a rather traditional structure of letters for his day. The main body of the letter was a response to particular problems in the church about which he had learned both from firsthand accounts and from a letter sent by the Corinthians to Paul. In chapters 1—6, he responded to problems he learned about from an eyewitness account; in chapters 7—16, he responded to enquiries by letter.

Although some believe that the Thessalonians may have written Paul, it is by no means certain. It is conceivable that Timothy himself brought back a letter (1 Thessalonians 3:1-6). After mentioning Timothy's visit, he very shortly began the formula for answering specific questions or addressing specific problems in the same way as he did in 1 Corinthians. (The usual way is with a *peri de* in Greek—"now concerning. . . ." See 1 Corinthians 7:1; 8:1; 12:1; 16:1 for examples. First Corinthians 15:1 clearly begins a new topic, too, but Paul only used a *de* to introduce it). And so, in chapters 4 and 5, he wrote about personal morality (1 Thessalonians 4:1-8), brotherly love (1 Thessalonians 4:9-12), those who had died (1 Thessalonians 4:13-18), "times and dates" (1

Thessalonians 5:1-11), and corporate life (1 Thessalonians 5:12-22). Most of these topics are introduced with *peri de* or *de,* that is, "but concerning . . ." or "but. . . ."

There is another feature of the structure of 1 and 2 Thessalonians that is noteworthy. Paul was given to using a literary structure called a triptych pattern. It is a structural device in which a topic is followed by some other material, which is in turn followed by the original topic—an A-B-A pattern. He uses this same pattern in Philippians (admonitions, examples, admonitions; see the comments on Philippians earlier in this work). In 1 Thessalonians, he wrote a rather traditional thanksgiving section typical of most of his letters (1 Thessalonians 1:2-10), the A part of the structure. He followed with a description of his ministry in Thessalonica (1 Thessalonians 2:1-12), the B part. He then restated the thanksgiving (1 Thessalonians 2:13-16), the A part repeated. This same pattern is repeated elsewhere: A—face-to-face visit desired (1 Thessalonians 2:17-20); B—Timothy's report (1 Thessalonians 3:1-8); A—Face-to-face visit still desired (1 Thessalonians 3:9-13). A—benediction (1 Thessalonians 5:23, 24); B—farewell (1 Thessalonians 5:25-27); A—benediction (1 Thessalonians 5:28). The same pattern is evident in 2 Thessalonians: A—thanksgiving (2 Thessalonians 1:3-12); B—man of lawlessness (2 Thessalonians 2:1-12); A—thanksgiving (2 Thessalonians 2:13-17). A—benediction (2 Thessalonians 3:16); B—farewell (2 Thessalonians 3:17); A—benediction (2 Thessalonians 3:18).

Beyond the A-B-A pattern mentioned above, 2 Thessalonians follows the same basic pattern as 1 Thessalonians and many other Pauline letters. Because of the shortness of the letter, the pattern is obviously compressed.

Given these considerations, then, an outline of the structure of 1 and 2 Thessalonians follows with some of these features noted:

1 Thessalonians

I. Greetings (1:1-10)
   A. Salutations (1:1)
   B. Thanksgiving prayer (1:2-10) [A]

II. Personal Relationship With the Church (2:1—3:13)
   A. Paul's Ministry in Thessalonica (2:1-12) [B]
   B. Thanksgiving Restated (2:13-16) [A]
   C. Face-to-face Visit Desired (2:17-20) [A]

D. Timothy's Report (3:1-8) [B]
E. Face-to-face Visit Still Desired (3:9-13) [A]

III. Exhortations About ... (4:1—5:11)
A. Personal Morality (4:1-8)
B. Brotherly Love (4:9-12)
C. A Completed Faith (4:13—5:11)

IV. Final Exhortations (5:12-28)
A. Exhortations on the Respectful Life (5:12, 13)
B. Exhortations on the Corporate Life (5:14, 15)
C. Exhortations on Personal Life (5:16-18)
D. Exhortations on Worship Life (5:19-22)
E. Conclusion (5:23-28)
   1. Benediction (5:23, 24) [A]
   2. Farewell (5:25-27) [B]
   3. Benediction (5:28) [A]

2 Thessalonians

I. Greetings (1:1-12)
A. Salutations (1:1, 2)
B. Thanksgiving (1:3-12) [A]
   1. Thanks to God (1:3, 4)
   2. God's actions (1:5-10)
   3. Paul's prayer (1:11, 12)

II. Coming of Jesus (2:1—3:5)
A. Man of Lawlessness (2:1-12) [B]
B. Thanksgiving (2:13-17) [A]
   1. Thanks to God (2:13-15)
   2. God's actions (2:16, 17)
   3. Their prayer (3:1-5)

III. Exhortations About ... (3:6-15)
A. Idleness (3:6-13)
B. Disobedience (3:14, 15)

IV. Conclusion (3:16-18)
A. Benediction (3:16) [A]
B. Farewell [3:17) [B]
C. Benediction (3:18) [A]

CHAPTER TWELVE

Greetings

1 Thessalonians 1:1-10

Salutation (1:1)

As noted earlier in this work, Paul is quite accustomed to using the typical format of letter-writing of his day. Once again, it must be remembered that these are not primarily theological treatises, but rather are real letters written to real people under particular circumstances. In order to understand the theological message inherent in them, the audience and the occasion need to be kept in mind along with the meaning of the words and the overall literary structure of the letter.

The only distinguishing feature of this salutation is that it is the shortest of all the letters attributed to Paul in the New Testament. It does, however, contain all of the elements characteristic of these greetings: names of the senders, name of the recipient, and the greeting proper. In four other letters, Paul listed others with him in the greetings: 1 Corinthians (Sosthenes), 2 Corinthians, Philippians, and Colossians (Timothy). In Galatians, he referred to "all the brothers with me" (Galatians 1:1). The Thessalonian epistles alone include Silas and Timothy.

Not too much is known about Silas, or "Silvanus" as some translations have the name (See RSV, KJV, and NIV footnote). He was chosen by the Jerusalem church to take the decision of the Jerusalem Council to Antioch (Acts 15:22), a choice that attests to his leadership there. He accompanied Paul on his second missionary journey (Acts 15:40), was put in jail with him (Acts 16:22, 23), and preached at Thessalonica and Corinth in a faithful manner (Acts 17; 2 Corinthians 1:19).

Timothy has already been mentioned in this work. (See the comments on Philippians 1:1 and Colossians 1:1.) It appears that Timothy stayed behind in Philippi when Paul and Silas went on to Thessalonica. He reappears with them at Berea, where he stayed with Silas while Paul went on the Athens. After joining Paul in Athens, he was sent to Thessalonica to check on their condition. It was his return with their news that gave occasion for the first letter to them.

The letter is addressed to the "church *[ekklesia]* of the Thessalonians" (1 Thessalonians 1:1). The form here is unique to the Thessalonian epistles. In other places, he called it the "church of God" (e.g., 1 Corinthians 1:2; 10:32; 11:22). More often than not, the word, either singular or plural, stands alone or is designated by location (e.g. "the church in Cenchrea," Romans 16:1). Just why Paul uses this formula in these letters is not clear.

The church is further designated by the phrase *in God the Father and the Lord Jesus Christ* (1 Thessalonians 1:1). This phrase is also unique in referring to the church. Perhaps he chooses this description because the church is still young and has not settled on a particular way to refer to itself. The word for church was a fairly common one and, in the early years, at least, some greater description of the church was needed. In later years, it became quite sufficient merely to refer to "the church." At any rate, Paul makes clear the nature of this assembly; he had just quoted a pagan poet back in Athens: "in him [i.e. God] we live and move and have our being" (Acts 17:28). That is the sphere of life for the church.

The church also exists in "the Lord Jesus Christ" (1 Thessalonians 1:1). "In Christ Jesus," "in the Lord," and "in Christ" are all common descriptions Paul uses when describing how Christians are brought into a new existence. In this place, he uses the full formula and links it with "God the Father." In fact, he combines the two several times in these letters (1 Thessalonians 1:3; 3:11-13; 5:18; 2 Thessalonians 1:1, 2, 8, 12; 2:16; 3:5).

The greeting is typical for Paul: "Grace and peace to you" (1 Thessalonians 1:1). (See the notes on Philippians 1:2; Colossians 1:2.) It combines the Greek and Hebrew form of greeting. *Grace (charis)* comes from the same root word used for greeting in Greek letters *(charein);* Paul changes the form and makes it fit his Hebrew sensibilities. *Peace (eirene)* was and is a typical Hebrew greeting, meaning an active and productive peace.

Thanksgiving Prayer (1:2-10)

With the notable exception of Galatians, Paul always includes a thanksgiving section in his letters. As noted in the section on the

164

literary structure of these epistles in the introduction, this section forms the first A part of a triptych (a three-part literary structure, A-B-A), which will reoccur in 1 Thessalonians 2:13-16.

There are two major reasons that give occasion for Paul's thanksgiving in this passage. One is found in 1 Thessalonians 1:3 and is the object of his memory: "We continually remember before our God and Father your work produced by faith, your labor prompted by love, and your endurance inspired by hope." The other is found in the next verse and is the object of his knowledge: "For we know, brothers loved by God, that he has chosen you."

Faith, Love, and Hope (2, 3)

These three have been very productive for the Thessalonians. It is helpful to note again the presence of these three: faith, love, and hope (in 1 Corinthians 13:13; Galatians 5:5, 6; Romans 5:1-5; Colossians 1:5; 1 Thessalonians 5:8). When these appear in the thanksgiving section of a letter, they may provide a clue to the problem within the church. In 2 Thessalonians, for example, Paul mentions faith and love but conspicously leaves out hope (2 Thessalonians 1:3), thereby previewing one of their significant problems that has developed since the first letter. There is obviously a different order of these three compared to the 1 Corinthians, Romans, and Galatians passages. Here, Paul uses the chronological order. Faith looks to the past work of God in Jesus Christ and accepts that work in Him. Love looks to the present and expresses what it means to be in Him. Hope looks to the future with confidence that His promises will be true for those who are in Him.

There may not be too much difference in meaning between the "work produced by faith" and the "labor prompted by love" (1 Thessalonians 1:3). Work *(ergou)* perhaps focuses more upon the product of the effort while *labor (kopou)* emphasizes the extent of the effort expended. At any rate, they very well may issue in the same result.

The relationship between faith and work was not the problem for Paul that it became for later theologians. His attacks on works as a means of salvation are well known: "For it is by grace you have been saved, through faith—and this is not from yourselves, it is the gift of God—not by works, so that no one can boast" (Ephesians 2:8, 9; see also Romans 4:1ff). But Paul never dismissed work as a component and consequence of faith. He wrote to the Ephesians immediately after the passage just quoted: "For

165

we are God's workmanship, created in Christ Jesus to do good works" (Ephesians 2:10; see also Romans 2:7; 13:3; 14:20; 1 Corinthians 3:14). This connection is supported by other portions of Scripture as well. In Hebrews 11, the great "faith" chapter of the Bible, almost every time the word *faith* appears, it is soon followed by a verb expressing action: "By faith Abel *offered* ..."; "by faith Noah ... *built* an ark ..."; "by faith Abraham ... *went*" (Hebrews 11:4, 7, 8).

At this point, at least, the Thessalonians still have hope for the future. Hope is the longing anticipation for the fulfillment of the promises of God. They still believe those promises are true; the day will come when such hope seems to abandon them (see 2 Thessalonians). At this point, however, their hope provides the means for enduring persecutions and hardships in the name of Jesus.

Chosen by God

There are few doctrines misunderstood any more than that of election. While there are many variations on the theme, the usual explanation is that God "chooses" or "enables" some to receive His message and thereby gain salvation. There is no human effort sufficient to posture oneself into God's favor. A careful examination of the topic, however, demonstrates this understanding to be questionable.

A complete exposition of the topic of election goes beyond the scope of this present work; a brief survey must suffice. Paul uses the word, indeed all of the New Testament writers use the word, in the same way that it was used at the time of Plato. It meant to choose a person or a thing for a particular function, to serve a predetermined purpose. Thus, elders (presbyters) were chosen to govern in the Greek city-state, or soldiers were chosen to serve in the army. The *purpose* for this choosing was always an important feature of the process.

With this understanding of the meaning of the word, it is helpful to look at two of the classic passages where it occurs in the New Testament. One is in Ephesians:

> For he *chose* us in him before the creation of the world to be holy and blameless in his sight. In love he *predestined* us to be adopted as his sons through Jesus Christ, in accordance with his pleasure and will.... And he made known to us the *mystery of his will*.... In

him we were also *chosen,* having been *predestined* according to the plan of him who works out everything in conformity with the purpose of his will, in order that we, who were the first to hope in Christ, might be for the praise of his glory. And you also were included in Christ when you heard the word . . . (Ephesians 1:4-13).

This rather long passage contains important information concerning Paul's understanding of election, which includes the following observations: (1) First of all, it should be noted who is among the chosen. Paul's use of pronouns all through Ephesians is important; the "us" or "we" pronouns refer to the Jews or sometimes specifically to the apostles and prophets. They are the ones, then, who are included as God's elect. (2) *Chosen* (Ephesians 1:4) and *predestined* are used synonymously. (3) The meaning of being "chosen" or "predestined" is the same as their use in Plato's day; that is, chosen for a particular service. (4) Paul says here that they (the Jews) were chosen to be holy (i.e., set apart for service) and blameless (Ephesians 1:4). (5) They (the Jews) were predestined to be adopted as God's sons. Israel was called God's son, holding a special relationship and holding a special function as son. (See Exodus 4:22; Jeremiah 3:19; Hosea 11:1.) (6) They (the Jews) were to know the mystery of His will. (See the comments in this work on Colossians 1:26, 27; 2:2.) The mystery is that Gentiles are included in God's plan (Ephesians 3:2-13) and Paul and the other "saints" have been made ministers of that mystery. They were "chosen" to proclaim the mystery of God.

Another passage that focuses upon the doctrine of election is Romans 8—11. Only a few of the pertinent passages can be examined:

For those God *foreknew* he also *predestined* to be conformed to the likeness of his Son. . . . Those he *predestined,* he also *called;* those he *called,* he also justified; those he justified, he also glorified. . . . Who will bring any charge against those whom God has *chosen?* (Romans 8:29-33).

This passage presents some of the same features that Ephesians 1 does. (1) While not as clear as the Ephesians passage, it still appears that the focus of this passage is the Jews. To some extent, there is the we-you [Jews-Gentiles] language. In Romans 7, Paul focused on knowing the law—certainly meaning the Jews.

167

(2) *Predestined* and *chosen* are used synonymously. (3) The meaning of being "chosen" or "predestined" is the same as their use in Plato's day; that is, chosen for a particular service. (4) They (the Jews) were predestined to be like the Son, that is, to function as the Son functioned, to perform some special service as the Son did.

In the next three chapters (Romans 9—11), Paul continued to describe how Israel was predestined—chosen—to serve as son. This decision was made by God's sovereign choice, just in the same way God chose Jacob instead of Esau: "in order that God's purpose in election might stand. . . . Just as it is written: Jacob I loved [or respected], but Esau I hated [or slighted]." Even Pharaoh was predestined, chosen, for a particular service (Romans 9:17, 18).

This rather long excursus on election should inform the understanding of Paul's phrase in 1 Thessalonians 1:4. Paul readily gives thanks for them because they were chosen—not arbitrarily chosen for salvation, but rather picked for a special service.

The reasons for this knowledge that the Thessalonians are among the elect are two-fold. One has to do with the experience of Paul and his companions; the other involves the responses to the message by the Thessalonians.

Paul claims to know of their election because the gospel he preached did not come "simply with words, but also with power, with the Holy Spirit and with deep conviction" (1 Thessalonians 1:5). Unlike some teachers, Paul's instruction went far beyond mere words. They preached a gospel that had power (Romans 1:16) sufficient to accomplish its purposes. Paul and associates were cognizant of that power when they preached in Thessalonica. They also experienced the Holy Spirit in this process of preaching. It is through the preaching of the Word that the Spirit does His work. Furthermore, they were fully convinced that they should be there in Thessalonica and preaching to them (i.e. "with deep conviction"). The unhappy experiences in Europe up to this place had not created doubts in their minds about what they were doing.

The second reason that Paul is convinced of their election is the Thessalonians' own actions in response to the gospel. That response was essentially two-fold and illustrative of the special purpose for which they were chosen. On the one hand, they became imitators of Paul, his associates, and Jesus himself (1

Thessalonians 1:6). While there is a significant range of meaning in that imitation, Paul did qualify it somewhat in the following verses: they experienced "severe suffering," but "welcomed the message with . . . joy" nonetheless. Furthermore, they "became a model" to believers in their territory (1 Thessalonians 1:7). It was through them, through the living out of their lives, that God affected His will in Macedonia. It was for that purpose they were chosen.

On the other hand, "the Lord's message rang out" from them (1 Thessalonians 1:8). They are fulfilling their elective purpose by proclaiming the gospel themselves. As is often characteristic of new converts, they are enthusiastic about communicating this newfound faith to others, even if they suffer for it. That is what it means to imitate Paul, to imitate Jesus, and to be chosen by God. They are models to believers and messengers to nonbelievers.

So effective is this preaching that Paul can say that their faith is "known everywhere" (1 Thessalonians 1:8). It is known far and wide that they have "turned to God from idols to serve the living and true God" (1 Thessalonians 1:9). Those untold missionary stories of such commitment and service would be helpful indeed. How they have been able to achieve so much in so little time is not clear, but because they are in a prime location, on the Egnatian Way, they could easily travel in either direction in the Empire. Since Paul is in Corinth, another strategically located city, he could easily hear of such activity. Aquila and Priscilla have recently come from Rome to Corinth; one wonders whether they brought him word of the Thessalonians' activities there (Acts 18:2ff).

Paul concludes chapter 1 by reminding them that a part of their reputation, in addition to abandoning idol worship, is the great hope they have: "to wait for his Son from heaven, whom he raised from the dead—Jesus, who rescues us from the coming wrath" (1 Thessalonians 1:10). He will have occasion to say much more about this hope later.

CHAPTER THIRTEEN

Personal Relationship With the Church

1 Thessalonians 2:1—3:13

This section focuses upon Paul's close friendship with, and love for, the people at Thessalonica. As such, it forms a transition from the opening thanksgiving section to the body of the letter.

Paul's Ministry in Thessalonica (2:1-12)

It is not clear what Paul's motivation is for spending so much time using his own personal examples. The Jews had opposed him fiercely in Thessalonica (Acts 17), but there is no evidence that there were serious challenges to his leadership within the church. It was not uncommon to use personal examples as a basis for exhortation in the ancient world, and that may very well be his purpose here. In that regard, then, 1 Thessalonians differs from 2 Corinthians in this important respect. Whereas in 2 Corinthians Paul used much autobiographical material to counter false teachers in the congregation, in 1 Thessalonians he uses it as a springboard for exhortation.

This passage is structured around another rhetorical device, the antithesis, which presents a contrasting or opposing set of parts. Each of these antitheses is introduced by the connecting word *for* (Greek, *gar*). In the first case, this ties this passage into the context of chapter one. In the remaining sets, the word ties the following antithesis into the second or contrasting part of the previous set. In other words, the second part of the antithesis is expanded into another antithesis, which further explains that second part. Moreover, all but one of these sets are introduced also by the phrase *you know*. (The information Paul presents to them is not new; he is reminding them of what they already know.)

This structure is not especially obvious as translated in the New International Version, partly because some important connecting words have been left out. Each series is introduced with the word *for.* The thesis is then stated (usually introduced by *you know*), and then the contrast or antithesis is stated (introduced by *but*). That is, each series follows this basic pattern:

Antithesis (set of contrasting ideas) Introduced: "For"
  1. Concept (Thesis) introduced: "You know"
        Concept stated.
  2. Contrast (Antithesis) introduced: "But"
        Contrast stated.

The chart on the opposite page, with the connecting words inserted in brackets, may help the structure to be more apparent.

The first antithesis contrasts the possibility of failure for the first visit ("was *not* a failure"; 1 Thessalonians 2:1) with that which made it a success, "we dared to tell you his gospel" (1 Thessalonians 2:2). Even though they had "suffered and [had] been insulted in Philippi" (1 Thessalonians 2:2), they were able to accomplish the primary purpose of coming to Europe and to Thessalonica; they could preach the gospel. The definition of failure for Paul is not personal reverses or frustrating circumstances. Failure is being prevented from preaching the gospel freely. It was "in spite of strong opposition" and "with the help of our God" (1 Thessalonians 2:2) that this experience was not a failure. Inasmuch as he was chosen by God ("elected") for the special purpose of preaching to Gentiles, that mission will be a successful one as long as he strives to do His will. No reverses, even imprisonment or death, can stop that purpose (cf. Philippians 1).

The second contrast (1 Thessalonians 2:3, 4) expands what Paul has just affirmed in the previous antithesis—the proclamation of his gospel to them (1 Thessalonians 2:2). There are three assertions in the negative part of this antithesis, all of which focus upon what was *not* characteristic of that gospel he had preached: "not . . . from error or impure motives, nor are we trying to trick you" (1 Thessalonians 2:3). One might wonder whether these denials are quotations from Paul's accusers who had followed him to Thessalonica (Acts 17:5ff). Paul does not spend a great deal of time refuting these accusations; they are not generally believed by the Thessalonians. These characteristics are applicable to some traveling teachers, but not to Paul and his companions.

First Antithesis: [For] (1 Thessalonians 2:1)
1. "You know" (1 Thessalonians 2:1)
    Concept: "our visit . . . was not a failure" (1 Thessalonians 2:1)
2. [But] (1 Thessalonians 2:2)
    Contrast: "we dared to tell you his gospel" (1 Thessalonians 2:2)

Second Antithesis: "For" (1 Thessalonians 2:3)
1. Concept: "The appeal . . . does not spring from error or impure motives" (1 Thessalonians 2:3)
2. [But] "On the contrary" (1 Thessalonians 2:4)
    Contrast: "we speak as men approved by God" (1 Thessalonians 2:4)

Third Antithesis: [For] (1 Thessalonians 2:5)
1. "You know" (1 Thessalonians 2:5)
    Concept: "We never used flattery, nor . . . put on a mask" (1 Thessalonians 2:5). "We were not looking for praise" (1 Thessalonians 2:6)
2. "But" (1 Thessalonians 2:7)
    Contrast: "we were gentle . . . like a mother" (1 Thessalonians 2:7)

Contrast (above) Expanded: [For] (1 Thessalonians 2:9)
1. "You remember" (1 Thessalonians 2:9)
    Concept: "our toil and hardship; we worked night and day in order not to be a burden" (1 Thessalonians 2:9)
2. "You are witnesses" (1 Thessalonians 2:10)
    Concept expanded: "how holy, righteous and blameless we were" (1 Thessalonians 2:10)

Conclusion: "For" (Greek, "Just as"; 1 Thessalonians 2:11)
1. "You know" (1 Thessalonians 2:11)
    "we dealt with each of you as a father" (1 Thessalonians 2:11)

They had been welcomed in Thessalonica. His point here is to remind them he was not like others; he does not need to argue the point. If the second part of this contrast does not directly counter the three negatives above, it at least does so indirectly. The phrase *approved by God (dedokimasmetha)* has a root meaning of "passed the test." In a similar way to those Greek leaders who were "put to the test" before they were accepted as leaders by the people, Paul and friends have been tested and proven worthy as leaders for God's cause. While other teachers are validated as effective by the praises of men, Paul says of their ministry that it was "God who tests our hearts" (1 Thessalonians 2:4).

The third antithesis of this section (1 Thessalonians 2:5-8) expands upon the latter part of the previous one ("We speak as men approved by God"; 1 Thessalonians 2:4). He begins "For" (not translated in the NIV, but in the Greek text and so translated in some other versions), which connects it to what immediately preceded. He also includes the frequently used *you know* again, emphasizing that this is not new information but rather a reminiscence. In the last contrast, he included a three-part denial that largely focuses on their message; here, he offers a three-part denial that focuses largely on their method: "never used flattery, nor ... put on a mask to cover up greed ... [nor sought] praise" (1 Thessalonians 2:5, 6). There were many traveling teachers who needed all three of these. The story is told of Corax and Tsias. Corax was a clever teacher of rhetoric, and Tsias was his student. When Tsias refused to pay for his instruction, Corax took him to court. His argument was that Tsias should pay for one of two reasons: (1) If he presented the better case, it simply proved that he had been taught well; therefore he should pay. (2) If he did not present a good case, the better case should win. Tsias argued: (1) If he presented a weak case, it proved poor teaching and he should not pay. (2) If he presented a strong case, the better case should win. Such cleverness as these rhetoricians was much admired and could bring those who mastered it great wealth. Paul had not been this kind of teacher to them, and they know as much.

The contrast to such self-seeking style is the way that Paul and his companions related to the Thessalonians "like a mother caring for her little children" (1 Thessalonians 2:7—the RSV more correctly has "nurse" for *trophos;* it could mean "nursing mother"). It was a manner which not only showed concern for them; they did not even insist upon what they had a right to: "as apostles ...

we could have been a burden to you" (1 Thessalonians 2:6). Elsewhere Paul maintains that those who live by the gospel may be supported by the gospel (1 Corinthians 9:3-14; 2 Corinthians 11:7-11). In Thessalonica, he did not exercise that right; a mother does not take pay from her children for her "motherly" treatment of them.

The next verse (1 Thessalonians 2:9, 10) begins much like another contrast, although the New International Version's omission of the word *for (gar)* obscures the similarity. And like the contrasts, this verse expands upon the second part of the previous contrast. But there is no antithesis here; there is no contrasting conjunction *(but)*. The tone is synthetic now, each point building on the last.

As every mother works for her children, they had "worked night and day" on behalf of the Thessalonians. The purpose of that work was that they might not "be a burden to anyone" (1 Thessalonians 2:9). Every Jewish child learned a trade, and Paul's was tentmaking (Acts 18:3). Though he received some help from the Philippians while he was in Thessalonica, it was not enough for his living expenses; so he worked. The Thessalonians need to understand how this example is *apropos* to their current situation.

Paul closes this section by underscoring his confidence that they understand his actions (1 Thessalonians 2:10-12). In fact, it is a divine understanding they have: "You are witnesses, and so is God" (1 Thessalonians 2:10). This time he changes the figure from the hard working, self-sacrificing mother to the encouraging and comforting father: "as a father deals with his own children, encouraging..." (1 Thessalonians 2:11, 12). The good mother works hard for her children; she is not lazy. The good father encourages and comforts his children; he is not negative. That is how Paul has treated them as well.

Thanksgiving Restated (2:13-16)

With this section, Paul completes the A-B-A structure he began in 1 Thessalonians 1:2-10 with the thanksgiving prayer. (See the comments on "Literary Structure" on page 160 above.) Before, he expressed thanks because of their faith, love, and hope and for their election by God for special service (1 Thessalonians 1:2-10). Now, after an exposition of his ministry to them (1 Thessalonians 2:1-12), he thanks God for their acceptance of the message he preached to them. He does not present another cause for thanksgiving; a slightly more literal translation of verse 13 might be "Because of this [*dia touto* (not translated in NIV); this phrase probably refers to all that has gone before: their acceptance of God and of Paul's ministry] we also thank God always, namely that [not another *because* as in the NIV], when you received. . . ." He is not adding new information, but merely restating what he has already established.

There is no doubt that Paul understands his own preaching as being a word or message, not originated by men, but rather coming from God himself. Not only is Paul's written communication done with the authority of God; the message he spoke was the very word of God. The Greek text says, "When you received the word of hearing [*logon akoes*, not "Word of God" as NIV], you accepted it . . . as the word of God" (1 Thessalonians 2:13). The word *received (paralabontes)* is used by Paul to refer to the acceptance of doctrine taught in some official way. (See 1 Corinthians 11:23; 15:1, 3; Galatians 1:9, 12; Colossians 2:6.) It was the living message of God handed down from one to another, initiated by God himself, which is the occasion for thanksgiving.

Paul reiterates that they "became imitators," though this time of the Judean churches rather than of Paul and his associates (1 Thessalonians 2:14). The point of imitation is that they both suffered at the hands of their countrymen. The Judean Christians were persecuted by Jews there; the Thessalonians were persecuted by their own countrymen, including perhaps local Jews there (Acts 17:5-9). The acceptance of Jesus as Lord does not ensure that the road will always be smooth; Paul is not acquainted with the contemporary gospel of prosperity characteristic of so many media evangelists.

Having drawn attention to the Jews, Paul denounces in the most explicit terms the Jews who killed Jesus and the prophets (1 Thessalonians 2:15, 16). Of course, it was by the instigation of Jews that the Roman authorities put Jesus to death. Their sinfulness has continued and is focused on the followers of Jesus, particularly Paul. Having rejected the Word themselves, they try to prevent the Gentiles from hearing and believing. In so acting, they have heaped "up their sins to the limit" (1 Thessalonians 2:16). The phrase is reminiscent of Jesus' warning to the scribes and Pharisees: "You build tombs for the prophets and decorate the graves of the righteous. And you say, 'If we had lived in the days of our forefathers, we would not have taken part with them in the shedding of blood of the prophets.' . . . Fill up, then, the measure of the sin of your forefathers" (Matthew 23:29-32). The idea here seems to be that there is a fixed limit of disobedience after which God responds with judgment. The same theme is emphasized in Genesis 15:16 and Daniel 8:23.

The consequence of their action is the wrath of God (1 Thessalonians 2:16). The tense of the passage is unexpected. The preceding remarks set the stage for a warning of the wrath to come in the future. However, Paul uses a past tense (rendered as a present perfect in the NIV), "the wrath of God has come upon them." In Romans 9:22, Paul described the wrath of God as a present, though incomplete, reality cast upon the Jews. Even though the wrath is to come at the end of all things, it is just as real as if it were experienced in the present.

Face-to-face Visit Desired (2:17-20)

After the short excursus on the Jews, Paul comes back to his main focus, the personal relationship with the Thessalonians. He starts another one of those three-part A-B-A structures, which demonstrates his rhetorical skill: A—he describes his desire to visit face to face (1 Thessalonians 2:17-20); B—he describes the motive for Timothy's visit and the subsequent good news from him (1 Thessalonians 3:1-8). A—he restates his desire to visit them face to face (1 Thessalonians 3:9-13).

His desire to see them is so great that the separation is described by terms that refer to being made an orphan, "We were torn away from you" (1 Thessalonians 2:17). Paul has made at least two attempts to see them; it is not "out of sight, out of mind" with them. Satan, however, has prevented him. Earlier on this missionary journey, he had been prevented from going into Bithynia, although by God and not Satan (Acts 16). How he knows the difference he does not say, nor does he say how he was prevented. It is possible that he was ill, or perhaps it was that "thorn in [his] flesh" (2 Corinthians 12:7), "a messenger of Satan," that was the barrier. At any rate, it is with great frustration that Paul has remained separated from his dear friends.

The reason for that great disappointment is what the Thessalonians mean to him. He calls them his hope, joy, and crown in which he will glory (1 Thessalonians 2:19). It may seem strange for Paul to call mere humans his hope or his joy. It has been pointed out earlier that hope is the longing for, or the anticipation of, the fulfillment of the promises of God. How do the Thessalonians fill that role? They do it in this way. Paul was chosen (elected) to be an apostle to the Gentiles. It is these Gentile churches, then, that serve as proof of his election. Their embracing of the gospel and their faithfulness under persecution give eloquent testimony to Paul's election as apostle to Gentiles. Yes, his election is sure; here in Thessalonica is a church to prove it. They are his joy and his crown of victory. In the same way that the victor at the games proudly displayed his laurel wreath as a symbol of that victory, Paul can display them as his symbol of victory. It is only natural, then, that Paul expresses such strong desires to see them again.

Timothy's Report (3:1-8)

There is a considerable amount of itinerary in this passage, which helps fill in the gaps of the account in Acts. While there is some disagreement about the sequence of events, the following scenario seems to be the most logical:

1. Thessalonica — Paul and Silas arrived here from Philippi (Acts 17:1-9). Perhaps Timothy was with them or came later.

2. Berea — Paul and Silas arrived here from Thessalonica (Acts 17:10-14). Timothy came sometime, either with them or later (Acts 17:14).

3. Athens — Paul went here alone (Acts 17:15). Silas and Timothy later joined him (not recorded in Acts; cf. 1 Thessalonians 3:2).

4. Macedonian cities (including Thessalonica). — Paul sent Silas and Timothy here from Athens (1 Thessalonians 3:2 for Timothy).

5. Corinth — After dispatching his comrades, Paul left Athens and came here for more preaching and to wait for them (Acts 18; 1 Thessalonians 3:6).

The purpose for sending Timothy to them is most clear. In 1 Thessalonians 3:1 and again in 3:5, he says they "could stand it no longer." That is, the question about how the Thessalonians were doing had paralyzed Paul from effectiveness at any other work. Timothy was "to strengthen and encourage [them] in [their] faith" and thereby sustain them in the face of trials. The trials were sure; they "were destined for them" (1 Thessalonians 3:3). Paul is again plain about the Christian life. His is not the modern gospel of success. Suffering and persecution prove to be the common experience. The realization of this experience should not be occasion for doubting the faith, but rather a confirmation of it.

Timothy's message was comforting and encouraging. Paul writes this letter soon after Timothy has arrived in Corinth ("Timothy has just now come to us"; 1 Thessalonians 3:6). There are four elements to his report. There are the issues of their (1) *faith* and (2) *love,* which Paul is pleased to hear. Then there are (3) the *memories* they have of Paul and (4) a *longing* to see him (1 Thessalonians 3:6). It may be insignificant that Timothy does not report on their *hope;* the triad of faith, love, and hope goes together frequently, as has been shown. In the thanksgiving section of 2 Thessalonians, hope is also omitted for commendation. Perhaps they have already begun to demonstrate some peculiar beliefs about Jesus' second coming.

The result of the report is of such a nature that Paul can say, "Now we really live" (1 Thessalonians 3:8). He frequently discusses dying and living in the Christian life, "For to me, to live is Christ and to die is gain" (Philippians 1:21). His awareness of the connectedness of the body of Christ, the church, is acute. When the church succeeds, he rejoices; when the church suffers, he is in pain. His focus of values is not narrow. He is concerned that the whole church be faithful. To hear, then, of the faithfulness and love of the Thessalonians is breath and life to him. The point here needs to be understood by the contemporary church. Christianity is not merely a personal matter. The Christian becomes part of a large, diverse body and, as such, bears a responsibility as a part of that body. John Donne (d. 1631) expressed this sentiment in the following lines:

> No man is a Island, entire of itself; every man is a piece of the Continent, a part of the main. If a clod be washed away by the sea,

Europe is the less, as well as if a promontory were, was well as if a manor of thy friends or of thine own were. Any man's death diminishes me, because I am involved in Mankind. And therefore never send to know for whom the bell tolls; it tolls for thee (Devotions, Meditation XVII).

Face-to-face Visit Still Desired (3:9-13)

Paul concludes this section, the final *A* part of the A-B-A triad, by restating his desire to see them face to face. He also gets to the real concern he has about the congregation. He does so in a remarkable rhetorical fashion. The New International Version rightly translates 1 Thessalonians 3:9 as a rhetorical question, and verse 10 as a statement of fact (unlike some other versions that make both questions). Paul reveals three concerns here. The first is the complete nature of their faith (1 Thessalonians 3:10). He has already commended them for their faith (1 Thessalonians 1:3; 3:6). Here he judiciously suggests that they have a way to go before their faith is complete; he wants to supply what is "lacking" in their faith. He will expand what he means by that phrase (used only here in the New Testament) in 1 Thessalonians 4:13—5:11. Before he does that, however, he continues with a prayer stating the very desires of his heart and also revealing two other major concerns. Of course, it is his great wish and prayer to see them face to face (1 Thessalonians 3:11).

He continues by wishing and praying for their "love [to] increase and overflow for each other and for everyone else, just as ours does for you" (1 Thessalonians 3:12). This is the second issue about which Paul is concerned, and he will expand upon this topic in 1 Thessalonians 4:9-12.

The third issue that is of some problem to the church is their personal morality: "That you will be blameless and holy . . . when our Lord Jesus comes with all his holy ones" (1 Thessalonians 3:13). Paul will expand upon this point in 1 Thessalonians 4:1-8.

So much time has been spent on the structure of this passage because it reveals the transition from the unusually long section on personal relationship with the church (chapters 2 and 3) to the exhortation or application section of the letter (4:1—5:11). These two sections together form what is known in Greek rhetoric as "chiasmus," the crossing of parallel phrases or clauses. The structure is more easily diagrammed than described:

A. "Supply what is lacking in your *faith* ..." (1 Thessalonians 3:10).
   B. "Make your *love* increase and overflow ..." (1 Thessalonians 3:12).
      C. "May he strengthen your hearts ... *blameless and holy* ..." (1 Thessalonians 3:13).
      C. Examples of how to be *blameless and holy* (1 Thessalonians 4:1-8).
   B. Exhortations to *love* "more and more" (1 Thessalonians 4:9-12).
A. Discussion of "what is lacking" in their *faith* (1 Thessalonians 4:13—5:11).

To see it in a more brief form:

A. Faith (1 Thessalonians 3:10)
   B. Love (1 Thessalonians 3:12)
      C. Holy Living (1 Thessalonians 3:13)
      C. Holy Living (1 Thessalonians 4:1-8)
   B. Love (1 Thessalonians 4:9-12)
A. Faith (1 Thessalonians 4:13—5:11)

It remains for the next chapter to see how Paul expands upon these three topics.

181

CHAPTER FOURTEEN

Exhortations Concerning Their Problems

1 Thessalonians 4:1—5:11

As seen from the remarks on Philippians and Colossians in this present work, Paul characteristically includes a major section in his letters that is often called the practical part, in which he focuses on daily issues of Christian living. The issues normally include problems that have arisen within the church. As seen in the discussion above, the issues at Thessalonica appear to have been relayed by Timothy after his quick visit there. Paul discusses (1) personal morality (1 Thessalonians 4:1-8), (2) brotherly love (1 Thessalonians 4:9-12), and (3) a completed faith (1 Thessalonians 4:13—5:11).

Personal Morality (4:1-8)

Paul very obviously makes the transition to the application section with the words "Finally, brothers" (1 Thessalonians 4:1). Actually, the Greek reads, "Finally, *therefore,* brothers." What he is about to say to them is not at all new information, but rather a repetition of "what instructions we [already] gave you" (1 Thessalonians 4:2). Paul presents the basis for this application, makes specific points of application, and then gives reasons for the application.

The basis for exhortations on personal morality is located in the will of God: "It is God's will that you should be sanctified" (1 Thessalonians 4:3). Though a short statement, there is a powerful truth here often missed by the contemporary world. What does it mean to be human? Mistakes and shortcomings are often overlooked or dismissed with the explanation, "Oh, he is *only* human." Being human is equated with being frail and fallible, given to error by very nature. There is found in the Bible, however, a different understanding of what it means to be human. The Genesis account affirms that to be human is to be made in the very likeness of God himself. Mankind is the crowning achievement of the creation process. Man and woman had the capacity to communicate with one another and with God. They had responsibility for all the rest of creation. They had the capacity to be creative (for example, in naming the animals). Furthermore, to be human was important enough for God to create a covenant people and through them to bless all the peoples of the earth. To be human was important enough for God to give up His own Son to death on a cross. To be human is not meant to be an excuse for any shortcoming or failure. Rather, it should be a high compliment to be called "human," that is, to be "sanctified" or "set apart."

The application of the exhortation (1 Thessalonians 4:3b-6a) focuses upon three areas. First, they "should avoid sexual immorality." The general world of Paul's day does not particularly look down upon sexual immorality; there is, in fact, a rather clear double standard in operation. Women are not permitted the freedom granted to men. Christianity, however, makes clear the expectation that sexual fidelity is expected for males as well as females. The church is not merely to mirror the values of the society around it; it is "set apart."

Second, the admonition is that each one "should learn to control his own body." The translation of this verse (1 Thessalonians 4:4) is a real enigma. The Revised Standard Version has "each one of you know how to take a wife for himself." A rather literal translation is "to know how to possess for himself his own vessel." It is not likely that Paul uses *vessel* for *wife* here. Furthermore, there is now evidence that the infinitive can very well be translated "to possess," and thus express the popular usage of the term in Paul's day. So *vessel* may very well be a synonym for *body* (see 2 Corinthians 4:7; 2 Timothy 2:21). One "possesses" his or her body and is not "possessed" by it.

The physical body is not something to be put down as evil; such was the attitude of ascetics during the Middle Ages. It is not a tomb, as Plato claimed *(soma sema;* "the body is a tomb," in Greek, a play on words). Rather, the body is a means, a "vessel" for the praise of God. It is not to control the actions, "not in passionate lust like the heathen" (1 Thessalonians 4:5), but instead be an example of holiness and honor. The physical *can* be spiritual. Spirituality all too often has become equated with nonphysical, a view that is more Platonic than Christian.

184

Third, Paul urges that "in this matter no one should wrong his brother or take advantage of him" (1 Thessalonians 4:6). Some take "this matter" to refer to business dealings, since the word used here often means just that. However, most see the context requiring that "this matter" refer to the sexual practices Paul describes here. The point, then, is that cavalier sexual practices, which are "like the heathen," do more than transgress some objective law. They also violate the very sensibilities of other human beings. Such practices suggest that humans are less than human.

Paul closes this section on personal morality with a brief mention of three reasons for these exhortations (1 Thessalonians 4:6-8). First, God will avenge these things: "The Lord will punish men for all such sins." The point of this reason is not just "fire and brimstone" on the unrighteous. The thrust is upon the return of Jesus. It is in His presence that unholiness cannot exist. It is not so much that He comes to punish, though that does become a definite consequence. No evil can stand in that day when He comes with such overwhelming righteousness and holiness. Therefore, in light of His holiness and in anticipation of His appearing, righteous and holy lives should be the order of the day. Only those lives can exist at His coming.

Second, such exhortation to holy living is consistent with His call: "God did not call us to be impure, but to live a holy life." The clear call of God was to a "holy" (i.e., "set apart") life. The call was initiated by God; mankind did not first choose God. Holiness began with God; mankind did not first decide to be holy. God has called mankind back to a position to be like God himself.

Third, whoever rejects this teaching rejects God himself. The church is not a democracy, but a theocracy. Behavior is not determined by a vote of the majority. It is God who determines the parameters of behavior and rejection of those is rejection of the God who decided the nature of holiness. Furthermore, it is God who gives the Holy Spirit (1 Thessalonians 4:8), and it is the Holy Spirit who helps produce such holiness within the individual (see Galatians 4:6; 5:16-26; 2 Corinthians 5:17; 1 John 3:24).

Brotherly Love (4:9-12)

The second focus of Paul's exhortations is the need for brotherly love, taking up the point made in 1 Thessalonians 3:12 and continuing the chiasmus. (See the comment on chiasmus on pages 180 and 181.) There are two dimensions of brotherly love in this section. First, Paul establishes the need for brotherly love in the life of the Christian community. There is nothing more characteristic of Christians than love for one another. Tertullian, a second-century author and apologist, wrote, "Behold how these Christians love one another" (*Apology,* 39). Most every Christian treatise, whether Scripture or not, includes a primary emphasis upon the necessity of love.

It is common enough, in fact, that Paul does "not need to write to you" (1 Thessalonians 4:9). They know of its importance and already "love all the brothers throughout Macedonia" (1 Thessalonians 4:10). Furthermore, they have "been taught by God to love each other" (1 Thessalonians 4:9). Paul never explains just what he means by the phrase *taught by God.* It is an unusual term *(theodidaktoi)* used for the first time in this place. It is easy to hear the phrase with much modern-day theology sounding in one's ears. Some frequently claim to be told by God one thing or another in some direct and mystical way. To understand the phrase in this way is to impose a meaning that is not there nor is consistent with the teaching of Paul or the rest of the New Testament. A possible meaning is that the new age had come, supplanting the law with love. Both Isaiah and Jeremiah spoke of a time when there would be no need for a human means of communicating God's will; God himself would be the teacher of all (Isaiah 54:13; Jeremiah 31:34). Paul may mean that they have been taught the nature of love by God through His own actions. Paul uses the methodology himself in the Thessalonian correspondence of teaching by example. He might very well quote John 3:16 at this point, "God so loved ... he gave...." God taught love by His own example of giving His Son for the sake of the world.

Paul not only encourages them concerning the need for brotherly love, but he also describes the nature of that love (1 Thessalonians 4:11, 12). This is the first real evidence that there may have been a problem in the church. It will later grow to greater proportions. (See 2 Thessalonians 3:11ff.)

There are three ways mentioned in 1 Thessalonians 4:11 by which love can be demonstrated. First, he says, "Make it your ambition to lead a quiet life." Another meaning is, "Be eager to be quiet." Though the specific nature of this problem is not known for sure, it may be that they are being most enthusiastic or overly eager in their day-by-day activities. A kind of restlessness characterizes their lives. That restless energy should be directed toward a quiet and peaceful existence. Second, Paul tells them "to mind your own business." Such restlessness as there must be gives occasion for unnecessary involvement in the affairs of other people. It is a problem that does not easily go away. Third, he encourages them "to work with your hands." Manual labor was not highly valued in Greek society; it was an activity reserved for slaves. Christianity casts it in a different light, however. It is useful and good (Ephesians 4:28). It is to be done as service to God (Colossians 3:17). Jesus himself worked with His hands (Mark 6:3). From this exhortation, it might be concluded that the Thessalonians have stopped working and have become dependent upon others, which casts them in a bad light in the community (1 Thessalonians 4:12; 2 Thessalonians 3:6ff).

A Completed Faith (4:13—5:11)

Paul here turns to the issue he raised earlier (1 Thessalonians 3:10) about his desire to "supply what is lacking" in their faith. This section, then, completes the three-part rhetorical figure described at the end of chapter 2. The major topic, and therefore the major deficit of their faith, is a more complete understanding of the coming of Jesus in great victory to fulfill His promises. There are clearly two separate aspects of that coming. One focuses upon the circumstances of those who have already died (1 Thessalonians 4:13-18). The other focuses upon the timing of Jesus' coming as it relates to their preparedness (1 Thessalonians 5:1-11). This passage holds special interest because it is one of the earliest New Testament records of Jesus' coming, and it contains Jesus' own word concerning that event (1 Thessalonians 4:15; it should be noted that the often-used phrase *second coming* is not used in Scripture to refer to this event).

There are two particular problems that complicate our present understanding of this passage. For one thing, Paul is obviously responding to a specific misunderstanding of the event and trying to correct that problem. Knowing the nature of that misunderstanding would certainly facilitate understanding various components of Paul's teachings. Since that kind of information is not absolutely clear, it is difficult to put all that he said in proper context. Moreover, Paul uses apocalyptic language, which cannot always be understood literally. The nature of the reality of the life in the world to come is difficult to describe in language that is so tied to a temporal world. In fact, it is even difficult to think about it, since thinking itself is temporal to a significant degree. For example, so much of thinking is located in time—yesterday, today, or tomorrow. Events are most usually identified in a context of time in relationship to other events that are located in time and space. Thus, both people and events have this temporal quality. However, life in the world to come is not tied to this temporal dimension. Paul described it thus: "Now we see but a poor reflection as in a mirror; then we shall see face to face. Now I know in part; then I shall know fully, even as I am fully known" (1 Corinthians 13:12). To try to describe this phenomenon "fully" or in a "face-to-face" way with great precision and clarity is futile. The reality of the event, according to Scriptural affirmation, is inescapable; the *exact* nature of the event is uncertain.

"Those Who Fall Asleep" (13-18)

The first dimension of faith that is lacking concerns the faithful ones who have already died. As noted above, it is not clear what the specific problem is with regard to them; it may be any one of a number of circumstances.

1. They may not know anything at all about the resurrection. To believe this, one must assume that Paul had not finished his teaching there before he was forced to leave. Yet the resurrection is at the heart of the gospel (1 Corinthians 15:20). It is a logical consequence of the resurrection of Jesus.

2. Some have suggested that the Thessalonians see death as the consequence of personal sin, and that has removed from them the joy of Jesus' coming. Yet Paul says nothing at all concerning the relationship of death and personal sin.

3. Another possibility is that the Thessalonians have stopped believing in the resurrection because of false teachings that have come since Paul left. Such occurrences happened in other places and at other times. (See 1 Corinthians 15.) However, there is not the note of warning in this letter that exists in letters where a Gnostic type of teaching had infiltrated the church (cf. 1 Corinthians and Colossians).

4. Perhaps the Thessalonians have stopped believing in the coming of Jesus. There is significant evidence that the early church expected an early return of Jesus. It might be supposed that, given the delay, they have begun to question the return itself. However, the return itself is not the focus of Paul's rebuttal

here; it is rather the situation of those who have died before the return.

5. Perhaps the most plausible suggestion is that the Thessalonians still believe that Jesus is coming to bring into being the new age, and they also still believe the resurrection of the dead. They have not, however, made any connection in these two events. While certainty about the exact nature of the problem in Thessalonians is not possible, Paul's response to their problem allows for this latter supposition.

His response to this first dimension of the problem is at least two-fold. First, he affirms that Jesus is Lord now; the office of lordship does not follow upon His return. Four times in three verses (1 Thessalonians 4:15, 16, 17), he calls Jesus "Lord" and uses the present tense. There is not some future event that qualifies Him for this title; He has the title right now. Peter affirmed as much on the day of Pentecost, "God has made this Jesus, whom you crucified, both Lord and Christ" (Acts 2:36). He is Lord over those who have "fallen asleep" and over those who still live.

Second, because of this fact about His present lordship, there is no reason to sorrow for the fate of those who have died. In spite of their deaths, Paul affirms that upon Jesus' return, "God will bring with Jesus those who have fallen asleep in him" (1 Thessalonians 4:14). The Revised Standard Version translates the passage: "Through Jesus, God will bring with him those who have fallen asleep." While there is a difference in the meaning of these two translations, the result is the same: those who have died will not miss Jesus' return. They will be at no disadvantage because they are not living on earth at the time of His coming. They will experience the same joy as those who are still alive.

This truth, that both those alive and those "asleep" will share in the glory of Jesus' coming, is even affirmed by His own word. "According to the Lord's own word, we tell you that we who are still alive, who are left till the coming of the Lord, will certainly not precede those who have fallen asleep" (1 Thessalonians 4:15). This statement from Jesus does not resemble any of His statements recorded in the Gospels. There were obviously many unrecorded sayings, and this is apparently one of them. (Another is in Acts 20:35, "It is more blessed to give than to receive.")

It is in the context of this passage that Paul gives the fullest account of Jesus' return:

> For the Lord himself will come down from heaven, with a loud command, with the voice of the archangel and with the trumpet call of God, and the dead in Christ will rise first. After that, we who are still alive and are left will be caught up together with them in the clouds to meet the Lord in the air. And so we will be with the Lord forever (1 Thessalonians 4:16, 17).

The passage has sparked much discussion and, at times, fanciful theories about what is called "the rapture" (from the Latin word *rapture,* meaning "caught up"). One must avoid either one of two extremes with this passage. One is taking it as so much rhetoric influenced by an antiquated world-view and therefore needing translation into a modern idiom. The technical term for this approach is "demythologizing," that is, taking away any supernatural character of the event and seeing in it only timeless truths. The other extreme is to take the passage as an attempt to present an agenda for the return of Jesus, a moment-by-moment account of those events. There is little doubt that Paul is describing an event that he believes will take place in space and time—a real event. It is also clear that his purpose is not to give the exact and complete chronology of the event.

The apocalyptic language used supports this understanding of the passage. For example, Jesus' coming is to be attended by a "loud command," "the voice of the archangel," and a "trumpet call." These three may very well be one great symbolic act; apocalyptic literature refers to trumpet-sounding shouts that precede God's judgments. (See Revelation 1:10; 4:1.) Furthermore, a trumpet blast is frequently associated with God's ultimate judgment (Isaiah 27:13; Joel 2:1; Zephaniah 1:14-16; Zechariah 9:14; 1 Corinthians 15:52). The point is that "those who have fallen asleep" will meet Jesus before those who live at His coming. However, both groups will then be together, and therefore equal in relation to Jesus. The conclusion of the matter, and the ultimate purpose for this discussion, is comfort and encouragement: "Therefore encourage each other with these words" (1 Thessalonians 4:18).

A point should be made about the phrase *those who sleep* because of the teaching by some of what is called "soul-sleeping," that is, the disembodied spirits of the dead existing in some intermediate state in a sleep-like trance until Jesus' return. Paul does not use the term in that way at all. The clear teaching of Scripture is that at death, the Christian comes into the everlasting presence of God (e.g. Philippians 1:23).

"Times and Dates" (5:1-11)

The second dimension of faith that Paul addresses here has to do with "times and dates" (1 Thessalonians 5:1). Again, the specific problem that gave rise to this section is not clear. Paul is certainly answering some specific question or issue that he has learned about from Timothy or perhaps from a letter. (See the *peri de* construction here and discussed earlier.) It does not seem very likely that they have been predicting precise dates and times of Jesus' return. They have been worried about the fate of those who have died before His return. It is a natural extension of that fear to wonder about their own status with regard to His coming. Will they die, too, before that great event? Will they be able to remain faithful until He returns? If the dead in Christ might miss it because they were dead, might the living miss it by being in the wrong place at the wrong time? How long should they wait? Some of these questions Paul anticipated in the previous section, but here he turns to the underlying assumptions of the others.

Paul does not answer the basic question of *when* with regard to the coming. He has already taught them about the inability to know that: "About times and dates we do not need to write to you" (1 Thessalonians 5:1). Rather, he focuses upon the *how* of the coming. If they know the *how* of the return, they can be encouraged and can live prepared for that event.

He uses two similes to describe how that day will come. First, it will come "like a thief in the night" (1 Thessalonians 5:2; see also Matthew 24:42-44; Luke 12:39, 40; 2 Peter 3:10; Revelation 3:3; 16:15). The point, of course, is that it will occur suddenly and unexpectedly. The consequence of this figure is always the need for watchfulness and anticipation.

The second figure describing how Jesus will return is "as labor pains on a pregnant woman" (1 Thessalonians 5:3). This figure also includes the idea of suddenness, but adds to it the idea of destruction for the unprepared: "While people are saying, 'Peace and safety,' destruction will come on them suddenly" (1 Thessalonians 5:3). The coming of Jesus will be sudden, unexpected, and with inevitable consequences.

Having dealt with the how of Jesus' coming (1 Thessalonians 5:1-3), Paul turns to the status of the Thessalonians in view of the "thief in the night" figures (1 Thessalonians 5:4-10). It is a status that should be reassuring to them in light of the assertions Paul has just made about Jesus' return. In an extension of the "night-day" figure, he affirms that they are "not in darkness." They are "sons of the light and sons of the day." They do "not belong to the night or to the darkness," but "to the day" (1 Thessalonians 5:4, 5, 8).

There is both an implicit and an explicit consequence included in this imagery. Implicitly, memory of the great prophetic tradition of the "day of the Lord" will be called to mind. The phrase *day of the Lord* was often used to describe an important component of God's relationship to His people. At times, the phrase was used to describe events in the past, such as the fall of Jerusalem, the fall of Egyptians to the Babylonians, or the near catastrophe of Jerusalem at the hand of Sennacherib, king of Assyria (Lamentations 1, 2; Ezekiel 13:1-9; Jeremiah 46:2-12; Isaiah 22:1-14). At other times, the phrase was used to describe future historical events (Zephaniah 1:1—2:3; Ezekiel 7:1-27; 30:1-9; Obadiah 1-21; Isaiah 13:1-22; Joel 1—3). Ultimately, it was used to refer to that great "day of the Lord" at the end of history (e.g. Zechariah 14:1-21; Malachi 3:13—4:6). The "day" was the time when God's presence became apparent. His will was effected, the righteous were blessed, and the unrighteous were destroyed in the light of His presence. It is natural, then, to see Jesus' return to earth as the "day of the Lord" when His presence becomes so apparent that no unrighteous persons can exist in that light. Thus, for them, it becomes a day of destruction.

The explicit consequence of the imagery of day and night/light and darkness is that, as ones who "belong to the day," the Thessalonians have nothing to fear. "God did not appoint us to suffer wrath but to receive salvation through our Lord Jesus Christ" (1 Thessalonians 5:9). Furthermore, they can be "self-controlled" (1 Thessalonians 5:6). They are not controlled by the evil forces of the night. Also, this status allows them to be "putting on faith and love as a breastplate, and the hope of salvation as a helmet" (1 Thessalonians 5:8). It is God's overwhelming presence that allows His followers to demonstrate these three important characteristics.

Before leaving this section, with its focus upon the return of Jesus, a note should be made about Matthew 24 (and Mark 13), since the apocalyptic teaching of Jesus recorded in those places agrees with the emphasis Paul makes here. It is not clear how Paul would have come into contact with this teaching, but he seems to have some familiarity with it.

Space does not permit an extensive investigation, but some clarification of this often misunderstood passage is helpful. Jesus' disciples had asked Him two, or maybe three, questions after hearing a prediction about the destruction of the temple. The first question was about that destruction of the temple (Matthew 24:3). Jesus answered this question in Matthew 24:4-35. He wanted them to know how to recognize the signs for that event; and He described them in cryptic terms for modern ears, but understandable ones for the disciples. He concluded His answer thus: "Even so, when you see all these things, you know that it [i.e., the destruction of the temple] is near, right at the door. I tell you the truth, *this generation* [emphasis mine] will certainly not pass away until all these things have happened" (Matthew 24:33, 34). He then answered the second/third question(s) in Matthew 24:36-51. He began this answer with an emphasis not translated in the New International Version: "But of *that* day and hour [i.e., the sign of His coming and the end of the age; cf. Matthew 24:3] no one knows, not even the angels of heaven, nor the Son, but the Father alone" (Matthew 24:36, NASB). Jesus then proceeded, as does Paul in the Thessalonians text, to describe *how* rather than when the coming will be. One of those ways *how* is as a thief in the night (Matthew 24:43). The emphasis is the same with Jesus as with Paul. The primary consequence of this coming is watchfulness.

Paul concludes this section on the return of Jesus with the cogent, "Encourage one another and build each other up, just as in fact you are doing" (1 Thessalonians 5:11). They have every reason to be encouraged based on this teaching of Jesus' return.

So do we.

CHAPTER FIFTEEN

Final Exhortations

1 Thessalonians 5:12-28

As Paul concludes this first letter to the Thessalonians, he makes an obvious change of topics at 1 Thessalonians 5:12. It appears that he is expanding the admonition of the previous verse to "build each other up." He proceeds to list four areas where such edification is possible and then closes with a benediction.

1. Exhortation on a respectful life (1 Thessalonians 5:12, 13).
2. Exhortation on the corporate life (1 Thessalonians 5:14, 15).
3. Exhortation on personal life (1 Thessalonians 5:16-18).
4. Exhortation on worship life (1 Thessalonians 5:19-22).
5. Benediction/conclusion (1 Thessalonians 5:23-28).

Exhortation on a Respectful Life (5:12, 13)

There is no exhaustive treatment in the New Testament concerning the organization and leadership in the early congregations. On the first missionary journey, Paul and Barnabas "appointed elders . . . in each church" (Acts 14:23). This leadership role may have been somewhat similar to that of the elder in the Jewish synagogue. In fact, a Christian church is even called a "synagogue" in James 2:2. (See the ASV or the footnote in the NASB.) Paul does not call these leaders "elders," but their work matches some of the work described elsewhere as the work of the elder: they "work hard among you, . . . are over you in the Lord and . . . admonish you" (1 Thessalonians 5:12; see also 1 Timothy 3:1ff and Titus 1:5ff). It may not be unfair to conclude that title was not so important in the early church as function was.

The word for "work hard" is related to the "labor prompted by love" mentioned in 1 Thessalonians 1:3. These persons work hard for the church because they love the church. They are also described as ones "who are over you in the Lord" (1 Thessalonians 5:12). This description is not an official title. Paul used the same

195

term in Romans 12:8 (fourth in a series of five functions done by people in the church who were leaders, but again it was not an official title). He called Phoebe by this same term in a slightly different form *(prostatis),* though not as an official designation. Interestingly enough, when applied to Phoebe, the word is translated "a great help to many people" (Romans 16:2). The more usual function of leadership is not maintained when it is applied to her, though there is no good reason not to be consistent. (See also 1 Timothy 3:4, 12; 5:17, where the leadership dimension of the word is inescapable.) The third task to be respected by the church is that of admonishing, a function most often done by leaders of the church. (See Acts 20:31; Romans 15:14; 1 Corinthians 4:14; Colossians 1:28; 3:16; 1 Thessalonians 5:14; and Titus 3:10.) The word means to bring back to mind, and may carry the force of a rebuke, though not necessarily. If the church is to be the force it needs to be in Thessalonica, and if the problems emerging there are to be resolved, the leaders must be respected. Any group whose leaders are not respected is doomed to failure.

Exhortation on the Corporate Life (5:14, 15)

Not only is the church to respect its leaders; each member is also to perform a ministry to the whole body. The mutual ministry of the body of Christ was frequently stressed by Paul. (See Romans 12; 1 Corinthians 12; Ephesians 4; Colossians 2.) Here he focuses upon four different functions for the church. Each one is necessary for a healthy corporate life.

(1) "Warn those who are idle" (1 Thessalonians 5:14). Paul uses the same verb here as in the twelfth verse *(nouthetein).* From later information, it appears that some are not prepared for Jesus' return; they have stopped working and are presuming upon the charity of others in the church. The problem will continue. (See 2 Thessalonians 3:6-11.)

(2) "Encourage the timid" (1 Thessalonians 5:14). Paul has a lot to say about the responsibility of the whole body to help the weak. (See Romans 14; 1 Corinthians 8.) Rather than be criticized, they need to be encouraged. It is the same word used of those who tried to encourage Mary and Martha after the death of Lazarus (John 11:19, 31). Paul himself had done this to the Thessalonians (1 Thessalonians 2:12).

(3) "Help the weak" (1 Thessalonians 5:14). The word *help* means "do not give up on" or "stick with to the end" in modern

parlance. Those who are spiritually immature need room to grow just as do the physically immature.

(4) "Be patient with everyone" (1 Thessalonians 5:14). This patience is one of the fruits of the Spirit (Galatians 5:22) and is a characteristic of God himself. Older translations may capture the uniqueness of the word even more with the rendering "longsuffering." Paul cited this characteristic as one of the outstanding features of love (1 Corinthians 13:4). One of the ways to be longsuffering is seen in the next verse, "Make sure that nobody pays back wrong for wrong . . ." (1 Thessalonians 5:15). Jesus taught the principle of nonretaliation (Matthew 5:38-48; Luke 6:27-36), and Paul emphasized it elsewhere as well. (See Romans 12:17. Notice the parallel themes in Romans 12, though they occur almost in reverse order when compared to 1 Thessalonians 5.)

Exhortation on Personal Life (5:16-18)

Paul moves here from focus upon church life to that of individual conduct and attitude. If the corporate life of the church will be what it ought to be, then the persons within the church must exhibit Christlike qualities. Paul presents to them three admonitions in quick succession.

(1) "Be joyful always" (1 Thessalonians 5:16). Even in the face of persecution and suffering, the Christian has the ability to find joy. It is one of the fruits of the Spirit (Galatians 5:22). Since joy is not the same as happiness nor dependent upon external circumstances, Paul can encourage them to joy, even in their bad times.

(2) "Pray continually" (1 Thessalonians 5:17). Constant prayer is a sign of a dependence on God rather than on personal resources. While Paul never treats the topic of prayer very extensively, he does encourage it frequently (Romans 12:12; Ephesians 6:18; Colossians 4:2).

(3) "Give thanks in all circumstances" (1 Thessalonians 5:18). The lack of a thankful spirit is characteristic of the pagan life (Romans 1:21). Since God works out His will in all circumstances, the Christian has the capacity to be thankful in all circumstances. The point is not to be thankful *for* all circumstances, but *in* all circumstances. The difference is significant.

Exhortation on Worship Life (5:19-22)

Paul next moves in his exhortations to the public worship of the church. He offers five short commands, the first two of which are negative. These admonitions probably come out of the context of specific problems and practices about which almost nothing is known except for these correctives. From the negative commands, "Do not put out the Spirit's fire" (1 Thessalonians 5:19), and, "Do not treat prophecies with contempt" (1 Thessalonians 5:20), it appears that the leaders were too restrictive in controlling the various expressions of the gifts of the Spirit. If so, the situation is the reverse of the one in Corinth, where the exercise of the gifts needed more control. A church must use all of the resources that come from the giftedness of its members if it is to be a vital body of Christ. It is even dangerous to criticize the preaching in the church (1 Thessalonians 5:20)! There is very possibly a connection between the undue concern with Jesus' return and the slack attitude toward the role of preaching in the worship of the church.

The positive admonitions, however, do not occasion an "anything goes" approach. They were to "test everything. Hold on to the good. Avoid every kind of evil" (1 Thessalonians 5:21, 22). The latter two of these commands follow from the first. After testing, that which is proven authentic is to be maintained and that proven false discarded. What the test is Paul does not say, but it is certainly an important function for the early church. In Robert Law's commentary on 1 John, *The Tests of Life: A Study in the First Epistle of St. John* (1909), he points out three tests in John's epistle: the social test (love), the doctrinal test (faith), and the moral test (obedience). This approach would surely be consistent with Paul's approach.

Benediction/Conclusion (5:23-28)

In this conclusion, Paul uses the three-part literary structure (A-B-A) that characterized the first three chapters. A—benediction (1 Thessalonians 5:23, 24); B—farewell (1 Thessalonians 5:25-27); A—benediction (1 Thessalonians 5:28). In the benediction, Paul prays for their sanctification. He explains his meaning further when he says, "May your whole spirit, soul and body be kept blameless at the coming of our Lord Jesus Christ" (1 Thessalonians 5:23). He has already prayed for this very result earlier in the letter (1 Thessalonians 3:11-13), though in different words. In 1 Thessalonians 4:3, he encouraged them to sanctify themselves and told them how to go about it. God has a part in the process as well as man. To be sanctified does not mean to arrive at a status of sinlessness, but rather be fitted in such a way to be used for the

198

purposes of God. Paul underscores, then, what he has already emphasized earlier in this letter.

In the farewell section, he makes three requests of them. He asks for their prayers on his behalf, a fairly common ending for his letters. (See Romans 15:30-32; Ephesians 6:19; Colossians 4:3; 2 Thessalonians 3:1.) As he prays for them (1 Thessalonians 5:23), he asks the same from them. They are then encouraged to "greet all the brothers with a holy kiss" (1 Thessalonians 5:26), another common request. (See Romans 16:16; 1 Corinthians 16:20; 2 Corinthians 13:12.) Kissing (men to men, women to women) is still a common form of greeting or farewell in some parts of the world today. It became "holy"; that is, it was appropriated by the church as a symbol of greeting, of brotherly concern, and of equality. The third request is "to have this letter read to all the brothers" (1 Thessalonians 5:27). This one is written in the first person ("I charge you . . .") and may have been written by the apostle himself, as was his custom (1 Corinthians 16:21; Galatians 6:11-18; Colossians 4:18; 2 Thessalonians 3:17). *Read* means to read aloud *(anaginosko)*. It became the practice to read aloud letters written by apostles and others who were with Jesus—in other words, those letters considered to be a part of the canon of Scripture. It is difficult for the modern world to realize that the Scripture of the early church was largely oral for most of the church and played a significant role in the corporate worship of the church. If worship of the church in the New Testament is to be recovered, it must include the public reading of significant portions of Scripture. The strong language Paul uses to encourage such reading attests to the importance he places on such activity.

The letter closes in typical Pauline fashion with a benediction prayer for grace. He used this same closing with slight variation in several other letters. (See Romans 16:20; Galatians 6:18; Philippians 4:23; Colossians 4:18; 2 Thessalonians 3:18). It is characteristic of Paul's spirit that his last words take his hearers to the very heart of the Christian gospel, the saving grace of Jesus Christ.

CHAPTER SIXTEEN

Greetings

2 Thessalonians 1:1-12

Salutations (1:1, 2)

This opening is very similar to that of 1 Thessalonians 1:1 with two minor additions. Paul includes *our* as a modifier to *Father* "in God *our* Father." He also includes the sources of grace and peace: "from God the Father and the Lord Jesus Christ" (2 Thessalonians 1:2). With these additions, the greeting is similar to those in some of his other letters. (See Romans 1:7; 1 Corinthians 1:3; Philippians 1:2.) See the comments above on 1 Thessalonians 1:1 and Philippians 1:1, 2 for other comments, as well as the "Introduction to 1 and 2 Thessalonians."

Thanksgiving (1:3-12)

The thanksgiving section also opens in a similar way to 1 Thessalonians. Once again in this present letter, Paul uses the A-B-A pattern that characterized parts of 1 Thessalonians. A—thanksgiving (2 Thessalonians 1:3-12); B—man of lawlessness (2 Thessalonians 2:1-12); A—thanksgiving (2 Thessalonians 2:13-17).

Some have detected a certain air of aloofness in Paul's statement, "We ought always to thank God" (2 Thessalonians 1:3) when compared to the warmer greeting in 1 Thessalonians 1:2. Yet it appears that, in some respects at least, the Thessalonians have responded to Paul's instructions in the first letter, and for that response he is indebted. The *ought,* then, does not make him more remote, but rather is proof of his thanksgiving for their positive response.

The cause for this outpouring of thanksgiving is two-fold. Their faith is "growing more and more," and their love for one another is "increasing" as well (2 Thessalonians 1:3). Both of these topics are addressed in the first letter. (See 1 Thessalonians 3:10, 12; 4:9, 10.) Their faith and love are so notable that they are occasions for Paul to boast to the churches of God about them. The object of that boasting is a steadfast endurance and faith in the face of persecution (2 Thessalonians 1:4). This endurance is not a passive resignation, but rather a stalwart and active confidence in the face of oppression. (See the comments on 1 Thessalonians 1:3 above.)

It is significant that Paul omits of any mention of hope in this thanksgiving. He included it in 1 Thessalonians 1:3 and wrote about it in the body of the first letter (1 Thessalonians 4:13ff). Based on the content of this short present letter, they had not received his words on hope as readily as those on faith and love. While faithful and loving to the extent that he can brag on them, they have a significant problem with hope, to the extent that Paul does not include it as a matter of thanksgiving.

From the thanksgiving statement, Paul turns to the issue of God's vindication of their suffering (2 Thessalonians 1:5-10). The passage serves as a transition from the opening thanksgiving to the main topic of the events surrounding the return of Jesus and the consequences of that return.

Paul begins this focus on God's vindication by asserting that it is plain that "all this is evidence that God's judgment is right" (2 Thessalonians 1:5). It is not at once clear what he means by "all this." He surely does not mean the persecutions and trials they endure. God does not vindicate the righteous by causing them to suffer. He does mean, however, that the patience and faithfulness with which they endure those trials provides the evidence of God's righteous judgment. There is a sense in which the righteousness of His saints in the face of persecution is the condemnation of God himself on the ungodly. The "day of the Lord" is seen as a time when God's presence is so great that He overwhelms the unrighteous by that very presence. In a similar way, He does that through these ones who are faithful. By virtue of His presence in their lives, they stand firm and faithful in the face of evil persecution and strife. That very act, then, is a condemnation of evil; they will not succumb to evil because the Spirit of God dwells within them. (See Philippians 1:28 for a similar emphasis.)

Paul moves on to a description of the method of this vindication (2 Thessalonians 1:6-10), which is seen in the outcome for the Thessalonians' persecutors (2 Thessalonians 1:6, 7), the outcome for others (2 Thessalonains 1:8, 9), and Christ's glorification (2 Thessalonians 1:10). Though the Thessalonians are undergoing suffering, it will not always be that evil ones are victorious. Paul assures them that "God is just: He will pay back trouble to those who trouble you" (2 Thessalonians 1:6). This view of God's bringing retribution upon people is not always a popular one. It is more pleasant to see Him as a God of mercy and love. The fact is that retribution is not His choice; it comes as the result of His overwhelming presence. Evil simply cannot exist when in that presence. As darkness is dispelled by the light, so is evil destroyed when the presence of God is realized. The assurance, then, is not so much that evil men will be destroyed and their crimes thus paid for. The assurance is rather that God's overwhelming righteous presence will come, and as a result, evil will be destroyed.

Because His presence will be dominant at that coming, those Thessalonians who reflect His character and purposes will benefit from the event (viz. "give relief to you who are troubled, and to us as well"; 2 Thessalonians 1:7). Then their holy lives will be affirmed and strengthened. The point is not that they are rewarded for their suffering, but rather are relieved of it.

In the next few verses, Paul provides several descriptions of the event (2 Thessalonians 1:7-10). The description is somewhat rambling and awkward grammatically, but vivid in its picture of the end of the ages. Paul draws heavily from Old Testament images of this event and, in so doing, interprets them here in a Christological sense. Jesus "fulfills" the Old Testament prophecies about the end of the ages. Following are the significant parts of this description with some of the Old Testament passages that use the same imagery:

"The Lord Jesus is revealed from heaven" (2 Thessalonians 1:7). "And the glory of the Lord will be revealed, and all mankind together will see it" (Isaiah 40:5). The word for revealed *(apokalypsis)* is also used in 1 Corinthians 1:7; 1 Peter 1:7, 13; 4:13. It means an uncovering of that which has been hidden. Most of the time, Paul used *coming (parousia:* 1 Thessalonians 2:19; 3:13; 4:15; 5:23; 2 Thessalonians 2:1 or *epiphaneia:* 2 Thessalonians 2:8). Here, however, His coming is a revelation for all to acknowledge.

"In blazing fire" (2 Thessalonians 1:7). "See, the Lord is coming with fire, and his chariots are like a whirlwind" (Isaiah 66:15). Several times God appears as a "fire" (Exodus 3:2; 19:18; Psalm 18:8; 104:4; Ezekiel 1:13; Daniel 7:9, 10). It is a fire that purifies and destroys.

"With his powerful angels" (2 Thessalonians 1:7). "Praise the Lord, you his angels, you mighty ones who do his bidding" (Psalm 103:20). See also 1 Thessalonians 3:13.

"Punish those who do not know God" (2 Thessalonians 1:8). "So I also will choose harsh treatment for them. . . . For when I called, no one answered . . ." (Isaiah 66:4; see also Psalm 9:17; 79:6; Daniel 7:13, 14). The Gentiles will feel His wrath at His coming.

"Who . . . do not obey the gospel" (2 Thessalonians 1:8). "Who has believed our message and to whom has the arm of the Lord been revealed?" (Isaiah 53:1). Those who will feel His retribution include not only those who have not heard, but also those who hear but do not obey.

"Punished with everlasting destruction and shut out from the presence of the Lord" (2 Thessalonians 1:9). "Go into the rocks, hide in the ground from the dread of the Lord and the splendor of his majesty" (Isaiah 2:10; see also Isaiah 2:19, 21).

"Glorified in his holy people" (2 Thessalonians 1:10). "In the council of the holy ones God is greatly feared" (Psalm 89:7; see also Psalm 68:35; 96:13). He is not just glorified "among" His holy people, but "in" them. They, too, are "glorified" at His coming.

Paul concludes the opening section of this letter with a prayer, a practice that is characteristic of many of the thanksgiving sections of other letters. It is appropriate following all that he said about the coming of Jesus. That event is not just a doctrine to be believed, a part of the creed. It always has a moral and ethical force to it. He, therefore, concludes this section with a two-fold object to his prayer. First, he prays that "God may count you worthy of his calling" (2 Thessalonians 1:11). They have been "called" to a special service, in this case involving persecution and oppression. Paul prays, with assurance of answer, that God will fit them for the tasks before them. The day will come when the wicked are punished and the righteous relieved. Until then, however, they must remain true with the help of God's Spirit. (See also Ephesians 4:1 and Philippians 3:4.)

The second object of Paul's prayer is that "he may fulfill every good purpose of yours and every act prompted by your faith (2 Thessalonians 1:11). The purpose of the suffering to which they have been called is not to satisfy some weakness in their character or to make them holier or to make them justified. God is not bringing revenge on them. Rather, it is through their witness to which they are called by the gospel that God effects His will. It is always God's will that people hear and respond to the gospel. Because of what the Thessalonians endure, they will be able to witness effectively of their faith.

When they live up to that calling and fulfill His purpose, then the final part of the prayer will come to be so: "The name of our Lord Jesus may be glorified in you, and you in him" (2 Thessalonians 1:12). Through their witness, others will come to recognize Jesus as "Lord" and thereby be prepared to receive Him as such when He comes again. As this is happening, the Thessalonians themselves are being "glorified" (2 Thessalonians 1:12). Their association with Him results in their own "glorification," that is, recognition of true character in their own lives. Although it appears from their unfortunate circumstances that "glory" has missed them, their real glory will finally be revealed.

CHAPTER SEVENTEEN

The Coming of Jesus

2 Thessalonians 2:1-17

Issues in this chapter are among the most controversial in all of the New Testament. There are a number of problems that render sure understanding very difficult. For one thing, the topic in the first part of the chapter (verses 1-12) is not found in other letters written by Paul; so it is not possible to compare what he says here with other comments about the topic. Furthermore, apocalyptic imagery is used throughout the passage. While common to the day and the audience, and apparently the focus of Paul's prior teaching, such language is foreign to contemporary audiences. Complicating the ability to understand clearly is the fact that the hearers, as well as Paul, understood from prior teaching what the problem was. In the intensity of the issue, Paul rushed his words out, not always paying careful attention to grammar or, at times, even completing his sentences (e.g., 2 Thessalonians 2:3).

What is clear is that the Thessalonians do not correctly understand the coming of Jesus, especially as it relates to their current suffering. The problem of the first letter was the status of those believers who had died before Jesus had come. By the time of this writing, however, their misunderstanding of that great event has expanded to other dimensions as well. They have been falsely taught that "the day of the Lord" has already come, and they have apparently missed it (2 Thessalonians 2:2). Paul's response is that it has not already come and will not do so until certain events precede it.

Man of Lawlessness (2:1-12)

Perhaps the easiest way to structure a study of this passage is to focus upon the significant questions that grow out of these verses.

What Is the Source of Their Error?

Paul says that they should not be upset or misled "by some prophecy, report or letter supposed to have come from us" (2 Thessalonians 2:2). The word translated "prophecy" is actually *spirit (pneumatos)*. A prophecy in the New Testament church was a special message that came through the inspiration of the Holy Spirit. Then, as today, not everyone who claimed to speak under the influence of the Holy Spirit spoke truth; these "prophecies" about the Day of the Lord were false. The "report" *(logos)* probably refers to an exposition of a truth generally known and accepted. Some are taking what is true but then misinterpreting it to the congregation. The "letter" mentioned as the source of misinformation might be a letter that has allegedly come from Paul, but in reality is from a false teacher. How helpful it would be to have that letter in order to understand this passage more accurately!

What Is the "Day of the Lord"?

See the comments on 1 Thessalonians 5:2 for a more detailed treatment of this topic. Briefly, the expression *the Day of the Lord* is an apocalyptic term that referred to events in past history, future history, and ultimately to the end of time when God's presence, His "coming," will be so real and obvious that no evil thing can exist in the light of that presence. Those who have been faithful, consequently, who have demonstrated His own character, will have their faith vindicated in the light of His presence and will see an end to their suffering. While there have been several "days of the Lord" throughout history, that *great* Day of the Lord has not come, in spite of false teaching to the contrary. It is not clear from the evidence here just what they think the *Day of the Lord* means. If Paul has taught them that times of suffering and lawlessness will precede that Day, it is possible that they believe their own suffering experiences fulfill that prediction. Since Jesus has not come following upon such "lawlessness," perhaps they have concluded (and some have taught) that the Day has already come. In more contemporary times, when certain religious leaders have predicted the exact day of Jesus' return—only to see it come and go as every other day—the reaction has been to explain it away. They justify such outcomes by claiming that Jesus came "spiritually," and only those who are so enlightened can know that. Some similar teaching and belief may exist at

Thessalonica. Whatever the case, it is clear that they have misunderstood what Paul has said about the Day of the Lord.

What Must Precede the Day of the Lord?

Paul is confident that the Day has not come because two events must precede it. "Don't let anyone deceive you in any way, for that day will not come until the rebellion occurs and the man of lawlessness is revealed" (2 Thessalonians 2:3). It is the identification of these events that is the occasion for so much speculation and disagreement. Each is now considered in turn.

The word *rebellion* is a translation of the Greek word from which the English word *apostasy* comes *(apostasia)*. Its earliest usage is in the context of a military rebellion. Later, it referred to a religious abandonment or apostasy (as in Acts 21:21, referring to the abandonment of the Law of Moses). Most of the time, the word has a religious connotation in Biblical passages (cf. Joshua 22:22; 2 Chronicles 33:19; Jeremiah 2:19; Hebrews 3:12). There arose in some circles of Judaism a belief that during the last days, there would be great oppression of the people of God and many of them would fall away from Him. It does not seem that Paul would use the term in merely a military sense given the strong religious connotation it has.

In both 1 and 2 Timothy, Paul wrote about apostasy in the "last days," and may very well have been referring to the same event as here in 2 Thessalonians. First, he wrote,

> The Spirit clearly says that in later times some will abandon the faith and follow deceiving spirits and things taught by demons. Such teachings come through hypocritical liars, whose consciences have been seared as with a hot iron. They forbid people to marry and order them to abstain from certain foods, which God created to be received with thanksgiving. . . . If you point these things out to the brothers, you will be a good minister of Christ Jesus (1 Timothy 4:1-6).

It is apparent that Paul was describing a time that he fully anticipated to occur in the lifetime of Timothy. After this warning, he advised him to "have nothing to do with godless myths and old wives' tales; rather, train yourself to be godly" (1 Timothy 4:7).

The same warning was given in 2 Timothy:

There will be terrible times in the last days. People will be lovers of themselves, lovers of money, boastful, proud, abusive, disobedient to their parents, ungrateful, unholy, without love, unforgiving, slanderous, without self-control, brutal, not lovers of the good, treacherous, rash, conceited, lovers of pleasure rather than lovers of God—having a form of godliness but denying its power (2 Timothy 3:1-5).

Once again this warning was for Timothy and the people to whom he ministered. Paul said of such people, "Have nothing to do with them" (2 Timothy 3:5).

While the terminology is different in these passages written to Timothy, it does appear that Paul was describing the same event as this one in 2 Thessalonians 2. Here, too, he describes an event that is contemporary with their own time. Although the "rebellion" has not yet happened, it seems that it could occur at any time. He has taught them these things before, and they know what is keeping this rebellion in check (2 Thessalonians 2:5, 6).

The second event that must precede the Day of the Lord is the revelation of the "man of lawlessness" (2 Thessalonians 2:3). Actually, the "rebellion" and the "man of lawlessness" seem to be two parts of a single event; the grammar of the sentence suggests as much.

Who or what is the man of lawlessness? Few questions about Scripture have provoked more speculation or creativity in trying to answer than this question. Suggestions as to his identity include the following: Satan, the beast of Revelation 13, any number of Roman emperors, Nero brought back to life, the pope, Belial, the dragon of Babylonian religion, the antichrist, Judaism, Hitler, Stalin, and an abstract power of evil. The list is impressive and, in most cases, illustrates an active imagination. The major problem with most of these suggestions is that they do not allow the Thessalonians to have understand who it is that Paul means. He seems to imply that they know quite a bit about this issue. "You know," he writes, "what is holding him back" (2 Thessalonians 2:6). Furthermore, he says that "the secret power of lawlessness is already at work" (2 Thessalonians 2;7). The phenomenon seems to have been relatively close to their own time.

What is known about the person from the text does not help too much to clarify exactly who it is. First, the phrase *man of lawlessness* is not common enough to be of any help. Obviously, he is someone who is seen as the archenemy of God. Second, he is also called "the man doomed to destruction" ("the son of perdition," RSV; 2 Thessalonians 2:3), a description that merely reveals his ultimate end. The Hebrew phrase *son of* does not always indicate a familial relationship, but rather indicates character or nature. Thus, it is his nature to be doomed from the very beginning. Third, "he will oppose and will exalt himself over everything that is called God" (2 Thessalonians 2:4). He does this when "he sets himself up in God's temple, proclaiming himself to be God" (2 Thessalonians 2:4). The specificity of this reference is difficult to deal with if the person of whom Paul speaks is someone yet to come in history, someone who will appear at the very end of time. It appears that Paul expects the Thessalonians to understand rather well from the cryptic description of the one of whom he speaks. The similarity with this description and with Jesus' discourse in Matthew 24 is obvious. There was a connection in the minds of the Jews of that day in the destruction of the Temple and the ushering in of the great "age to come" when God rewards His people and punishes those who have persecuted them. Of course, Jesus made a distinction in the two events. (See the comments on 1 Thessalonians 5 above.) It may be that Paul is implying here that the Temple has not yet been desecrated in fulfillment of Jesus' prediction. Until that happens, Jesus will not return. The point is not to give them a sign of Jesus' return. Nor is he by any means suggesting that they should not expect the imminent return of Jesus. There is no reason to think that all of these events cannot happen very quickly and in their own lifetime. The point of his argument here is to prove that the coming of Jesus has not occurred; there are events that have not yet happened that must precede that coming.

Who Is the Restrainer?

A final question to be considered here is who, or what, is holding back this man of lawlessness (2 Thessalonians 2:6). The answer to this question, of course, is dependent upon how one answers the previous question. The same kind of variety is offered: Paul, the Holy Spirit, Jesus, God, the Roman empire, and many other suggestions. This restraining force over the man of lawlessness is described both as a man (2 Thessalonians 2:6) and an abstract force (2 Thessalonians 2:7). He will be "taken out of the way" to allow the man of lawlessness to promote his evil schemes

(2 Thessalonians 2:7, 8). There can be no more certainty about the identity of this person (or power) than the other perplexing questions in this chapter. One is inclined to agree with Augustine (fifth century), who said, "I admit that the meaning of this completely escapes me" (*City of God,* 20).

The consequence of this evil is that many will be deceived and will meet their destruction because of the activities of this man of lawlessness. "The coming of the lawless one will be in accordance with the work of Satan displayed in all kinds of counterfeit miracles, signs and wonders, and in every sort of evil that deceives those who are perishing" (2 Thessalonians 2:9, 10). They do not perish, however, because they have no choice in the matter. Paul makes it clear that the responsibility is theirs: "They perish because they refused to love the truth and so be saved" (2 Thessalonians 2:10). If they do not want to believe, then they will find themselves deluded by counterfeit truth (2 Thessalonians 2:11).

Thanksgiving (2:13-17)

Paul concludes this chapter, and the last A part of the A-B-A triad, with a thanksgiving. He is especially thankful for them at this point because they are chosen by God. A slightly preferred translation here is "chosen as firstfruits" rather than "from the beginning ... chose you" (2 Thessalonians 2:13; see NIV footnote). See the comments about election and being chosen in the comments on 1 Thessalonians 1:4. They are the firstfruits, not in the sense that they were the first converts in Europe, but rather that they are the first ones chosen for the special purpose of demonstrating God's grace in their community. As they do this work of election, the result of God's choosing, then, is salvation "through the sanctifying work of the Spirit and through belief in the truth" (2 Thessalonians 2:13). Notice that this election is consistent with the understanding of it presented earlier. It is election for service that results in salvation of many people. It does not mean that some are arbitrarily chosen for salvation. "Belief in the truth" is necessary for that salvation to be effected through the sanctifying work of the Holy Spirit. Paul repeats this very idea in the next verse. "He called you to this through our gospel, that you might share in the glory of our Lord Jesus Christ" (2 Thessalonians 2:14). Again, there is the sense in which the "choosing" of Christians for service puts them in the same category as Jesus, who is the model of service. In this sense, they "share in the glory" of Him. The conclusion of the thanksgiving, then, is a repetition of what he said before: "Stand firm and hold to the teachings we passed on to you, whether by word of mouth or by letter" (2 Thessalonians 2:15). The relationship between thought and actions is once again emphasized. How one thinks issues in how he or she acts. The letter mentioned here is presumably 1 Thessalonians.

Paul concludes this thanksgiving section with a prayer for the Thessalonians (2 Thessalonians 2:16, 17). In structure, it is reminiscent of some of the prayers found in 1 Thessalonians (e.g., 1 Thessalonians 3:11ff). He affirms here that he has received both love and encouragement as well as a foundation for hope. It is with confidence then that Paul can pray that they receive encouragement and strength in all that faces them. The word *encouragement* comes from the same word *(parakalesai)* from which the word *Paraclete* is taken, a term used for the Holy Spirit—often translated Comforter. (See John 14:16.) The Paraclete was a person in the ancient world who would accompany another to court, stand by his side, and whisper in his ear what to say to the jury. (The word literally means called alongside of.) As the Thessalonians face persecution and trial, God will be their Paraclete, their strength and encouragement.

CHAPTER EIGHTEEN

Closing Exhortations

2 Thessalonians 3:1-18

Their Prayer (3:1-5)

The next section serves as a conclusion to the previous discussion about the persecution the Thessalonians will face. Paul is aware that he, too, is to undergo persecution, and he asks for their prayers for him, also. He made such requests frequently (Romans 15:30-32; 2 Corinthians 1:11; Philippians 1:19; Colossians 4:3; 1 Thessalonians 5:25). In almost every one of these instances, he prayed for the spread of the gospel and his part in it. He is quite conscious of the impact that the prayers of the churches can have on his own ministry of evangelism among the Gentiles. In this particular case, the object of prayer is quite specific. He wants them to pray for the spread of the gospel and its subsequent reception. But he also wants their prayers for his deliverance from adversaries. He calls them "wicked and evil men" (2 Thessalonians 3:2), and seems to have a specific group in mind. He has come through some difficult and discouraging times since he arrived on the European continent and needs the support and prayers of these friends.

Paul continues with assurance that God will be faithful to help the Thessalonians through their crises. He will protect them "from the evil one" (2 Thessalonians 3:3). It is not clear whether the phrase *(apo tou ponerou)* refers to a person, "the evil one" (as in the NIV), or "evil" in general (as in the KJV and RSV). Either is possible, and either may fit the context.

Not only will God strengthen them for their upcoming trials, but Paul himself has confidence that they will continue to act in the right way. "We have confidence in the Lord that you are doing and will continue to do the things we command" (2 Thessalonians 3:4). The confidence is warranted because they are "in the Lord"; they do not have to rely on their own resources. While he speaks this with conviction, he also speaks it with tactfulness. If they are to hear what he has to say in the pointed exhortations to follow, they must know that they have access to the power of the Lord to accomplish his admonitions. Although they have serious problems that need to be addressed, Paul is convinced that they have the means to respond. He sums up this confidence in the conclusion of this wish/prayer: "May the Lord direct your hearts into God's love [i.e., God's love for mankind, in the normal Pauline usage] and Christ's perseverance" (2 Thessalonians 3:5). They will need both in order to respond positively to these exhortations.

Exhortation About Idleness (3:6-13)

Paul begins bringing this letter to a close by focusing upon a problem he just touched upon in the previous letter, the problem that some of them are not working. (See 1 Thessalonians 4:11, 12; 5:14.) The instances in the first letter are rather mildly addressed, but here they are approached most directly. In the first letter, they are instructed to "warn those who are idle" (1 Thessalonians 5:14); here they are to "keep away from every brother who is idle" (2 Thessalonians 3:6). One might suppose that the more gentle treatment Paul suggested in the first letter has not been effective.

Their problem is not merely that they refuse to work, but—additionally—they refuse in direct contradiction to the teaching about work that Paul has given to them. He says they do "not live according to the teaching you received from us" (2 Thessalonians 3:6). While that teaching is not explicit here in this passage, it surely dealt with the Christian view of work. Work (that is, manual labor) was not always widely admired in the Greek world. The Greeks saw such activity as tasks for slaves and not for "thinking" men. They preferred to sit around and philosophize; working with one's hands was only for those people who could not use their minds for the more noble pursuits of life.

While Christianity does, in fact, value the pursuits of the mind, it also gives a high place to the value of human labor. Work is not meant to be a curse upon man and woman, but rather a source of enjoyment for them. When Adam and Eve were placed in the garden, they were given the task "to work it and take care of it" (Genesis 2:15). It is true that because of sin's coming into the world, work would not always be a pleasant experience (cf. Genesis 3:17), but it never has become a curse itself. God still intends for mankind to work and to find fulfillment in that labor.

Not only did Paul teach the Thessalonians about the value of work; he demonstrated through his own efforts that value. "We were not idle when we were with you, nor did we eat anyone's food without paying for it. On the contrary, we worked night and day, laboring and toiling so that we would not be a burden to any of you" (2 Thessalonians 3:7, 8). Paul is not hesitant to use himself as a model for the Thessalonians to imitate. He spent considerable time on this subject in the first letter, both in terms of offering an apology for his own ministry among them as well as providing an example for them to follow. (See 1 Thessalonians 2:1, 3-12; 3:3; 4:1, 2; also 1 Corinthians 4:16 and Philippians 4:9). In many ways, they had imitated Paul (1 Thessalonians 1:6), but some were lacking in this important dimension of the Christian life.

Paul and his colleagues had given them this example of work, but not because these preachers were required to work. He made it clear that he could have expected them to support them in the preaching of the gospel. ("We did this, not because we do not have the right to such help, but in order to make ourselves a model for you"; 2 Thessalonians 3:9.) He made this very same point even more strongly to the Corinthians (1 Corinthians 9). Those who preach the gospel have the right to live by the gospel. Paul, however, deliberately chose to be responsible for his own welfare in this matter. It was not his custom to take funds for his own needs from the churches where he preached. He followed this practice in order to be free from any responsibility to them, in order to be above suspicion of wrong motives, and in order to give others an example of service.

The corrective for this problem is two-fold, one directed toward those in error and one for the rest of the church. To the former, he simply says "to settle down and earn the bread" which they are eating (2 Thessalonians 3:12). It would appear that he is in no mood to hear excuses or to make allowances in the matter. He had taught them during his time there, "If a man will not work, he shall not eat" (2 Thessalonians 3:10). To the latter, he said, "Keep away from every brother who is idle and does not live according to the teaching you received" (2 Thessalonians 3:6). This command has often been taken to mean that they are to excommunicate these idlers, but that is not what Paul says. As strongly as he feels about the issue, he still calls these erring ones "brothers" (2 Thessalonians 3:6). The point is that the rest of the church is not to reinforce this errant behavior, and the way to avoid reinforcement is to refrain from having an association with them in the particular way that he means.

The cause of all of this idleness is not at all clear. Many believe that it has resulted from their misunderstanding about the coming of Jesus: if Jesus' coming is imminent, then why go on working? If His coming is very soon, there is no point to planting a garden since there will be no one around to enjoy its harvest. While the theory sounds plausible, there is no indication, by anything that Paul says, to indicate this connection. Another possibility is that some of them have been abusing the love feast associated with the Lord's Supper. While it is to be a meal where all share equally (thus *koinonia,* fellowship or participation), some may have seen the practice as a way for a free meal without sharing in any of the expense of it. The Didache, an early second century document of the church, instructed how to deal with such situations:

> If he who comes is a traveler, help him as much as you can, but he shall not stay with you more than two days or, if necessary, three. If he wishes to settle down with you and has a craft, let him work for his bread. But if he has no craft, make such provision for him as your intelligence approves, so that no one shall live with you in idleness as a Christian. If he refuses so to do, he is making merchandise of Christ (Didache 12:2-5).

It may be this very kind of situation that Paul has in mind in this text.

Exhortation About Obedience (3:14, 15)

The concluding exhortation in the letter is a comprehensive one that applies to all that he has said: "If anyone does not obey our instruction in this letter, take special note of him. Do not associate with him, in order that he may feel ashamed. Yet do not regard him as an enemy, but warn him as a brother" (2 Thessalonians 3:14, 15). There are two dimensions of this closing instruction. First, the church is to deal decisively with those who flagrantly and consciously continue to ignore such teaching as Paul has dealt with in the letter. He mentions two responses. They are to avoid association with such people. It is not clear exactly what he means. Obviously, he does not mean to avoid any contact at all, because another one of the decisive ways to deal with these people is to "warn" them; they cannot be warned if there is no contact at all. Perhaps the association of which he speaks has to do with the common meal that was characteristic of the early church. At any rate, the "association" that is to be avoided is one that will be clear to the erring ones; they will have clear understanding that they are being so disciplined by the church.

A second dimension to this exhortation is the purpose for such action as advocated here. The goal of non-association is not to keep the church pure. Paul does not seem to fear for the purity of the church. Rather, the goal of this drastic action is the reclaiming of the erring ones who are behaving in these unacceptable ways. While they are acting in ways that are clearly wrong, and that wrong must be pointed out by the church, they are still brothers who need to be restored to a place of harmony in the body of Christ once again. Whatever implication this passage has for the contemporary church, it must take into consideration decisive action, a purpose of restoration, and treatment as brothers.

Conclusion (3:16-18)

This conclusion, as others we have seen above, follows the A-B-A pattern here once again: A—benediction (2 Thessalonians 3:16); B—farewell (2 Thessalonians 3:17); A—benediction (2 Thessalonians 3:18).

While Paul generally concluded his letters with some mention of the hope for peace, it certainly does not appear to be a perfunctory gesture in this instance. If this church, torn by disorder and disharmony, is to realize peace, it will have to be a peace that comes from Jesus himself. (See Romans 15:33; 16:20; 2 Corinthians 13:11; Philippians 4:7, 9; Colossians 3:15; 1 Thessalonians 5:23.)

Paul may have personally signed most of his letters, though he explicitly mentions it only here, in 1 Corinthians 16:21, and in Colossians 4:18. It was his custom to use a secretary, called an amanuensis. The practice is all the more important here, since someone had tried to forge a letter in his name (2 Thessalonians 2:2), and he wants them to see his own handwriting, which they presumably will recognize.

The final benediction (2 Thessalonians 3:18) is identical to 1 Thessalonians 5:28 except for the addition of *all,* which he included also in 1 Corinthians 16:24 and 2 Corinthians 13:13. Not even those ones rebuked so harshly by Paul are excluded from his final benediction.

SUGGESTED READING

Philippians

Barth, Karl. *The Epistle to the Philippians.* J. R. Leitch, tr. Richmond, VA: John Knox Press, 1962.

Beare, F. W. *A Commentary on the Epistle to the Philippians.* New York: Harper and Bros., 1959.

Doty, W. G. *Letters in Primitive Christianity.* Philadelphia: Fortress, 1973.

Ellis, Earle E. *Paul and His Recent Interpreters.* Grand Rapids: Eerdmans, 1961.

Hendriksen, William. *Philippians* (NTC). Grand Rapids: Baker, 1962.

Lightfoot, J. B. *St. Paul's Epistle to the Philippians.* London: Macmillan, 1894.

Loh, I-J. and E. A. Nida. *A Translator's Handbook on Paul's Letter to the Philippians.* Helps for Translators, 19. Sttutgart: United Bible Societies, 1977.

Maclaren, Alexander. *Expositions of Holy Scripture: Second Corinthians, Chapters VII to End, Galatians and Philippians.* New York: George H. Doran, n.d.

Martin, R. P. *The Epistle of Paul to the Philippians* (TNTC). Grand Rapids: Eerdmans, 1959.

_____. *Philippians* (NCB). Grand Rapids: Eerdmans, 1980.

_____. *Carmen Christi: Philippians 2:5-11 in Recent Interpretation and in the Setting of Early Christian Worship,* Rev. ed. Grand Rapids: Eerdmans, 1983.

Moule, H. C. G. *The Epistle to the Philippians.* Cambridge: University Press, 1897.

Muller, J. J. *The Epistles of Paul to the Philippians and to Philemon.* Grand Rapids: Eerdmans, 1955.

Sanders, J. T. *New Testament Christological Hymns: Their Historical and Religious Background.* Cambridge: University Press, 1971.

Schmithals, W. *Paul and the Gnostics.* J. E. Steely, tr. Nashville: Abingdon, 1972.

Scott, E. F. "The Epistle to the Philippians." *The Interpreter's Bible.* G. A. Butterick, et al, eds. New York: Abingdon, 1955.

Colossians

Barclay, William. *The All Sufficient Christ: Studies in Paul's Letter to the Colossians.* Philadelphia: Westminster, 1963.

Craddock, Fred B. *The Pre-existence of Christ in the New Testament.* Nashville: Abingdon, 1968.

Demarest, Gary. *Colossians: The Mystery of Christ in Us.* Waco: Word, 1979.

Efrid, J. M. *Christ, the Church, and the End: Studies in Colossians and Ephesians.* Valley Forge: Judson, 1980.

Erdman, Charles R. *The Epistles of Paul to the Colossians and to Philemon.* Philadelphia: Westminster, 1933.

Gutherie, Donald. *New Testament Introduction.* Downers Grove: IVP, 1970.

Harrison, Everett F. *Colossians: Christ All-sufficient.* Chicago: Moody, 1971.

Lightfoot, J. B. *Saint Paul's Epistles to the Colossians and to Philemon.* 1879 edition, reprinted. Grand Rapids: Zondervan, 1961.

Lohse, Eduard. *Colossians and Philemon.* William R. Poehlmann and Robert J. Karris, trs. Philadelphia: Fortress, 1971.

Lucas, R. C. *Fullness and Freedom: The Messages of Colossians and Philemon.* Downers Grove: IVP, 1980.

MacDonald, H. Dermot. *Commentary on Colossians and Philemon.* Waco: Word, 1980.

Macknight, James. *Macknight on the Epistles,* Vol. 3. Grand Rapids: Baker, 1969.

Maclaren, Alexander. *The Epistles of St. Paul to the Colossians and Philemon* (The Expositors' Bible). W. Robertson Nicoll, ed. New York: George H. Dorarn, n.d.

Martin, Ralph P. *Colossians: The Church's Lord and the Christian's Liberty; an Expository Commentary with a Present-Day Application.* Grand Rapids: Zondervan, 1972.

O'Brien, P. T. *Colossians, Philemon*. Waco: Word, 1982.

Robertson, A. T. *Paul and the Intellectuals: The Epistle to the Colossians*. Nashville: Broadman, 1959.

Sanders, Jack T. *The New Testament Christological Hymns: Their Historical Religious Background* (Society for New Testament Studies Monograph Series). Matthew Black, ed. Cambridge: University Press, 1971.

Schweizer, E. *The Letter to the Colossians: A Commentary*. A. Chester, tr. Minneapolis: Augsburg, 1982.

Simpson, E. K., and F. F. Bruce. *Commentary on the Epistles to the Ephesians and the Colossians* (NIC). Grand Rapids: Eerdmans, 1957.

Stewart, James S. *The Gates of New Life*. Grand Rapids: Baker, 1972.

Taylor, Louis H. *The New Creation: A Study of the Pauline Doctrines of Creation, Innocence, Sin, and Redemption*. New York: Pageant Press, 1958.

Thomas, W. H. Griffith. *Studies in Colossians and Philemon*. Grand Rapids: Baker, 1972.

Trevethan, T. L. *Our Joyful Confidence: The Lordship of Jesus in Colossians*. Downers Grove: IVP, 1981.

Wuest, Kenneth S. *Ephesians and Colossians in the Greek New Testament for the English Reader* (Word Studies in the Greek New Testament, Vol. 13). Grand Rapids: Eerdmans, 1954.

1 and 2 Thessalonians

Bailey, J. W. *The First and Second Epistles to the Thessalonians*. Nashville: Abingdon, 1955, pp. 243-329.

Best, Ernest. *A Commentary on the First and Second Epistles to the Thessalonians*. New York: Harper and Row, 1972.

Bruce, F. F. *1 and 2 Thessalonians*. Waco: Word, 1982.

Calvin, John. *The Epistles of Paul to the Romans and to the Thessalonians*. R. MacKenzie, tr. Edinburgh: Oliver & Boyd, 1960, pp. 329-423.

Demarest, G. W. *1, 2, Thessalonians, 1, 2 Timothy, Titus* (The Communicator's Commentary). Waco: Word, 1984.

Friskney, Tom. *Thirteen Lessons on I, II Thessalonians*. Joplin: College Press, 1982.

Hendriksen, William. *I and II Thessalonians* (NTC). Grand Rapids: Baker, 1955.

Hiebert, D. E. *The Thessalonian Epistles: A Call to Readiness.* Chicago: Moody, 1971.

Hobbs, H. H. *1 and 2 Thessalonians.* Nashville: Broadman, 1972.

Kelcy, R. C. *The Letters of Paul to the Thessalonians.* Austin: R. B. Sweet, 1968.

Lightfoot, J. B. *Notes on the Epistles of St. Paul.* London: Macmillan, 1895.

Lyons, G. *Pauline Autobiography: Toward a New Understanding.* Atlanta: Scholars Press, 1985.

Marshal, I. H. *1 and 2 Thessalonians* (New Century Bible). Grand Rapids: Eerdmans, 1983.

Milligan, G. *St. Paul's Epistles to the Thessalonians.* London: Macmillan, 1908.

Morris, Leon. *The First and Second Epistles to the Thessalonians.* Grand Rapids: Eerdmans, 1959.

Reese, J. M. *New Testament Message: A Biblical-Theological Commentary.* Wilmington: Michael Glazier, 1979.

Philippians, Colossians, 1, 2 Thessalonians Combinations

Barclay, William. *The Letters to the Philippians, Colossians, and Thessalonians.* Philadelphia: Westminster, 1959.

Calvin, John. *Commentaries on the Epistles of Paul the Apostle to the Philippians, Colossians, and Thessalonians.* J. Pringle, tr. Grand Rapids: Eerdmans, 1948.

Fields, Wilbur, *Philippians-Colossians-Philemon* (Bible Study Textbook Series). Joplin: College Press, 1969.

Gaebelein, Frank E., ed. *The Expositor's Bible Commentary,* Vol. 11: Ephesians—Philemon. Grand Rapids: Zondervan, 1978.

Hunter, Archibald. *The Letter of Paul to the Galatians; The Letter of Paul to the Ephesians; The Letter of Paul to the Philippians: The Letter of Paul to the Colossians* (Layman's Bible Commentary), Vol. 22. Richmond: John Knox, 1959.

Lenski, R. C. H. *The Interpretation of St. Paul's Epistles to the Colossians, to the Thessalonians, to Timothy, to Titus, and to Philemon.* Minneapolis: Augsburg, 1946.

Parker, Joseph. *The Epistles to the Colossians and Thessalonians* (Practical Commentary on the New Testament), Vol. 1. W. Robertson Nicoll, ed. New York: Eaton and Mains, 1905.